D0872097

SHIFTING CONTEXTS

The Generation of Effective Psychotherapy

BILL O'HANLON
JAMES WILK

Foreword by
JOHN H. WEAKLAND

Authors are listed alphabetically.

THE GUILFORD PRESS
NEW YORK   LONDON

For Anne and Rachel,
and for Patricia and Patrick,
who shifted our contexts.

© 1987 by Bill O'Hanlon and James Wilk
Published by The Guilford Press
72 Spring Street
New York, NY 10012

All rights reserved

No part of this book may be reproduced, stored in a retrieval system, or transmitted in any form or by any means, electronic, mechanical, photocopying, microfilming, recording, or otherwise, without written permission from the Publisher.

Printed in the United States of America

Last digit is print number 9 8 7 6 5 4 3

Library of Congress Cataloging-in-Publication Data

O'Hanlon, Bill.
   Shifting Contexts.
   Bibliography: p.
   Includes index.
   1. Psychotherapy.   I. Wilk, James.   II. Title.
RC480.W55   1987   616.89'14   86-26986
ISBN 0-89862-677-3

CONTENTS

FOREWORD

If I were a writer of promotional blurbs—and there do seem to be quite a few such in the therapy field these days—I might try to proclaim that O'Hanlon and Wilk have produced a work presenting the greatest revelations since the New Testament, or at least since the last published work on psychotherapy. But as those who know me would testify, that is not my style, and in any case I think this book deserves better than that. So I will instead just set out why I think their work deserves the close attention of two kinds of people: those who are seriously interested in and curious about the nature of human problems and problem resolution, and those practicing therapy who are interested in improving the effectiveness and efficiency of their work—plus the rare ones who are both.

Shifting Contexts is primarily concerned with the study and application of "clinical epistemology." O'Hanlon and Wilk take considerable space and pains—though not in a painful way; in fact their style is clear and often, as befits authors interested in language, includes charming literary touches—to make plain what they mean by this term. I will therefore not attempt to summarize their own statement, but rather restate their subject as it appears from my own viewpoint: Human beings do not behave, including those behaviors they label as "problems," on the basis of realities alone, but always on the basis of realities (that is, observable words and actions, what the authors call "video descriptions") plus interpretations they make of their own and others' behaviors. O'Hanlon and Wilk's work is concerned with making this interaction plain, with how interpretations usually are crucial to the existence and persistence of problems, especially when the interpretations exist as unrecognized "presuppositions" (by patients *or* therapists), and with how negotiation between therapist and client can bring to awareness and alter interpretations so that problems are resolved—with or without alterations in observable behavior.

On the significance of this endeavor, I both agree and disagree with the authors. I agree that this is a fundamental matter for therapy. I would not, however, agree it is *the* fundamental matter, primarily because I believe that effective therapy involves considering and dealing with a number of factors which are interrelated more systemically than hierarchically—*all* are fundamental, in a sense. To seek *the* fundamental factor in therapy is like seeking *the* cause of a problem. And I do not believe that no significant prior attention has been given to the uses and abuses of language, to interpretations versus observable behavior, in the field of therapy. For example, these matters are central, though not necessarily explicit, in all that has been written about the framing and reframing of behaviors. But this book is special in its explicit, organized, and comprehensive focus on the interrelationships between language, behavior, and interpretation, and the central relevance of this for the nature and resolution of human problems.

One critical note in conclusion: While the authors do include many useful general statements about putting their analytic viewpoint into practice, and many more specific "mini-examples" of this, they do not—despite my previous recommendation to them—include any more extended examples, such as one or more transcripts of a complete session or a whole case. I can only hope that enough of us will buy their book to encourage them to produce a sequel that will fill this need.

John H. Weakland

PREFACE

'Such nonsense . . . I've never heard of it!'—Gordon Pask

When the invention of the steam engine was first announced in the last century, a distinguished Irish scientist and wit is reported to have remarked, "It works *in practice* O.K. . . . but does it work *in theory?*"

Sooner or later in the professional life of every agent of change, in every field of human endeavor, there comes an experience of achieving results beyond what theory would have led one to believe was possible. Occasionally—very occasionally—such glimpses of the richness of the possibilities lead to the revision of our theoretical view. Science advances, and whole new realms of possibility are opened up. More often, the changes that have been achieved more rapidly or more sweepingly than received opinion would have allowed, are swept under the carpet, dismissed as flukes, explained away, and soon forgotten—as much by the unwitting, would-be innovator as by the carping skeptics looking on.

The field of psychotherapy is no exception. Every psychotherapist we have questioned on this point has confessed to isolated experiences of achieving the desired therapeutic results in a single session. Perhaps a longstanding, serious problem that has resisted all previous therapeutic efforts suddenly dissolves in the first "assessment" interview, and the client's life is subsequently transformed. But the case that didn't fit the prevailing theories of change simply remained an oddity, a curiosity, an unexplained anomaly, rather than a basis for questioning the accepted theoretical limits to what is possible. And until someone could provide a theoretical framework admitting of such possibilities, thousands upon thousands of such "flukes" would continue to be regarded as just that—flukes.

This book began with the recognition that one-session "flukes" ought to be no more inexplicable than three-session flukes or ten-session flukes or 357-session flukes. We set out to see whether there was any reason, in principle or in practice, why one-session psychotherapy could not become the norm. More importantly, as the possibilities realisable in practice were inevitably far greater than the possibilities allowed for in theory, we wanted to find ways of freeing therapy from the self-imposed, limiting assumptions made, often tacitly and unwittingly, by both therapists and their clients.

This book is therefore about effecting desired change as swiftly as possible by questioning and shifting one's own pre-suppositions. As such, it is necessarily minimalist in orientation. The emphasis is always on bringing about the maximum desirable transformation through the minimum necessary intervention, not—we hasten to add—so that all psychotherapy can wrap up after the first session, but so that we can make ourselves as useful as possible to our clients. Sometimes, the only intervention that turns out to be necessary is to shift the way we or our clients talk about the presenting complaint.

This is a practical book aimed at practising therapists. It is not aimed at therapists of any particular school of thought; indeed, it is our fondest ambition for this book to find a place on every therapist's bookshelf—Freudians and behaviorists, systemic family therapists and Jungians, cognitive and Rogerian therapists alike. Irrespective of a therapist's theoretical orientation or style of therapy, this book is aimed at making that therapist's clinical work more effective. It is thus intended to be inclusive rather than exclusive. So long as a therapist is more committed to making a positive contribution to the clients' lives than to furthering the cause of some particular therapeutic ideology, this book should prove to be of some value. And we think that that includes the overwhelming majority of therapists.

As every therapist has to operate on the basis of *some* set of presuppositions, the key is to learn to operate with freedom at the level of one's own presuppositions. Put more crudely, have you got a theory or has the theory got you? And if you're stuck with a theory, doesn't your client get stuck with it too? By moving away from the presuppositions and presumptuousness of theory's ever shifting sands to the firmer ground of uninterpreted description, we are attempting to introduce *certainty* into psychotherapy for a change.

For those who are interested in how we got here, some of the story is in the main text of the book and much of the rest can be gleaned from the Afterword. But if, like us, you are less interested in how things got to this point and more interested in what to do now, we offer plenty for you to be getting on with.

If, much of the time, we tend to take a conceptual approach, rooted in the fertile soil at the confluence of three great streams of modern thought—Epistemology, Cybernetics, and General Semantics—our discussion is no less practical for all that. For our preference is, wherever possible, to provide a *context* within which a therapist can generate her own effective therapeutic approach, her own possibilities for action. The therapist's job is, after all, a similar one: to create a context within which the client can generate his own possibilities, and see his way clear to taking the action he needs to take to solve his own problem in his own inimitable way. And how to do *that* is, above all, the subject of this book.

ACKNOWLEDGMENTS

So many people have contributed so much to both of us over the years—to our learning, to our thinking, to our practice, and above all to the shift in our own epistemology—contributions which inform and color every page of this book. To attempt to acknowledge them all would soon produce another volume. We hope that we have been, and continue to be, sufficiently good about acknowledging our gratitude to them in daily life, where we can offer more in the way of specifcs than a mere name on a printed page.

We would, however, like to give special mention to some of the many individuals who read earlier versions of the manuscript and offered their thoughts and criticisms. This book has gone through so many revisions, and has been so long in evolving, that we shall mention here only those whose comments have made a personally attributable difference to this work, including some who did not actually read the manuscript but made specific contributions in other ways. Inevitably, we have left some out whom we would have wanted to mention, but here goes: Judy Auer, Jeff Bogdan, Phil Booth, Bob Britchford, Michaela von Britzke, Peter Bruggen, Jessica Buck, David Calof, Greg Case, Rennie Childress, Steve de Shazer, Patricia O'Hanlon Hudson, John Jones, Brad Keeney, Alan McConville, Suzanne Markle, Bill Minier, Larry More, Joe Roe, Brian Roet, Keith Stoll, Stacey Vornbrock, John Weakland, Seymour Weingarten, Anne Wilk, Howard Williams, and Jeff Zeig. We would also like to thank the Editors of *The Journal of Strategic and Systemic Therapies* and publishers Brunner/Mazel for permission to incorporate material (Wilk 1982, 1985) that first appeared elsewhere.

The person we want to acknowledge most of all, however, is Dr. Jim Warner of South Molton, Devon, who has saved this book from being a rather dreadful one and who, we hope, has helped turn it into a rather good one. His thoughtful criticisms, comments, suggestions, marginal jokes, and painstaking editorial labor on the original manuscript helped slow us down by at least a year, largely because we thought he was, most of the time, right. You, the reader, owe as much as we do to Jim's generous and well-aimed efforts. We have, however, not always deferred to Jim's better judgment, and the astute reader will no doubt spot some of the places where we have ignored his—and others'—sober advice, occasionally, perhaps, at our peril.

James Wilk
Bill O'Hanlon

If, then, there is to be any fruitful development in the science of psychotherapy, as well as in the lives of those whom it intends to help, it must be released from the unconscious blocks, unexamined assumptions, and unrealized nonsense problems which lie in its social context.—Alan Watts

Each generation criticizes the unconscious assumptions made by its parents.—Alfred North Whitehead

BEYOND BELIEF
Getting from There to Here

Regardless of one's theoretical orientation, successes and failures sooner or later compel the therapist to question presuppositions and factors relating to change.—Claudio Angelo

We both began our careers in psychotherapy using models that were traditionally favored at that time to treat individuals with pathological (either "neurotic" or "psychotic") psychological, emotional, and behavioral problems. These approaches were based on certain well-established principles and "facts" about human beings, about the origins and functions of symptoms, and about appropriate treatment procedures. Faced with real human dilemmas and suffering, we rapidly became aware that the approaches we were using were not as effective as we had hoped. Thus, we began to search for more effective ways of assisting people to resolve the dilemmas that brought them to therapy.

During that search, we studied and practiced many different techniques and approaches. We noticed that as we shifted the way we approached therapy—as our models, our intervention techniques, and even our way of assessing the presenting complaint shifted—there were corresponding shifts in the kinds of responses and results we obtained. It gradually became clearer to us that the way we viewed and approached our clients and therapy had more to do with successful results than did the clients, their histories, their personalities, or their presenting complaints. We began to doubt more and more that there were any solid "problems" out there at all. We became convinced that problems are very negotiable, and that therapists play a large part in the definition and even the creation of the quandaries dealt with in therapy. What therapists discuss, ignore, ask about, or don't ask about; how they make appointments; who is included in the sessions; and so on—all these factors seemed to affect the definition of the problem, the perceived 'causes' of the difficulties, and the length and the results of therapy. Family therapists "discover" such problems as "entrenched coalitions" and "enmeshment," and the clients are affected by these determinations, for better or worse. Behavior therapists "discover" that the troublesome behavior that results from "learning" or "rewards" is the problem to be treated, and their clients end up with that problem, which is either successfully resolved by treatment or not. A client may seek therapy from a psychodynamically oriented therapist from whom he[1] learns that he has "low self-esteem" and must "work on that." We contend that these are not discoveries at all, but creations that are negotiable and that will affect the course of therapy and its eventual outcome.

BEYOND BELIEF: APPROACHING CERTAINTY IN PSYCHOTHERAPY

Belief is not the beginning but the end of all knowledge.—Johann Wolfgang von Goethe

We were each working independently, thousands of miles apart, and knew nothing of each other's work. Gradually, however, after several long telephone calls that were initially arranged with a view to organizing some training courses in England, we began to discover some remarkable similarities in our evolving orientations to psychotherapy. One of us (O'Hanlon) visited England to teach a workshop series in 1982, and it was then that we both realized that one of our shared preoccupations was with a phenomenon not unfamiliar to many therapists: namely, that of the "one-session cure." Why, we began to ask ourselves, do such rapid changes sometimes occur, and why do they not happen more often?

We resolved to devise ways and means so that we and others could achieve such quick successes with greater frequency and predictability. This book is a result of that resolution. Since the project began, we have worked together to provide the clearest description we could of how to make psychotherapy as

---

1. To solve the perennial pronoun "problem," we have decided to switch fairly randomly between "he/him" and "she/her" throughout the text.

effective as possible, and how to make one-session therapy a more regular event that could from time to time be expected. We have continued to test these conceptions and descriptions in our own clinical work, both to fine-tune them and to challenge the previously unexamined "beliefs" we have held (and doubtless still hold). It seems to us that many therapists "believe" their models, unquestioningly confusing map and territory, and fail to notice when the models don't produce results in therapy. Sometimes they even blame failures on a client's "pathology," or explain away the lack of results by attributing this to a client's "resistance" or a family's "homeostasis." We are firmly committed to verifying our conceptions in the proving grounds of clinical work, and hope and expect that the reader will do this too. We expect to continue to clarify our understanding and revise our clinical approach as we continue to do therapy and teach other therapists.

We hold that there are realms of certainty in clinical work and realms that are unverifiable and uncertain. We believe that the blurring of the distinction between these realms is the source of much confusion and lack of results in therapy. We want to introduce certainty into psychotherapy: certainty as to the nature of the presenting complaint, certainty as to when and whether results have been obtained, and certainty as to what must always remain in the realm of uncertainty in therapeutic work.

THE PURPOSE OF THE BOOK

Our purpose in writing this book is to demystify and redefine the process and goals of psychotherapy, to question and challenge current presuppositions (unexamined, implicit assumptions) about the nature of human dilemmas and their resolution, and to enable therapists to produce lasting results in the briefest possible time.

BEYOND PSYCHOLOGY

Sometimes when we tell people we meet that we do psychotherapy, they express some concern that we will analyze them. When we assure them that we don't analyze people, they can't imagine what we get paid to do. "Analysis" is in the realm of psychological theory. We are committed to moving psychotherapy beyond psychology—that is, beyond any attempt to explain *why* people behave as they do. We hold that psychotherapy is a distinct discipline in its own right, and that much of psychology not only is irrelevant to producing desired results in psychotherapy, but may at times be a positive hindrance to obtaining those results. Our views on the irrelevance of psychology to psychotherapy are discussed further and become apparent—and, we think, obvious—as the book progresses.

HEADING FOR CHAPTER ONE

Why have we used the term "clinical epistemology"? When we first told our friends and colleagues that we were writing a book on clinical epistemology, they groaned and assured us that we would only sell two copies: one to each of our mothers. As we have endeavored to make this book as accessible to clinicians and as relevant to clinical work as possible, we were hesitant to use the term at all. We did not want to put off the very readers for whom we were writing this book—those who want to make a difference in their day-to-day practice of psychotherapy. At several points in the course of writing the book, we considered censoring the word "epistemology" and omitting all reference to the subject. In the end, however, we decided it was the most descriptive term for the territory we cover, and so we have retained it. We believe, rightly or wrongly, that only in the context of epistemology does the essence of what we are trying to get across stand out clearly from what might otherwise be mistaken for mere differences in "technique" or approach.

We are clinicians and want this book to be read and used by other clinicians, and so we have endeavored to make this a practical book. But we do not want to overlook the rather far-reaching implications of what we are saying, and for that we need to provide a context. We will explore a terrain that is perhaps new, but at the same time strangely familiar. For the realm of clinical epistemology involves the very context in which we exist, not only as therapists, but as men and women engaged in the daily business of making sense of our world and of ourselves, and then acting according to our fallible—and often flawed—understandings.

CHAPTER ONE

SHIFTING PRESUPPOSITIONS
Clinical Epistemology and Clinical Practice

Every form of psychology or psychiatry rests upon some kind of philosophical presuppositions. The only error is not to be aware of these assumptions; the only illusion is to deny them.—Rollo May

The trouble is not with what the author does say, but with what he does not say. Also it is not with what he knows he has assumed, but with what he has unconsciously assumed. We do not doubt the author's honesty. It is his perspicacity which we are criticizing. Each generation criticizes the unconscious assumptions made by its parents. . . . —Alfred North Whitehead

What the therapist knows, understands, or believes about a patient is frequently limited in character and often mistaken.—Milton H. Erickson

Shifts in a therapist's methods of gaining knowledge and alterations in what the therapist "knows" can radically affect the process and outcomes of therapy. Epistemology is the study of the justifiability of claims to know. The examination of what therapists and clients think they know, what they can know with certainty, and how they know what they know constitutes the area in which clinical epistemology pursues its quarry.

RELATIONSHIP AND RELEVANCE OF EPISTEMOLOGY TO CLINICAL WORK

Are there such "things" as symptoms? Problems? Can the "cause" of presenting complaints in therapy be determined? Do people "have" personalities? Is there such a phenomenon as symptom substitution? Could any empirical evidence lend support to the alleged existence of this phenomenon?

The examination of the issues that these and other questions raise can have profound implications for therapeutic work. The language and actions of both clients and therapists reflect their underlying assumptions. The words we use to describe our and others' actions, experience, and perceptions are the primary means we as therapists have of discerning and challenging these assumptions.

EPISTEMOLOGICAL PRESUPPOSITIONS

When a person makes any epistemological claim (any claim to know something), this claim—whether it is true or false, asserted or denied—presupposes a considerable number of other statements, upon whose truth both the truth and falsity of the claim depend. For example, the claim that John is depressed, or that depression is the result of repressed anger, or that John's depression is the cause of his present low self-esteem, or that John's depression serves a stabilizing function in his marriage, or whatever, presupposes many things. Whether a person asserts or denies an epistemological claim, we can infer that the person believes in the validity of these presuppositions. This belief is implicit in the sense that the person may never have given serious thought to the matter of whether or not the presupposition (assumption) in question was true. Yet the truth (or falsity) of her explicit statement logically rests upon the validity of the assumption that it presupposes.

We use the term "epistemological presuppositions" to speak generally of certain assumptions that are often found to be presuppositions of particular epistemological claims—for example, assumptions like "Feelings can cause actions," "Symptoms serve a homeostatic function for the family system," or "Anger is a quantity or substance that can be released or dissipated by giving expression to it, or that can cause harm if 'bottled up' inside a person." By being able to discuss these general assumptions involved as presuppositions in specific epistemological claims, we can subject these assumptions to criticism in their own right; and if they are found to be dubious, we can lay down guidelines for regarding as inadmissible any epistemological claims that involve these assumptions as presuppositions. Epistemological presuppositions are defined and discussed with somewhat more rigor in Appendix I.

Which sets of epistemological presuppositions one holds in general as fundamental assumptions, and which sets one regards as invalid or otherwise unacceptable, will play a large part in setting the standards or forming the principles by which one appraises the reasonableness of any claim to know something. If one does not assume that emotions such as anger are quantities or substances and that there is a certain amount that a person has at any given time, or if one does not assume that natural events such as storms are omens sent by the gods, then such statements as "He has a lot of unexpressed anger inside him" or "The reason for the recent storms is the gods' displeasure at the building of the freeway," will not be regarded as false. Rather, consideration of the truth or falsity of these statements does not even arise, because the truth or falsity of each rests on the truth of invalid assumptions. The truth or falsity of "The present King of France drives a Mercedes" does not arise if there is no present King of France. One's assumptions about what can be known at all—about the existence of certain classes of entities about which someone claims to have knowledge, and about certain general posited relationships that one deems to hold in the world, and so on—will form an important basis for how one appraises the reasonableness of epistemological claims. An entirely different set of assumptions will produce an entirely different epistemological analysis.

The relevance in the clinical realm of both the client's and the therapist's epistemological presuppositions to both therapeutic understanding and intervention would seem to be quite considerable. Gregory Bateson was fond of quipping that one cannot *not* have an epistemology, and this would apply both to therapists and to clients. Both the client's and the therapist's respective epistemological presuppositions cannot *not* influence how they decide what the situation "is" clinically, how they decide how one might ascertain the relevant details of the clinical situation, what they think needs to be done, whether anything can be done, how to go about doing it, how long this ought to take, how they will know when they are finished, and so on.

In the clinical realm, shifts in epistemological presuppositions can lead to interventions that would not otherwise have occurred to the therapist. The outcome of these interventions may result in further shifting of the therapist's presuppositions, leading to yet further innovative therapeutic interventions.

THE CALL FOR CLINICAL EPISTEMOLOGY

As far as we know, the term "clinical epistemology" was first suggested by Richard Rabkin (1977, pp. 182, 194, and 206–207) as the name for "a new field," but he gave hardly any hint at all as to what such a field might be, except that it would somehow be concerned with how various psychological problems involve different ways of knowing, and that a "clinical epistemology" would involve an analysis of the way in which individual problems are part of an interactional context. Keeney attempts to understand Rabkin's proposal in Batesonian language as investigating the habits of punctuation that enable clients to construct a particular world of experience (1982, p. 157; 1983, pp. 27–28).

Paul Dell (1982, p. 37) proposes that a "clinical epistemology" is "badly needed by the mental health field," and he suggests that it would be the culmination of a study of "the matter of pathology," by which he seems to mean *classes* of problems that are dealt with in psychotherapists' offices. Dell, again, isn't giving many hints as to what he thinks a "clinical epistemology" would be, but he seems to suggest that it would involve looking at individual and systemic problems in terms of individuals' "epistemological errors," a concept of Bateson's. Bateson frequently referred to the notion of epistemological errors (1978, 1979), by which he meant epistemological presuppositions that do not "fit" with the way the world actually is (where "fit" had a biological/evolutionary connotation). These "false premises regarding the nature of the self and its relations to others" (1978, p. 238) and to the world, and actions arising from these premises, were in Bateson's view the essence of psychological and social "pathology." One example of such a premise would be the idea that it is possible for one part of a system to unilaterally control another part, and attendant attempts to use power to enforce control; another example would be the belief in lineal chains of causality and attendant actions ignoring "the fact of circuitry." This idea has clearly intrigued Dell, and he refers to it in a number of places in his own writings; it seems to be closely tied up with the proposed "clinical epistemology" that he feels is badly needed. There also seems to be a connection here, in Dell's conception, with Bateson's ideas on the "personal epistemology"—the body of habitual assumptions, including epistemological presuppositions—from which a person operates, and which Bateson equated with what has usually been called "character structure."

Ever attuned to problems of recursiveness and of the influence of the observer, Bradford Keeney, in his own call (explicitly echoing Rabkin's) for a new field of "clinical epistemology"—again, largely left unspecified as a proposal for future development—puts the emphasis on the epistemology of the therapist rather than that of the client. He considers the requirements for an "epistemological method applicable to the therapeutic setting," and sees this as involving essentially a "teasing apart" of "the levels inherent in one's attempt to understand a phenomenon" (1983, p. 28). First, according to Keeney, there is a question of what "primary distinctions" the therapist draws to discern his "raw data"—the process of abstracting selected "facts" from what the therapist can "learn" about the client and the client's situation. Second there is the drawing of distinctions to organize those raw data—the kinds of patterns he looks for in the "data" he has abstracted out. And, third, "once the therapist has drawn distinctions that carve out his data and patterns that organize these data, he can step back and examine what he has done. In other words, he recalls that he, as an observer, has drawn these distinctions and that there are other ways of discerning data and patterns of organization" (1983, p. 28). In this process, "the therapist's knowledge can be constantly recycled and modified in order that he may know how to act" (p. 28).

Keeney goes on to consider the "epistemological knots" that arise from the way therapists or clients themselves (1) make tacit assumptions about an experience or situation (say, a transitory episode of ordinary unhappiness); (2) go on to describe it in terms of their assumptions ("depression"); (3) use the description to explain "it" (the behavior, mood, etc., is "caused by depression")—a form of pseudoexplanation essentially involving saying that an item of simple action is caused by a class of action; and (4) respond to "it" in terms of this nonexplanatory explanation, initiating problem-solving behavior that "may serve to escalate a mere case of natural unhappiness into the experience of 'clinical depression'" (pp. 33–34). Keeney thus proposes this function for clinical epistemology: "Clinical epistemology examines how human dilemmas are created and perpetuated by these epistemological knots" (p. 34). Keeney's proposal for a clinical epistemology is a proposal for a field that would examine "patterns within social contexts that organize the recursive, vicious cycles [sic] surrounding symptomatic experience" including, in particular, "the confounding of different recursive orders" that occurs through semantic confusion between what something is and what the therapist or client says it is (pp. 34–35).

Let us return to our discussion of the effects on perception and action in psychotherapy, of shifts in the therapist's epistemological presuppositions. Throughout the behavioral sciences, and above all in the psychotherapy field, there is to be found a vast and most extraordinary array of sharply contrasting and frequently conflicting presuppositions forming the basis of how clinicians know, think, decide, and act when dealing with psychotherapeutic problems. Many of these presuppositions have become part of our culture, and many are held by clients and are clearly presupposed by the statements they make in therapy interviews. To reiterate what we have said earlier, neither the therapist nor the client can *not* operate from certain epistemological presuppositions, and these presuppositions will influence their views on how to find out about the situation, what the situation is, whether anything can be done to resolve the situation, what needs to be done to resolve it, how to go about that, how long it's expected to take, and how they will know they are done.

It seems to us that there is a need for a clinical discipline devoted to (1) identifying the client's and therapist's epistemological presuppositions; (2) discerning the effect on thought and action of holding those presuppositions; and (3) deliberately bringing about a shift in those presuppositions in order to further therapeutic outcomes. At the present time, epistemological confusion and clinical uncertainty reign in the psychotherapy field. At such a time, and at a time when so many of psychotherapy's most cherished presuppositions have been challenged, giving rise to new forms of therapy that have in turn produced results challenging still other cherished presuppositions, such as discipline seems clearly called for.

CLINICAL EPISTEMOLOGY: SHIFTING PRESUPPOSITIONS AND EFFECTIVE CLINICAL PRACTICE

Knowledge is produced in response to questions. And new knowledge results from the asking of new questions; quite often new questions about old questions.—Neil Postman and Charles Weingartner

There is something fascinating about science. One gets such a wholesale return of conjecture out of such trifling investments of fact.—Mark Twain

A cartoon poster shows a starry-eyed elephant looking fondly, if somewhat disappointedly, at a mouse that has arrived to court her. The elephant is saying, "You are the answer to all my prayers. Uh . . . , you're not what I prayed for exactly, . . . but I guess you're the answer." This book is our answer to a call for clinical epistemology. Intrigued by Rabkin's proposed new term, and spurred on by excitement over the earlier papers of Dell and Keeney (the later ones had not yet appeared), we set to work constructing a clinical epistemology, drawing largely on our attempts—already well under way—to synthesize a new way of looking at the therapeutic process. This new approach made what had seemed (to our older way of thinking) our rather unexpected therapeutic results appear, on the contrary, to be natural, understandable, and expectable. This book attempts to lay down the foundations for a new field of clinical epistemology. Although it may (or may not) have turned out to be very different from what Rabkin, Dell, Keeney, and others had in mind when calling for it, this book is, for all that, our answer.

The substance of this book constitutes our "long answer" to the question, "how do you define 'clinical epistemology'?" The "short answer," however, might be given as follows:

> Clinical epistemology is the conceptual analysis of the effect on psychotherapeutic practice and outcome of shifts in a therapist's presuppositions about the nature of human beings, the human mind, human difficulties, and the resolution of those difficulties. The clinical application of this conceptual analysis involves bringing about therapeutic resolutions of difficulties by altering a client's presuppositions, either directly or indirectly, thereby creating a context for effective psychotherapy. Thus, in applying clinical epistemology to therapeutic practice, we examine and challenge both therapists' (i.e., our own) and our clients' implicit beliefs and unexamined assumptions and conclusions about their "problems," about what (if anything) caused them, and about what will resolve them.

Clinical epistemology, as a field of study and as a clinical approach, is thus designed to be a double-edged sword. For clinical epistemology is both (1) a kind of descriptive epistemology of clinical psychotherapy, mapping out the relationship between a therapist's epistemological presuppositions on the one hand, and therapeutic practice and outcome on the other hand; and (2) a clinical application of this conceptual analysis, in which the therapist applies a parallel procedure to the therapeutic negotiation of psychotherapeutic problems, bringing about shifts in a client's epistemological presuppositions in order to facilitate the client's reaching her desired therapeutic outcome. The results of this clinical application of the approach, in turn, influence the therapist's own epistemological presuppositions, leading to shifts in his practice. This, in turn, influences the way in which the therapist examines and challenges the client's presuppositions, resulting in different outcomes again. At still another level of recursion, the therapist's observations of the effect, on practice and outcome, of shifts in the therapist's own presuppositions can contribute to the further honing of the descriptive/conceptual edge of clinical epistemology as a discipline.

As an essentially clinical rather than an academic discipline, clinical epistemology is intended not as an evolving body of theory or research, but as an evolving set of practical, clinical procedures, though what is perhaps most distinctive about clinical epistemology is that it *reveals* the way in which theory, practice, and research are inextricably intertwined. As de Shazer writes in a closely related connection (1982b, p. 71), "From this perspective, these activities are seen as intertwined in such a way that the traditional linear progression from theory to research to practice is reconceived as but three faces of the same 'thing.'" And as Keeney remarks (in his foreword to de Shazer, 1982a, p. viii), these "three faces are recursively intertwined."

This book attempts to map out the essential concepts and procedures of clinical epistemology as we presently conceive them. Since we began conducting training courses in clinical epistemology, separately and together, in 1982, our own understanding and practice of clinical epistemology have evolved considerably. In teaching this material and attempting to persuade our students and trainees to shift their own presuppositions in order to achieve similar results with their clients, our own ways of presenting this material have changed in response to our students' questions, comments, challenges, understandings, and misunderstandings. We have been sensitive to our successes and failures in enabling trainees to apply clinical epistemology in their own practice. As our ways of teaching clinical epistemology evolved, so our ways of conceptualizing and writing about it evolved. The new ways of conceptualizing refined our practice, led to further descriptive generalizations for our teaching, and so on. The process, needless to say, is still going on.

In addition to providing what we believe to be the essential conceptual and clinical tools for the practice of clinical epistemology, we tentatively offer, in Chapter Seven, a variety of more specific practical approaches (and "techniques") that we have so far found useful as working methods. These are confined to a separate and (in our view) less essential chapter, as these working methods are heavily influenced by our backgrounds and training, and seem much more subject to revision than the basic principles that are discussed in the other chapters.

Essentially, what we are presenting is a set of approaches for achieving therapeutic results through a process of teasing out and challenging epistemological presuppositions, a process we conceptualize as a process of negotiation (mapped out schematically in Chapter Four). Both the therapist's and the client's epistemological presuppositions are reflected in their language and actions. Their language and actions give clues about the unstated assumptions without which neither their language nor their actions make sense. The process of negotiation that we describe throughout this book is a means of teasing out and altering those unstated assumptions.

The different schools and theories of psychotherapy vary greatly in their epistemological presuppositions, though a number of widely divergent therapeutic approaches share many presuppositions in common. Everything the therapist does in an attempt to reach the client's desired outcome rests ultimately on these assumptions. Yet there is something exceedingly curious about these presuppositions. In the first place, there is the most widespread disagreement among psychotherapists about the validity of these assumptions. For almost every assumption, there is some therapist, somewhere, who does not hold that assumption; and for each and every one among the vast majority of these assumptions, there are *large numbers* of therapists who consider it invalid. In the second place, one is hard put to find a single one of these assumptions that rests upon any empirical evidence whatsoever. *They are merely assumptions.* The main apparent exception would be the behavior therapies, whose more explicit assumptions come from a body of theory indeed supported by experimental evidence. However, the theory and experimental methods themselves rest on a number of epistemological presuppositions, which also underlie the explicit assumptions of the behavior therapies; these presuppositions are themselves merely assumptions that cannot be justified empirically. Of course, this is also the situation in the natural sciences, nor could it be otherwise, as one must start with *some* unverifiable assumptions. The widespread consensus regarding these assumptions in the natural sciences, however, contrasts sharply with the utter disagreement prevailing in the psychotherapeutic field. And it gets worse: For the most part, throughout the psychotherapeutic literature, there is hardly a single "fact" to be reported anywhere amidst all this theory—at least, a fact that is not presented exclusively through the distorting lens of the epistemological presuppositions peculiar to the particular theory of psychotherapy held by the individual writer.

Clinical epistemology attempts to deal with the underlying assumptions of the psychotherapies in such a way as to get "underneath" current approaches to excavate the foundations on which they rest.

We attempt in this book to provide a clear set of guidelines for teasing out and appraising epistemological presuppositions. In order to be clear about what presuppositions are involved that can be negotiated, it is important to distinguish clearly between those epistemological claims that are more certain and those that are less certain.

The set of standards we propose for separating the epistemologically surer wheat from the epistemologically more negotiable chaff involves a distinction we present in the next chapter between "facts" and "meanings." The facts are what we can all agree on, even while we approach those facts from widely divergent epistemological presuppositions. For despite the divergent presuppositions with which the psychological field in particular is rife, we all seem to share a set of minimal epistemological presuppositions in common (perhaps by virtue of being human beings, or as native speakers of an Indo-European language, or whatever—the question of what the common ground is would be a matter for "experimental epistemologists" and semanticists). This minimal set of presuppositions, however they might be characterized, seems sufficient to enable fairly universal agreement at what we call the level of "video descriptions"—the level of sensory-based observations and sensory-based descriptions. Whatever can be described at this level, we call "facts," and on the facts there can be fairly broad consensus. ("The cat is on the mat" will do, for example, if we can specify "mat" in sensory-based terms we can all agree on, but "The cat is lazy" won't do.) Whatever is not in the realm of "facts" we call "meanings." "Meanings" are negotiable in a way that the "facts" are not, and the negotiation involves drawing out successive layers of presupposition as described throughout this book.

Our epistemological principles for appraising the warrantability of claims—based on the facts–meanings distinction—thus involve our keeping constant the minimum that needs to be kept constant (what we can all agree on), and allowing the rest to vary. Our own presuppositions, it will gradually become clear, we try to keep to an absolute minimum. One cannot *not* operate from presuppositions, but our own approach is to avoid unnecessarily bringing in presuppositions that would limit what is possible for the therapist or the client.

And so this book, inevitably, also reflects our own epistemology—in particular, our own preferred set of assumptions on which our clinical knowledge in each session ultimately rests. Many of the approaches we present are, of course, recursively bound up with our own set of presuppositions, nor could it be otherwise. We believe that our own set of presuppositions constitutes the optimum set of presuppositions for generating effective psychotherapy. Being clinical epistemologists, we have examined, re-examined, and challenged them ruthlessly, but we may not have been ruthless enough. And when the question of how little "ruth" has been settled, the question of how much truth will remain, and on that we have no copyright. So when and if the discipline we are putting forward evolves further in the hands of other clinicians and thinkers as well as ourselves, perhaps the recursive process cut by the double-edged sword will result in ever greater "fit" between our presuppositions and the real possibilities "out there." For this book is only intended to be a *first* word on clinical epistemology, not the last.

CHAPTER TWO

SIFTING FACTS FROM MEANINGS
The Observation/Description
Frame

The properties commonly ascribed to any object are, in the
last analysis, names for its behavior.—Charles Herrick

NO AGREEMENT ON THE BASICS

The only justification for our concepts and systems of concepts is that they
serve to represent the complex of our experiences; beyond this they have no
legitimacy. I am convinced that the philosophers have had a harmful effect
upon the progress of scientific thinking in removing certain fundamental
concepts from the domain of empiricism, where they are under our control,
to the intangible heights of the *a priori*.—Albert Einstein

Many different models of psychotherapy have been proposed
and employed over the past 100 years or so. In other disciplines—medicine, physics, mathematics, and so on—there may
be considerable disagreement on specific approaches and theories, but there is nevertheless a good deal of basic agreement on
generally accepted data; in other words, there exists in thcsc
disciplines an established body of demonstrated knowledge
that has been accepted by the majority of those working in that
discipline, regardless of their own particular theoretical orientation. By contrast, psychology and psychotherapy have made
little progress toward consensual agreement about the basics.
There is little certainty in psychology and psychotherapy. In
these fields, a book written 100 years ago has nearly the same
chance of being "accurate" as a book written last year. In part,
this lack of a developing consensus has been made possible by
the widespread confusion in psychology and psychotherapy

17

between the facts (the basic data to be accounted for and acted upon) on the one hand, and theoretical constructs, interpretation, conjecture, and often downright metaphysical speculation on the other hand.

Psychology and psychotherapy have so thoroughly intermingled the empirical and the theoretical that it has become virtually impossible to put theory to the test, because it is unclear against what "objective" data a theory could be checked. Most of the theories that abound in psychotherapy, even in the most "scientific" approaches to experimental psychology, rest entirely on the presuppositions that dictate what are to count as data, and what the data can be taken to be data for. The "data" of even the most austerely behaviorial approaches can be seen, on inspection, to consist not of observables, but of observations interpreted through a very particular and often rather dubious theoretical lens. One can observe a dog salivating, for example, but one cannot observe a "conditioned response," however clearly the latter may be "operationally defined" (cf. Colapinto, 1979). In the absence of methodologically valid attempts at empirical verification, one theory is about as good as another. In psychotherapy, the choice between one theory and another, like the choice between one sort of theory and another, essentially boils down in the end to a matter of taste (cf. Colapinto, 1979).

We want to bring a greater degree of certainty into psychotherapeutic work, and to make the rational, critical discussion of therapeutic work possible. What we propose is an assiduous attempt to distinguish clearly between what is in the realm of verifiable fact and what is not, and to use descriptions of what is observable and verifiable as the basic data for assessment and intervention. Almost all other approaches to psychotherapy, including behavior modification, go far beyond such descriptions; they make attributions of cause or meaning, and blur the distinction between what is observable, on the one hand, and what is imposed on the data by the observer through adherence to a particular theoretical framework, on the other hand. Therapists of all schools tend to speak about their own rather parochial abstractions as if they were speaking about observables. The behavioral therapists and theorists have attempted to bring certainty into clinical work by gathering "baseline" descriptive data and monitoring observable changes from those data, but they remain wedded to a theoretical base that soon heaps a greater load of attributed theoretical significance upon the backs of these observations than the observations will bear. The theoretical constructs of the behaviorists may seem, aesthetically speaking, relatively dry and clinical compared to the more colorful and elaborate interpretations of the "psychodynamic" theorists and practitioners, but they are no less in the realm of theory for all that, and are equally full of unverifiable speculation.

GETTING THE FACTS

What is in the realm of experience we may positively know. What is not capable of experience must remain in the realm of speculation.—A. P. Gouthey

In general, when we speak of "the facts" in this book, we shall be using the term "the facts" in such a way that it would *not* be redundant to speak of "true facts." When we speak of confining oneself to "the facts," we mean "factual statements," which may or may not turn out to be "true statements." A factual statement is one that is expressed in a form that makes it susceptible to verification through checking against sensory observations "in certain obvious ways (looking, listening, touching, counting, etc.) and therefore may turn out on inspection to be false" (Postman, 1976, p. 204). A factual statement is simply one that is confined to description of observable events (or events that at least once were observable) and is (or at least once was) susceptible to verification (Postman, 1976). "The cat is on the mat" is thus a factual statement even if it isn't true (i.e., even if the cat is not on the mat), and the statement "The Empire State Building is 27 miles high" is factual in our sense, even though it is false. The point is that it would be possible (or would at one time have been possible), at least in principle, to find out, through sensory verification, whether it is true or false. As Postman points out (1976, p. 204), the phrase "He is tall" does not count as a fact in this sense, since "tallness" is a relative term and hence cannot be verified unless explicit criteria are first supplied.

In gathering information in therapy, "Johnny then threw a temper tantrum" would not be a factual statement, as there is no indication of what on earth a temper tamtrum might be; the term does not refer to observables as such. However, "Johnny then stamped his foot on the floor five times and screamed for 2 minutes" would be much more safely back in the realm of "the facts." Even if the mother who reported this "fact" were mistaken, and Johnny actually at that point went up to his room and played with his toys (and it was on another occasion that Johnny had performed the behavior described), the statement is more clearly in the realm of the observable and verifiable than the statement about a "temper tantrum." While the therapist will want to ensure, as far as possible, that the statements are accurate, the first order of business is to obtain factual statements that could in principle be determined, or could once have been determined, to be accurate or not.

As a rule of thumb, facts can be thought of as "video descriptions"—descriptive statements based on observation, which neither contain nor presuppose any information that could not in principle be derived without interpretation from a video with a soundtrack. In short, "facts" are statements that do not go beyond what could be picked up on a video with sound. In our "getting the facts," as in a court of law, any "conclusionary statements" are ruled out of court. For example, a video camera cannot "see" somebody kill somebody; at most it can record, for example, one person pointing a gun in the direction of another person, a loud report, some red substance trickling from the shirt of the second person, smoke curling upward from the barrel of the gun, and so on. "Video descriptions" are thus observational statements that are (as nearly as possible) purely and objectively descriptive, including only those descriptive features that are objectively indisputable by anyone, irrespective of the particular presuppositions and interpretations one may bring to those observations. We assume, of course, sincerity and candor on the part of the hypothetical observers. The facts are thus neutral descriptions, in the sense that they are descriptions we can all agree on.

"Getting the facts" is the touchstone that we use to initially assess the presenting complaint in therapy and to monitor the results of our interventions. (There is some disagreement in the field as to what constitutes successful results in therapy, but, as will be seen, we judge results solely on whether or not the client has achieved the outcome requested or desired. In our approach, the outcome is, in turn, judged according to behavior observed, or else reported in the form of video descriptions.) In "getting the facts," it is as if we had a colander with specially shaped holes that allowed all interpretations, attributions, characterizations, predictions, evaluations, presuppositions, hypotheses, and so forth, to slip through, and that retained only the "hard" facts. Or, to change the metaphor, the process is a kind of distilling process or filtering process in which we filter out or distill out all the impurities (presuppositions, interpretations, etc.) and leave only a clear filtrate or distillate of facts that are "pure" facts in our sense.

NEGOTIABLE AND NONNEGOTIABLE REALMS

Now we are not saying (as some behaviorists do) that one should ignore the "meanings"—that is, "all the other stuff" the client attaches to the facts—but that the facts and meanings should be clearly distinguished. The facts of the matter, if they are indeed accurate, are not negotiable: They are what is happening or has happened. Some of these facts can be changed through the client's actions, but none can be put to rights merely by discussing them. The meanings, on the other hand (both those of the client and those of the therapist), are negotiable, and this is why it is so important that they be sifted from the facts.

"There's no getting 'round the facts," but what the client makes of these facts is something else again. The constructions the client places on those facts are very negotiable indeed; in this negotiable realm of meanings, the therapist can begin to intervene by means of the information-gathering process in the therapeutic session. It is essential, therefore, that the therapist distinguish (for herself) nonnegotiable fact from negotiable meaning—most importantly, the unspoken presuppositions about those facts that limit the client (and potentially the therapist) unnecessarily. If the therapist wittingly or unwittingly takes on board the client's presuppositions, which is particularly easy to do if the therapist already happens to hold those same presuppositions, the therapist is restricting both herself and the client. If too many presuppositions are taken on board, the therapeutic ship is sunk. With the aid of the "getting-the-facts" frame, the therapist leaves her own and her client's options as open as possible. In our view, not only does failing to distinguish between the negotiable and the nonnegotiable realms make for severe restrictions on what is possible for the client, but it is the source of much uncertainty and, frankly, downright foolishness in psychotherapy.

In simple terms, we are saying that there are two major aspects to the presenting complaint: the "doing" and the "viewing" of the difficulty—in other words, the actual performance of the difficulty and the interpretations the client and therapist make about it (i.e., how they talk about it). In the approach to psychotherapy we are presenting, the "doing" is to be *ascertained* by the assessment process of gathering the facts, and the "viewing" is to be *altered* through the interaction between therapist and client from the very moment the therapeutic encounter begins. The "doing," once again, is not very negotiable (i.e., while the client is sitting in the therapist's office, there is not much that will change about the actual performance of the difficulty), but the highly negotiable "viewing" of the difficulty will be determined by the nature of the interaction between therapist and client right there in the office.

We return to this matter in considerable detail in Chapters Four and Five. In the meantime, let us just point out that a large part of the altering of the viewing of the difficulty comes about through the "mere" process of the therapist's separating the facts from the interpretations in the client's reporting of the presenting complaint and/or subsequent reporting of the situation in further sessions.[1] As Postman and Weingartner (1969) write, " . . . Korzybski's concern with keeping conscious 'connection' or correspondence between language and verifiable

---

1. It is to this aspect of the therapeutic process that Postman and Weingartner (1969) refer when they make use of the distinction between "denotation" or (Korzybski's) "extensional meaning" (referring to observable processes occurring "outside" our skins) and "connotation" or "intensional meaning" (referring to processes occurring "inside" our skins) (Postman, 1976, p. 215), a distinction corresponding (in some ways) to our distinction between "facts" and "meanings." Note that Postman and Weingartner point out that "with increasingly abstract or general words (i.e.

referents is, for all practical purposes, paralleled by the process of psychotherapy. In this process, which is largely 'just talk,' the purpose is to foster closer and more accurate correspondence between the patient's language and externally verifiable meanings . . . '' (p. 108). We should add that in our own view, as will become apparent, psychotherapy is aimed at much more than this, but we cannot overstate the therapeutic importance of assisting the client to sift the facts from the meanings attributed to those facts.

HANDLING SUBJECTIVE EXPERIENCE

After all, it is not possible to talk about "the mind" in terms other than metaphorical.—Neil Postman and Charles Weingartner

It seems that I am pointing out to myself what I am feeling, as though my act of concentration was an "inward" act of pointing, one which no one else but me is aware of, this however is unimportant. But I don't point to the feeling by attending to it. Rather, attending to the feeling means producing or modifying it. (On the other hand, observing a chair does not mean producing or modifying a chair.)—Ludwig Wittgenstein, The Brown Book

The point is well made in the story of the three umpires. The first umpire, being a man of small knowledge of how meanings are made, says, "I calls 'em as they are." The second umpire, knowing something about human perception and its limitations, says, "I calls 'em as I sees 'em." The third umpire, having studied at Cambridge with Wittgenstein himself, says, "Until I calls 'em, they ain't."—Neil Postman

Experience is not what happens to you, but what you do with what happens to you.—Aldous Huxley

From the beginning, much of the attention, thought, and talk of psychotherapists and their clients has been concerned with the clients' subjective experience. Among all but the most staunch behaviorists, the clients' thoughts, ''feelings,'' internal images,

---

those farther removed from operationally verifiable referents), the direction of meaning shifts accordingly from 'outside' to 'inside.' . . . The primary semantic distinction made in kinds of meaning is between connotation (intensional, subjective, personal meaning) and denotation (extensional, objective, social meaning). . . . As a semanticist would say, the process of psychotherapy is aimed at shifting the patient's word choices from those having highly intensional, connotative meanings to others carrying more denotative meanings'' (p. 108).

and so on have been considered to be matters of some importance for therapy; in most approaches, subjective experience
occupies the center of the clinical stage. Therapists of different
schools have disagreed over what constitutes the royal road to
subjective experience. However, we maintain that, whatever the
route chosen, however long and tortuous, or short and direct,
therapists have only been led up the garden path for all their
wanderings.

In our view, to alter the metaphor slightly, the clinical pursuit of subjective experience has been a blind alley for psychotherapists. It has also been, along with the blurring of the distinction between facts and meanings, the second chief cause of
the uncertainty prevailing in the psychotherapy field and in the
psychotherapy session. The reason for this is twofold. First,
therapists and clients alike have reified subjective experience
and have spoken of it in pseudo-objective terms, as if it could
somehow be "introspected" and described in much the same
way as external events could be observed and described; this
has led to all kinds of imaginary obstacles for clients and therapists. Second, in our view, subjective experience is for the most
part irrelevant to effective psychotherapy.

It is in view of the fundamental irrelevance of the topic to
our discussion that we touch on the topic only very briefly
here. Detailed discussion is more a matter, too, for a book on
the philosophical foundations of (and in particular the epistemology of) psychotherapy, than for a book like the present one
on the effective clinical *practice* of therapy.

The problem is that if someone is asked to describe his
subjective experience, he is being asked to produce a metaphor;
and he cannot describe subjective experience without altering
it in the process, along the lines of the chosen metaphor. Every
hypnotherapist who works with pain knows that if she can get a
patient to describe his pain differently, she will thereby alter his
subjective experience of it and can sometimes thereby eliminate
the pain altogether.

Now what are we including under this rather sweeping
abstraction "subjective experience"? Well, bodily sensations
would certainly be included. Thoughts very probably would
also be included, where these are understood to indicate
"thinkings," not "ideas." For example, "What do you think of

the following thought? We could move the fireplace over there instead," is an instance of offering a suggestion, not of describing a subjective experience. Visual images, perhaps including hallucinations, might be included, but not ideas described in visual terms (i.e., not "I was just picturing how the fireplace would look over there—what do you think?"). Olfactory or gustatory sensations, images, memories, or hallucinations might generally qualify here; auditory hallucinations or memories (e.g., remembering the ringing sound that European telephones make) would probably fit in all right; but statements or avowals of emotion, in our view, would not even come close to "making it" as subjective experience.

EMOTIONS

The question of the epistemological status of the emotions and the place of the emotions in psychotherapy are two major topics to which we do not address ourselves in detail in the present work, but on which one of us (Wilk) has worked extensively (his work will be presented in a separate publication). Although the word "feelings" is used (in English) to apply to emotions, emotion statements are not descriptions of internal sensations, and arguably are not primarily descriptive at all.

What is relevant here is to note that where internal bodily sensations are purportedly associated with the avowed emotion, the "description" of the sensation is rarely free of added attributions of meaning or cause; or presuppositions; or explicit interpretations about the import of the sensation, its "name," and so on. In our process of "getting the facts" in the psychotherapeutic session, we would rule out of court any such statement as "Then I suddenly felt depressed" in favor of a more neutral description or avowal of bodily sensation, such as "Then I suddenly had a sinking sensation here in my chest." Alan Watts has noted, "It seems that if I am afraid, then I am 'stuck' with fear. But in fact I am chained to the fear only so long as I am trying to get away from it . . . When I am aware of this feeling without naming it, without calling it 'fear,' 'bad,' 'negative,' etc., it changes instantly into something else, and life moves freely ahead" (1954, p. 117). Sometimes no particular bodily sensations are involved at all, and the client uses the term "depression" or "fear" to refer to certain behavior or thoughts.

So as a first stage in the distilling process, emotion statements would be distilled down to neutral descriptions or avowals of bodily sensations, free of attributions or presuppositions of meaning, or to reports of thoughts or (our ultimate preference, of course) video descriptions of behavior. Then the statements about bodily sensations or thoughts would themselves be put through our distilling process as we shall describe. The main thing is, on the first distillation, to separate out as much as possible of the attributed meanings—the negotiable "stuff". In this way, we attempt (if we may again change the metaphor) to gradually reduce the nonnegotiable area, which eventually shrinks into a tiny point like the picture on the screen when the television set is turned off. In handling emotion statements in psychotherapy, this first distillation, then, consists in getting emotion statements specified down to particular thoughts, neutral ("meaning"-free) descriptions or avowals of bodily sensations, and video descriptions of behavior.

It remains for us to clarify briefly how we handle thoughts, bodily sensations, and other categories of subjective experience.

SENSATIONS AND IMAGES

Once we have bodily sensations specified down to neutral descriptions or avowals,there is nothing left that is negotiable except the way in which the sensations are described. But this is very negotiable indeed. If we choose to pursue this at all (which is not often), we pick such descriptions apart and get down to finer and finer detail, always questioning the generality of the descriptions ("Is it always a sinking sensation just there, or is it sometimes lower down, or more to one side? Is it like a fairly lightweight object sinking in the air, or like a heavy object sinking at the same rate in a dense, viscous fluid?"). Each time we ask such questions for specifying further, and in ever greater detail, we are not seeking information at all. Rather, we are asking our clients to produce new and different metaphors, and all the time we are altering not only how the subjective experiences are described, but the very experiences themselves. In a 1962 workshop, Milton Erickson used a charming illustration to put this process in a nutshell:

> Whenever you start picking things apart, you destroy them. You destroy their value. A pretty girl is very kissable. Look at that pretty girl and you see she has such a kissable face. But look closer and, of course, her eyes are a little too close together—her ears are a little bit too large—her nose is slightly long—her chin is pretty heavy—that lower lip is really too thick—her mouth is really too wide. Who wants to kiss her once you pick that face apart! You pick a pain apart, you pick gagging apart, you pick nausea apart, you pick fear apart, you pick anxiety apart—all in exactly the same sort of way. (Erickson, in Rossi, Ryan, & Sharp, 1983, p. 118)

All the while, we challenge any attributions of meaning or cause, using absurdity if necessary. ("How does that sinking sensation differ from the sinking sensation you sometimes get with indigestion, or from eating too quickly?") Where we are ultimately leading the clients and ourselves is to the most important question of all: "So what?" A bodily sensation is not, in and of itself, a problem. And so we can get away from the distracting irrelevancies and get down to the facts of the client's "problem," the genuinely "nonnegotiable stuff" that may need to be altered. On the very rare occasions when they come up (rare because we rarely ask questions about them), visual images, olfactory and gustatory experiences, and the like are handled in the same way.

Two of the psychotherapist's most important questions, in our view, are "How do you know?" and "So what?" The former is especially helpful when dealing with negotiable meanings attached to the facts or to sensations; the latter is especially helpful when dealing with (what we have eventually reduced to) neutral descriptions or avowals of sensations—literally "feelings."

It might be emphasized at this point that, during our questioning, we try to avoid giving clients the impression that we are being sarcastic or critical, or that we are not taking their problems seriously.

THOUGHTS

Cognitive therapists and rational–emotive therapists seem to have attached considerable therapeutic importance to "thoughts." Generally, there appears to be a fair measure of agreement among these therapists with Plato's metaphorical assertion that "When the mind is thinking, it is talking to itself." Thinking seems to be regarded by most of these therapists as a kind of "talking to oneself" or "subvocal speech," and this inner dialogue is supposed to be the source of psychological problems and symptoms. We have two chief quarrels with this approach. First, we think that the extent to which people talk to themselves tends to be overestimated; second, the importance of this tends to be vastly overrated. Describing thinking as talking to oneself is clearly a mere metaphor. In our experience, thinking usually goes by too fast and is too difficult to pay heed to for any "transcription" of it to be possible with any degree of accuracy, particularly in retrospect. The "translation" (to use another metaphor) is at best very loose indeed. People certainly do (in our opinion) sometimes soliloquize silently, but just how important is this?

Thoughts do not determine behavior, any more than do sensations. Having a certain thought or a certain sensation per se does not cause one to do anything at all. Clients, of course, often come in believing that thoughts and sensations do have such power. So long as they believe this, it will be, in their experience, just as good as if thoughts and sensations had such power. There will tend to be in the client's experience, then, a fairly habitual if not constant conjunction of the particular thought or sensation and the particular behavior in question. Of course, for any given thought or sensation followed by any given behavior (such as craving a cigarette followed by lighting up a cigarette), it is equally possible to have that sensation or thought and not to do that behavior but to do something else instead. We will return to this matter later.

While clients may come in believing thoughts to be powerful determinants of behavior, therapists would do well to avoid being trapped by this presupposition. Clients can, as far as we're concerned, have any thoughts they darn well please, and this needn't restrict their behavior, nor need it make for any problems in their lives. Where clients are specifically troubled by certain repetitive, "obsessive" thoughts, this can often be eliminated by eliminating the associated problems. Alternatively, therapists might challenge the presupposed but highly negotiable link between thought and behavior (thus making the thoughts a "so what?" matter, and therefore less subjectively "powerful"), or by otherwise getting the clients to stop trying to get rid of the thoughts.

Now, while we regard clients' "talking to themselves" as very unimportant for therapy, we regard their talking to the therapist as of the utmost importance. This is the talk in which we are interested. These are the thoughts (now in the sense of "ideas," if you will) that interest us. We have no clinical interest in any thoughts our clients have had before they come to see us, or in any thoughts they may have afterwards. By and large, we have no interest in any talk they talk to themselves, and certainly where we do deal with such (silently soliloquizing) "talk," we are aware that we are in "metaphor land" and not gathering data on anything. We are interested in the clients' "thoughts" in our offices, by which we mean "what the clients have to say about the matters under discussion," and our interest here is not to gather information as such but to alter the "viewing" of the difficulties. But this is the subject of some later chapters.

PURSUING TRUTH AND RELEVANCE: INTRODUCING DOUBT

True science teaches, above all, to doubt and be ignorant.—Jules Henri Poincaré

And so when a patient comes to me, I have all the doubts. I doubt in the right direction. The patient doubts in the wrong direction.—Milton H. Erickson

The trouble ain't that people are ignorant; it's that they "know" so much that ain't so.—Josh Billings (Henry Wheeler Shaw)

To summarize, what we do pursue are the facts (the nonnegotiable, uninterpreted, potentially verifiable, observationally based descriptions—i.e., video descriptions—of the client's situation), so that these facts can be separated out from the negotiable meanings attributed to those facts by the client. We seek video descriptions that are accurate, for often the client can be mistaken. ("Are you sure?" is another good question, often nearly as important as "How do you know?" and "So what?") In addition, however, to "true facts" (accurate factual statements), we "pursue the truth" in two further ways:

1. $X = X$ *in place of* $X = Y$. We reject the client's negotiable attributed meaning equivalences in favor of acceptable (nonnegotiable) tautologies. Thus we would agree with the client to substitute indisputably valid simple tautologies of the form $X = X$ (e.g., "Five dollars is five dollars," "Reading the paper is reading the paper," and "Love is love") in place of the client's rather dubious equivalences of the form $X = Y$ (e.g., "Five dollars is a lot of money," "His reading the paper was his way of showing he just didn't care," and "Love is never having to say you're sorry").

2. *Covering all possibilities; valid ignorance-claims.* We reject (negotiable) conjectures (assertions without evidence), causal attributions, and predictions in favor of one of two things:

a. *Valid claims of ignorance.* Thus we would elicit the client's admission that she doesn't know or can't be sure what such-and-such means, or what caused it, or what will transpire. We call such admissions "valid claims of ignorance"—valid because we would not accept statements from the client claiming that she does not know things that she logically couldn't *not* know.

b. *Acceptable (nonnegotiable) tautologies in the form of statements covering all possibilities.* We may obtain the client's agreement that, for example, "Either the car will start in the morning or it won't," "He'll go back to school or he won't," "He's given up completely on the marriage or else he hasn't," or "Either the reason he's not going to school is because he's being bullied, or else it's not," in place of the corresponding unequivocal predictions, conjectures, or causal attributions.

Thus, in our "pursuit of the truth" in psychotherapy, we are seeking to end up with, on one side, (1) "the facts"—accurate video descriptions; (2) tautologies (usually of the form "$X = X$" or "P or not-P"); and (3) valid claims of ignorance. On the other side, we have all of the highly negotiable meanings.

To pursue the truth, however, is not quite enough: We must also pursue relevance. For example, it may be true that a client was breast-fed as a baby, but is this relevant? And if so, how? Clients say all kinds of things that are not objectionable except for the fact that they are not relevant. Usually clients take this relevance for granted in ways that make life rather complicated. A classic example was a client who was challenged as to why she thought that sitting at home every evening feeling lonely (because she had few social contacts) would end up in her "having a nervous breakdown." She replied, "Because I've had nervous problems before. You see, several years ago my mother died; then about 3 years later I started having problems sleeping and my GP had to prescribe some sleeping medication." That was it. No other clues. What is the relevance of some sleep problems a few years before to fears of (literally) going crazy with loneliness? And, more extraordinary still, why slip in the information about her mother dying 3 years before the sleep problems, and in the same breath? Clients often volunteer information that they think is relevant, and unless the therapist asks, "Is this relevant?" they may take the therapist's silence (or patient pursuit of the matter) as confirmation of the relevance of the irrelevant. Occasionally a client will offer to fill out her account by recounting some "traumatic" experience from her childhood. If we quickly interrupt her with "Is this relevant?", we often get a response like "Well, I don't really think so, but I thought *you* might think so," accompanied by a sigh of relief when we shrug our shoulders and indicate that we can't be sure, but, on the face of it, we don't see any grounds for supposing a connection.

We believe that therapists and clients often get into countertherapeutic vicious circles by attaching relevance to, and spending time dealing with, issues each believes the other regards as relevant or important, taking as evidence for this the other's apparent willingness to continue this line of discussion. Imagine any two people coming together, each with the agenda of talking about whatever the other person thinks is a relevant and interesting topic of conversation, using conversational cues to guide them. They may spend hours or years talking about matters of no relevance or interest to anyone, just by trying to be "polite." And is this not precisely the situation that arises when a "nondirective" (particularly a "let the patient free-associate'') therapist meets up with a client who doesn't know how to "do" therapy and has no idea (except as derived from popular conceptions of psychiatry) what is relevant to the therapist? Such a client might take the therapist's silence as a sign that he is on the right track and is therefore saying things relevant to the solution of the problem. No wonder, then, that therapy's first effect on the client's handling of his problem is often to get him to give up hope of ever resolving it through some simple action. The simplest problem can, through this vicious circle, soon start to look incredibly complicated.

The way out of this vicious downward spiral of uncertainty and mutually fabricated complexity is through the therapist's pursuit of truth and relevance: going for "facts" (video descriptions), tautologies, and valid claims of ignorance; bracketing-off the "meanings" for further negotiation (see Chapters Four and Five); and freely asking "Are you sure?," "How do you know?," "Is this really relevant?," and "So what?"

One of the therapist's most important tasks in psychotherapy is the introduction of doubt. Clients come in to therapy certain of all kinds of things that "ain't so"; they are full of doubts about what they can do now, or may be capable of doing in the future, or can ever stop doing, or can ever do differently from the way they've always done it. As Erickson has said, they doubt in the wrong direction. One might say that people have the kinds of problems for which they end up going to psychotherapists because they assume things that are terribly limiting—about their lives, about life, about their minds, their husband or wife, their children, their families, their past, their present, their future, the things they want to do, and the things they don't want to do. To top it off, they assume that they need to get themselves "fixed" before they can solve their problems; that is when they decide to seek a therapist's help. And so we sift from the clients' words those little nuggets of fact and start negotiating the rest, introducing doubt all the while. We get the clients doubting in the right direction. We share T. H. Huxley's sentiment of being "too much of a skeptic to believe in the impossibility of anything."

CHAPTER THREE

PSYCHOTHERAPY CHANGES NOTHING
The Bottom Line

Indeed, it often seems absurd to reeducate patients when all that may be needed may be a redirection of their endeavors, rather than a change or a correction of their behavior.— Milton H. Erickson

A picture held us captive. And we could not get outside it, for it lay in our language and language seemed to repeat it to us inexorably.—Ludwig Wittgenstein

The way out is through the door. Why is it that no one will use this method?—Confucius

One of our central contentions in this book is that psychotherapy changes nothing. By this, we mean that even "successful" psychotherapy *does* (in fact) change nothing, *can* (in principle) change nothing, and (for a successful outcome) *need* change nothing.

People often come to us with long-standing serious complaints, experiencing much distress in their lives; during the process of therapy, they find their problems resolved. They then leave to get on with their lives, free of the complaints. Now many people might say that something has changed. Colloquially speaking, this is quite appropriate; yet it is our contention that nothing has really changed. We maintain that psychotherapy has nothing whatsoever to do with changing anything or anyone. When we say that even successful psychotherapy can, does, and need change nothing, we are saying that there is "nothing in the world" that changes as a result of psychotherapy. In "nothing in the world" we include "nothing in the client or his family either."

The picture therapists and clients alike usually have of the "change process" (a picture we ourselves used to hold) is that at some time before therapy there was something in the world (or in the clients themselves or in their families) that at some time after therapy is still in the world, only in a changed state. In other words, something that was around before therapy is still around after therapy, only it is now significantly different in some way.

This is what we deny.

As a man walks along he can suddenly or gradually change his step, but this only means that at some particular point in time he was walking one way and now at some later point in time he is walking in another way. There is not something in the world called "his step," which was in the world at both points in time, only with something different about it. Likewise, a woman can change her serve in tennis as a result of successful instruction, but this simply means that she typically used to serve that way and now typically serves this way, not that there is some mysterious abstract entity in the world (which we call "her serve") that somehow has undergone a transformation between then and now. And again, people can change their styles of cracking eggs or telling jokes without there being some mysterious something in the world called "his style of cracking eggs" or "her style of telling jokes" that has somehow undergone an alteration over time; rather, they simply don't crack 'em the way they used to.

What happens during the process of the interpersonal influence we call psychotherapy—if all goes well—is not that something changes, but rather that the client used to act in certain ways in certain contexts and now acts differently in otherwise similar contexts. (To say that "therefore something must have changed" is to beg the question, and to commit an elementary error in reasoning not unlike that of "the person who, upon being told that the thermometer outside the window read 98 degrees, remarked, 'No wonder it's so hot!'" [Postman, 1976, p. 141].)

"I used to do it that way, now I do it this way." What has changed? Have those "yellings" been transformed or muted if a father used to yell at his kids and now he doesn't? Or perhaps it is his *propensity* to yell that has undergone a change. Were there certain propensities of his in the world that are still in the world now, only in a different condition—such as "inoperative"? Heaven help us. We can posit (i.e., make up) all the "inventities" we like—muted yellings, inoperative propensities, subdued strivings, strengthened egos, and even altered interactional patterns—but the bottom line is that our clients used to do THAT and now they don't, or else they did not use to do THIS and now they do, or else they used to do it THATAWAY and now they do it THISAWAY.

Nothing needs to be changed. Nothing needs to be fixed. Nothing needs to be added. Nothing taken away. Nothing ventured. Nothing gained.

We agree that often our clients may well hold certain views at one point in time and may hold other views at some later time, and they may evaluate something or other one way at one time and evaluate it another way at a later time. We may even agree that we prefer the opinions they put forward and the evaluations they make later to the ones they had proffered earlier, and that the new ones may make a more positive contribution to their lives. But "to change one's mind" is a figure of speech meaning "to hold a different opinion now to the opinion one held earlier," and has nothing to do with a "mind" undergoing a change.

Everything's just fine the way it is. And "if it ain't broke, don't fix it." Nobody needs to be repaired. All the parts are there and in fine working order. They don't even need a different arrangement. This is our starting point in psychotherapy.

THE BOTTOM LINE

Given such a starting point, however surprising, it is perhaps not so surprising, then, that we contend the following: The only way for a client to do something different, or to do what he (already) does differently, is for the client to do something different or to do what he already does differently. That's it. That's the bottom line. (Remember that here we are talking about a way of thinking about therapy, not of *doing* therapy. We probably wouldn't discuss this view with our clients.)

In our seminars, we often remind participants of the obvious—that the only way to do something different is to do something different. Whatever else may happen, the only way for the so-called agoraphobic to go out of the house regularly is for her to go out of the house regularly. That's it. The only way for the physically fit 11-year-old to stop doing bowel movements in his pants is for him to stop doing bowel movements in his pants. That's it—that's the bottom line. And the only way for the smoker to stop smoking is for the smoker to stop sticking one end of the cigarette in his mouth, or to stop setting fire to the other end, or to stop inhaling through it. That's all. And, yes, the only way for the heroin addict to stop shooting up is to stop shooting up. And so on. One of our trainees had an 82-year-old client who expressed this point rather succinctly: "If the floor is dirty, it has to be washed." And it won't get washed until somebody washes it.

This is not, in our view, a trivial point. Neither is it, to our chagrin, either "common sense" or received opinion. And we appreciate that at this point the reader may well still be skeptical as to the usefulness of this doctrine, and/or its validity, and/or the breadth of its applicability across the range of psychological, emotional, and behavioral complaints with which clients come to psychotherapists for help. But we assert that this principle holds for all such presenting complaints, and not only for those of a more obviously behavioral nature. We attempt later on to show how this is so.

NAIVE PSYCHOLOGY: NO CAUSE FOR CHANGE

Upon the whole, I am inclined to think that the far greater part, if not all, of those difficulties which have hitherto amused philosophers, and blocked up the way to knowledge, are entirely owing to ourselves—that we have first raised a dust and then complain we cannot see.—George Berkeley

We have noticed a pervasive notion in the field of psychotherapy—that a person must change in some way in order to behave differently. This is the picture of alteration over time that we discussed earlier. You might call it a picture of therapy as involving the person in a "state change," like that of water becoming steam. This picture involves a view of human beings in which an individual is seen as having (1) a "real" nature[1] (2) that is revealed more or less, sooner or later, actually or potentially to oneself or others,[2] (3) and that can be (and can sometimes be revealed to be) damaged or otherwise imperfect[3]; (4) it may therefore give rise to problems,[4] and (5) it needs to change[5] if these problems are to be resolved. This view involves positing (i.e., making up) all kinds of extraordinary "inventi-

1. For example: personality, belief system, system of introjects, unconscious, subconscious, position, character, psychodynamics, identity, repertoire of behavior, response hierarchy, psychopathology, repertory of resources, place in the wider system, set of skills, self, Self, role, mind, neurosis, stage of development, personal history, adaptation to reality, psychosis, ego structure, characteristic ways of relating, psyche, emotional life, set of personal constructs, self-concept, self-image, self-esteem, temperament, set of cognitive structures, attachment, representational system, position on the problem, inner world, motivation, dependence, internal objects, pattern of object relations, autonomy, lack of autonomy, will, degree of individuation, parts, traits, needs, fixation points, anxiety level, developmental forces, state of being, essence, level of awareness, developmental gaps, complexes, conflicts, stress, life script, inadequacy, maladaptive ideation, cognitive organization, defense mechanisms, structure of defenses, repressed material, latent defects, affective structures, pathogenic ideas, identification, and so on and on and on.

2. For example: in behavior, experience, thoughts, communications, dreams, slips, symptoms, relationships, interactions, choice of career or partner, "the transference," family functioning, test scores or responses, diagnostic profiles, and so on.

3. For example: distorted, delayed, regressed, damaged, traumatized, mature or immature, scarred, limited, maladaptive, pathogenic, functional or dysfunctional, blocked, weakened, precocious, rigid, fragmented, retarded, undifferentiated, repressed, neurotic, psychotic, pathological, or what have you.

4. For example: difficulties, problems, conflicts, complaints, symptoms, lack of adjustment, personal unhappiness, psychosomatic or somatic illness, success or failure, troublesome behavior, relationship difficulties, psychopathology, symptomatic acts, criminal acts, depression, anxiety, alienation, confusion, crises, phobias, and so forth.

5. For example: alter, evolve, expand, grow, develop, improve, change, mature; be fixed, repaired, cured, straightened out, healed, redirected, reformed, rebuilt, strengthened, differentiated, redefined, transcended, neutralized, enhanced, increased or decreased, integrated or reintegrated, raised or lowered, transformed, confronted, synthesized, reconditioned, reorganized, reconsidered, re-educated, and so on.

ties," and is contrasted with what we call "naive psychology."[6]

Naive psychology is a view of human beings in which people are seen as doing some things and not doing other things, as using their skills or not, as knowing some things and not knowing other things, as seeing things one way or seeing them another way, and as dealing with life's difficulties more or less successfully or not. Naive psychology is naive enough to suppose that if one wants to know people's "real" reasons for doing something, the best thing is to ask them (though they may not tell you or may not recall), and that people don't necessarily have a reason for everything they do. Naive psychology is also naive enough to suppose that the metaphors of "developing" and "maturing" are inappropriately applied to human beings except in the physical sense, or (occasionally) in a very colloquial sense. In other words, from the standpoint of naive psychology, "psychological development" is a fiction.[7]

Only if we actually believe literally in the "inventities" of most of recent psychology and psychotherapy can we make sense of the question, "What is it that has changed?" when someone has achieved a successful outcome in psychotherapy. If, however, we don't happen to take seriously any of the current "inventities" of psychology and psychotherapy (ego structure, superego, developmental gaps, response hierarchy, contingencies of reinforcement, self-image, etc.), we are hard pressed to say what is any different now from the way "it" was before. All we can say is that the person used to do such-and-such and had a lot of difficulty in her life; now she doesn't do that any more, but does this instead, and her life goes a lot better. Does anything need to be different about her for her to do something else, apart from the fact that now she does something she didn't used to do? If a person is experiencing difficulties in his life (including what would be termed "psychological

6. David Calof suggested the term "naive psychology" in a discussion in December 1983. We have since heard that the term is used, albeit in a different sense, in social psychology.

7. Peirce's doctrine of "contrite fallibilism" (his answer to Freud's "psychopathology of everyday life")—namely, that people are fallible (capable of simply making mistakes), and that the most one can do afterwards is to be contrite about them—is certainly compatible with naive psychology.

symptoms"), what reason have we to believe that there must be a cause for the problematic behavior, let alone that this cause must be dealt with before the person can do something different? Or what reason have we to believe that there must at least be some reason behind the problematic behavior, or some function that it serves? We assert that if a person is, for example, a "chain-smoker," the "reason" or "cause" for this is that he lights up one cigarette just as soon as he has finished the last. The same holds true of "thumbsuckers" (reason or cause: they suck their thumbs a lot), "nailbiters" (they bite their nails), "bingers" (they keep on bingeing on food), "anorexics" (they don't eat), "alcoholics" (they drink more alcohol than they or other people think they ought to), "agoraphobics" (they don't go out), and so on.[8]

People, we find, do things that don't work. And they go on doing them. They have all sorts of excuses, reasons, explanations, attributed causes, and all sorts of funny ideas about why they don't just do something different. They are nonetheless perfectly capable of doing something different without any help from us. And, when psychotherapy is successful, that's just what they go out and do. And they are pleased with how much better their life goes once they do. And the funny thing is, they then don't have their "problem" any more. And nothing has changed.

"A picture held us captive"—the picture of the therapeutic process as the bringing about of some mysterious change in some equally mysterious aspect of a person, so that she might now do what she needs to do to solve her problem. This picture resembles the client's initial complaint that she can't do such-and-such "because" or "until." The more awesome the "inventity" in question, and the more monumental the corresponding task involved in changing it, the longer therapy will take. But if psychotherapy is seen as not involving changing anyone or anything, but as getting the client to see her way to doing what

8. To our knowledge, the only leading psychotherapist to base his psychotherapy on naive psychology (though few of his commentators have fully appreciated this) was Milton Erickson. Erickson himself drew attention to this point in a number of places, stating, for example, that "all of what I do boils down to simple commonsense psychology" (in Beahrs, 1982, p. 64).

needs to be done to solve the problem, and if the therapist does not interpolate any theoretical obstacles between the client and the client's goal, the client can reach that goal very rapidly indeed. Closely related to this picture (of therapeutic outcomes being reached if and only if something changes) is the picture of the role of "causes" in the mental life of human beings. In his classic paper, "A Plea for Excuses," philosopher J. L. Austin (1957) made the following remarks about the lingering, limiting "pictures" of how things happen, which are wrapped up in our notion of "cause," for example:

> "Causing," I suppose, was a notion taken from a man's own experience of doing simple actions, and by primitive man every event was construed in terms of this model: every event has a cause, that is, every event is an action done by somebody—if not by a man, than by a quasi-man, a spirit. When, later, events which are *not* actions are realized to be such, we still say that they must be "caused," and the word snares us: we are struggling to ascribe to it a new, unanthropomorphic meaning, yet constantly, in searching for its analysis, we unearth and incorporate the lineaments of the ancient model. . . . Examining such a word historically, we may well find that it has been extended to cases that have by now too tenuous a relation to the model case, that it is a source of confusion and superstition. (pp. 202–203)

And as Austin notes earlier in this same discussion:

> Going back into the history of a word, very often into Latin, we come back pretty commonly to pictures or models of how things happen or are done. These models may be fairly sophisticated and recent, as is perhaps the case with "motive" or "impulse," but one of the commonest and most primitive types of model is one which is apt to baffle us through its very naturalness and simplicity. We take some very simple action, like shoving a stone, usually as done by and viewed by oneself, and use this with the features distinguishable in it as our model in terms of which to talk about other actions and events: and we continue to do so, scarcely realizing it, even when these other actions are pretty remote and perhaps much more interesting to us in their own right than the acts originally used in constructing the model ever were, and even when the model is really distorting the facts rather than helping us to observe them. In primitive cases we may get to see clearly the differences between, say, "results," "effects" and "consequences," and yet discover that these dif-

ferences are no longer clear, and the terms themselves are no longer of real service to us, in the more complicated cases where we had been bandying them about most freely. (pp. 202–203)

Then, too, in a similar way, we suppose that, surely, "something needs to 'change,'" and this word snares us as well. There is nothing necessarily wrong with using the *word* "change," so long as we do not attach to it the old picture, the old model that can make psychotherapy such a laborious business. Approaches to psychotherapy that are epistemologically unsound, of course, can and do produce beneficial results at times. We are pointing toward making therapy more effective and not such a laborious or time-consuming process.

BENEVOLENT SKEPTICISM: BEGINNING AT THE END

Now your patients come to you and tell you their problems. But do they tell you their problems or do they tell you what they *think* are problems? And are they only problems because they *think* that the things are problems?—Milton H. Erickson

The method of invention, as Edgar Poe demonstrated in his "Philosophy of Composition," is simply to begin with the solution of the problem or with the effect intended. Then one backtracks, step by step, to the point from which one must begin in order to reach that solution or effect.—Marshall McLuhan

What we call the beginning is often the end
And to make an end is to make a beginning.
The end is where we start from.

—T. S. Eliot

In our approach to our clients, we add to the usual (in our view necessary but by no means sufficient) blend of "empathy, warmth, genuineness, and unconditional positive regard," a fair measure of another, more important, ingredient—which we might call "benevolent skepticism." Our attitude, though rarely expressed overtly in such bald terms, is one of "You've got to convince me you've got a problem." Given our starting point (nothing needs to be changed, everything's in order, our client needs simply to do something different or differently), and given the bottom line in such matters (the only way for someone to do something different is for her to do something different), naturally we are bound to be puzzled about this particular person's appearance in our office seeking help with a particular matter. How can we help? That is (in the privacy of our own minds) the question. What help is needed? "If you don't want to do that, then, for cryin' out loud, DON'T DO THAT!" That's the bottom line.

And so we begin at the end. Since we are unburdened by any of the claims of current psychology and psychotherapy, we begin with our own "naive" presupposition (again, in the privacy of our own minds) that there isn't anything preventing clients from going out and solving their problems right now; they merely think there is. So we ask, once we can see what simple action needs to be taken by the client, "Well, why not just do *this*?" And then we get the objections, and we work backwards from there. In so doing, we are involving ourselves in a process of negotiation in which we gradually disabuse clients of the self-imposed limitations that otherwise keep them and ourselves not prisoners of fate, as Franklin D. Roosevelt once said, but only prisoners of our own minds.

We understand that the person in our office is experiencing distress in his life and wishes to get on with his life without such distress, without the limitations or restrictions he believes he 'has', and we accept his request for our help. But as to the need for any help to reach his goals, or as to the question of whether he has got a problem as such—here we are (lovingly, compassionately, benevolently) skeptical. You've got to convince me you've got a problem. Ours is an attitude that says, "You've got to convince me that what you're after is not already well within your reach and, potentially, imminently, eminently within your grasp."

CHAPTER FOUR

TALKING THERAPY
Language Limits

Effective results in psychotherapy . . . derive only from the patient's activities. The therapist merely stimulates the patient into activity, often not knowing what that activity may be, and then he guides the patient and exercises clinical judgement in determining the amount of work to be done to achieve the desired results.—Milton H. Erickson

What we think, or what we know, or what we believe is, in the end, of little consequence. The only consequence is what we do.—John Ruskin

[We] are all somewhat in love with our ways of talking about the world, whatever deformities such talk might have, and it takes some doing to convince any of us that our favorite sentences often betray our best interests.—Neil Postman

According to the old joke, anyone who chooses to consult a psychiatrist ought to have his head examined. Our discussion thus far leads us to propose an updated version: "Anyone who chooses to consult a psychotherapist ought to do something different."

A person consults a psychotherapist in order to resolve the "problem" with which he comes in. But what does this mean? He is in some way dissatisfied with his life as it is, either because there is something he does in his life that he doesn't want to do, or something he doesn't do that he would like to do, or something he does but would like to do differently. Thus, in a sense, the client is in the therapist's office because he wants to do something different or differently in his life. This is, we may say, his goal. Now ultimately, the only way to do something different or differently is to do just that—to go out and do something different or differently. And for there to be a successful outcome in psychotherapy, that's exactly what the client will need to do sooner or later. So the therapist's job is to get the client to go out and do something different or differently—to leave the therapist's office and take whatever action is necessary to eliminate the problem.

Psychotherapy, as we see it, is essentially a problem-solving process consisting of verbal negotiation between client and therapist. The two most fundamental items on the table for negotiation are (1) whether there even is a "problem" as such to solve, and (2) how that problem is to be defined. Whatever the client's presenting complaint and whatever the psychotherapist's orientation or approach to conducting the therapeutic interview, the therapist cannot avoid playing a decisive role in determining the outcome of the implicit negotiation of these two issues. The outcome of that negotiation will in turn influence the nature of the ensuing course of therapy, and, ultimately, its outcome. Most importantly, there is not some right answer to the question of whether there is a problem or not, nor (and this may be more obvious) is there a right or wrong way to define the problem, even if it is agreed that a problem exists. For these are matters not for investigation, but for negotiation, and whatever "answers" therapist and client mutually agree upon, they will both be right; the future course of therapy will often "confirm" their rightness.

The grocer and the customer at a Hong Kong vegetable market do not conduct a joint investigation to determine the true price and correct amount of carrots or cabbages to be sold. They negotiate an agreement to proceed on a particular basis (i.e., they make a deal), and the price and the amount are whatever they decide them to be. And so it is in the negotiation between every therapist and every client of whether there is a problem and, if so, how it is to be defined.

The client comes in with a goal, which may or may not at first be explicitly defined, and an implicit or explicit belief that she cannot presently achieve it—that is, a belief to the effect that there is some "problem" about achieving it. In our approach to psychotherapy, no sooner do we "get the facts" of the situation than we propose an action the client can take to reach that goal—an action that is something she can go out and do right now (or we would not propose it in the first place). But when, starting at the end, we begin by saying to the client, "Well, why not just do *this*?", we get various objections, and it is these objections that are the grist for our therapeutic mill. For these objections are the self-imposed limitations that stand (as it were) between the problem and its solution.

In the therapeutic negotiation process, the therapist "removes" the client's self-imposed limitations by negotiating with the client to alter the way the client talks about the "problem" and how to solve it. We have often found that some very simple action on the client's part was all that was needed to eliminate the problem, and that that action was invariably well within the client's capability. Once we start "getting the facts" of the situation and discussing with the client what needs to be done to eliminate the difficulties, it becomes clear that the only thing that makes the situation problematic for the client is the way the client talks about it.

To return to a distinction we introduced earlier, the "doing" of a difficulty can only be altered by the client's leaving the therapist's office and doing something different, and the desired result will be achieved if and only if the therapist can get the client to do that. But, again, all that may be necessary to persuade the client to alter the "doing" of the difficulty may be to alter, in the therapists's office, the "viewing" of the difficulty—that is, to alter how the client talks about the facts of the situation. It is, in our view, not the facts of the situation that are problematic; what is problematic is the client's (and potentially the therapist's) way of talking about those facts.

In the first part of this chapter and in Appendix II, we discuss some of the general ways in which talk can be problematic, and how ways of talking about a problem can prematurely close off possibilities of solving it. Later in this chapter, we attempt to map out the negotiable and nonnegotiable areas of discussion in psychotherapy, and to outline the general procedure for dealing psychotherapeutically with the self-imposed limitations proffered by the client in the course of the session.

PART ONE:
PROBLEMS: IN A MANNER OF SPEAKING

Since the concepts people live by are derived only from perceptions and from language and since the perceptions are received and interpreted only in the light of earlier concepts, man comes pretty close to living in the house that language built.—Russell F. W. Smith

Every language conceals within its structure a vast array of unconscious assumptions about life and the universe, all that you take for granted and everything that seems to make common sense—the long forgotten history of thought itself, still coercing the living to think along the old-established ways.—N. J. Berrill

People make themselves, or are made, "closed" systems for many reasons, most frequently because they are unaware of the extent to which they are languaging systems, and being unaware, lock themselves into predetermined decisions by limiting their language resources.—Neil Postman and Charles Weingartner

It should not be surprising that we consider talk to be of paramount importance in therapy, when one considers that the therapeutic process consists almost entirely of talk. Psychotherapy, whatever else it may be, is "talking therapy," a "talking cure." But talk is not only the therapeutic agent; it is also the patient. If we make metaphoric use of the "medical model" at all in describing the therapeutic process, we could say that what the therapist (with her talk) is "treating" is the client's talk—how the client talks about "the problem."

The presenting complaint does not somehow have an objective existence as a thing in itself, independent of the acts of presenting it and complaining about it to others including (most importantly for therapy) the therapist. It is not as if a client experiences something in his life called "the problem" and then comes in to the therapist's office and reports on it, much as a botanist or zoologist returning from the field might objectively report on some newly discovered species of flora or fauna, or as the client might be able to describe his stereo system, refrigerator, or Jack Russell terrier. Reporting on his terror is not the same kind of thing as reporting on his terrier; both reports may be full of presuppositions and attributions that are not inherently tied in with the bundles of facts, but the presuppositions in his report about his pet dog are not an integral part of the dog in the same way as the presuppositions in his report of his pet fears are very much an integral part of those fears.

There are not certain entities floating around in the universe called "problems" that occasionally come to light and then need to be solved or otherwise dealt with. Something isn't a problem until someone defines it as such and sets about trying to solve it. (And how one defines it will have more than a little to do with how one goes about trying to solve it.) In the same way, an issue isn't a "cause" until someone labels it as such and takes up the banner; a law isn't a law until it's been passed; a piece of paper with a check mark next to "yes" isn't a vote unless a ballot has been called and the piece of paper has gone into the ballot box; and a legal verdict does not exist apart from the process of arriving at it through courtroom procedure. The "therapeutic problem" does not come into being until the therapist and client begin talking together about how to solve "it." Until that point there are certain facts of the client's situation, and the client may set certain goals for herself and not reach them, but there is not yet a therapeutic problem, any more than there is a question until someone poses one.

The client has a goal and does not achieve it—she experiences difficulty achieving it. This factual state of affairs we may call "the difficulty," and this means "the doing of the difficulty," and this doing must be replaced by some different action if the client is no longer to experience difficulty achieving the goal. "The viewing of the difficulty"—how the client, or therapist and client, talk about the "doing of the difficulty" (i.e., the nonachievement of a certain goal)—is "the problem," because there is no problem inherent in the facts, in the "doing." It is not a problem that to get different results, sooner or later the client has to do something different. "The problem" is a purely verbal matter—it is, we may say, an artifact of the discussion between therapist and client. *The therapeutic problem to be worked on does not exist outside the therapist's office*; it is a product of the client's and therapist's talking together. It is created verbally and solved verbally. And how it is formulated will determine how (indeed whether) it will be solved.

PREMATURE CLOSURE

The folly of locking the stable door after the horse has bolted is well known; less well-known but more relevant to psychotherapy is the folly of locking the stable door *before* the horse has bolted, and then roaming the countryside in search of the presumedly "missing" horse (even to the extent of ending up in a therapist's office hoping to find it *there*). Clients' initial formulations of their problems are typically such as to close the door on solving them before they begin. Part of the therapist's job is to negotiate a formulation of a problem that renders it soluble. Again, we can speak of this very "closure" as being "the problem": If the various options available to a client had not been ruled out from the start, the client would not be in a therapist's office complaining of having run out of options.

Clients can introduce premature closure into a situation either behaviorally or verbally. Behaviorally, they can simply fail to take advantage of opportunities that present themselves: Either they restrict their range of behavior by operating within certain unnecessary assumptions, or they simply continue to operate in rigid patterns that do not contain the behavioral options necessary to reach the goal.

> The picture that most readily comes to my mind is that of an experiment conducted many times with minnows and pike. Both species are put in a large fish tank but are kept separate from each other by a glass shield. The pike, being very fond of eating minnows, go for them immediately but, of course, bump into the glass partition. The pike keep trying—five times, ten times, in some cases, many more. Then, they give up. At that point, the glass partition is removed so that the minnows swim freely amidst the pike who are hungrier than ever. What happens next? The pike will not eat the minnows. Pike will even starve to death under such conditions. (Postman, 1976, pp. 103–104).

Another metaphorical illustration of behavioral closure is the children's game of "Blind Men's Obstacle Race," in which the children are lined up at one end of a room and have to race to the other end. Numerous obstacles (chairs, cushions, stools, etc.) are placed across their path, and the children are then blindfolded. On a given signal, the race begins. Unbeknownst to the children, however, all the obstacles have been quietly removed. It is great fun to watch the children groping their way across the room, and then to note their expressions when the blindfolds are removed (Warner, 1984). (Although in both of these examples the closure happens to be introduced by assuming the continued existence of obstacles that once were there but are now no longer relevant, this is merely coincidental; more often, in the case of therapeutic complaints, the obstacles were never there in the first place.) Behavioral closure is more fully discussed in Chapter Eight. But it should be noted here (and with these two examples kept in mind) that behavioral closure, when discussed in the therapy session ("Why not just do this?"), will usually present in the form of verbal closure—the client rules out available behavioral options by the way the situation is described.

In other words, we may, for heuristic purposes, describe the facts of the client's situation in terms of behavioral closure, and simply introduce a behavioral task assignment of some kind that will disrupt the rigid, limiting pattern (see Chapter Eight). But as soon as therapist and client start discussing the behavioral closure and the alternative options that the therapist (but not the client) sees as available, note what happens: Unless the client simply says, "Great idea! Fine! That solves it; how much do I owe you?", the client will be proffering objections that, taken together, can be described as verbal closure—ruling out possibilities through a verbal formulation of the situation. And all of our talk of "sifting facts from meanings attributed to those facts" is simply talk about alternative ways of talking, sifting forms of language that are less negotiable from forms that are more negotiable, and negotiating ways of talking more suited to effective action.

THE ALL-PERVASIVENESS OF METAPHOR

Numerous writers, including, most recently, Postman (1976) and Lakoff and Johnson (1980), have argued that, in a certain sense, all language is metaphorical, and often in the subtlest ways. Postman, for example, draws attention to the way in which simple verbs such as "is," "has," and "does" "are in fact powerful metaphors which express some of our most fundamental conceptions of the way things are" (1976, p. 123). As he points out, our beliefs that there are certain things that people "have," other things that people "do," and still other things that they "are" reflect the structure not of reality, but of traditional ways of talking. Lakoff and Johnson's essay provides a panoramic survey of the variety of metaphors that make up our language, a guided tour that could profitably be undertaken by every would-be psychotherapist.

The way in which this feature of language can bring about a powerful kind of verbal closure is that every metaphor breaks down *somewhere*; otherwise, the form of speech would not be metaphorical but literal. Therefore there are always more possibilities than are allowed for in the metaphor. To describe one thing in terms of another is all very well, but limits our thinking to the range of possibilities inherent in the imported model, the chosen metaphor, as Austin discusses in the passage quoted in Chapter Three. If the metaphor is not perceived to be a mere metaphor, it may be used to provide a pseudoexplanation. Consider Lakoff and Johnson's example (1980, pp. 28–29): The metaphorical frame "The mind is a brittle object" can give rise to such phrases as "Her ego is very fragile," "You have to handle him with care since his wife's death," "She is easily crushed," "He broke under cross-examination," "The experience shattered him," "I'm going to pieces," and "His mind snapped." Such figurative expressions are fine so long as they are recognized as such and are not taken to be "self-evident, direct descriptions of mental phenomena" (p. 28), as they often are, in which case they can limit our choice of responses unnecessarily (as in the first three examples above) or can serve as pseudoexplanations (as in the last four examples). As Lakoff and Johnson point out, "He cracked under pressure" has actually been employed by journalists (and one should add, by nonjournalists) as an explanatory account of why, for example, a city supervisor went armed to the San Francisco city hall and shot and killed the mayor.

The metaphor of issues or questions having sides, as in "Let's consider both sides of this question," arbitrarily limits us to mutually exclusive alternatives. Even if we say "There are many sides to this issue," we are still confining ourselves to either–or thinking, because "even if you conceive of an issue as octagonal, there is the implication that for every side there is its opposite, that if this is true, then that cannot be" (Postman, 1976, p. 201).

The metaphor of emotions as entities or as feelings may have many unfortunate consequences, of which perhaps the clearest illustration is the example of the metaphor of anger as boiling water and steam, as in a pressure cooker ("He was starting to simmer with anger," "She was rapidly reaching boiling point," "I was getting all steamed up," "I was ready to explode," etc.). Adhering to this metaphor, many people actually believe that if they don't get their anger out ("express" it), it will somehow build up inside them, with possibly dangerous consequences to themselves or others. Thus they "express" their anger, and often find that the more they express the more there is to express; this "confirms" for them just how much anger they had had dammed up inside needing to be released. And they go on trying to get rid of their anger by expressing it as often as they can, whereas the (formal and informal) empirical evidence seems to suggest that often the more people speak and act angrily, the angrier they feel. This evidence suggests a metaphor of anger as something produced rather than released by the process of expression (cf. also Tavris, 1982).

Still other difficulties arise in still other ways, such as when different people in a situation are operating on the basis of different metaphors for the situation. Postman (1976) gives this example: "The doctor who thinks of his profession as a priestly craft will naturally think his 'parishioners' arrogant if they ask too many questions or seek to penetrate the mysteries of his ministrations. The patient who thinks of himself as a 'customer' will naturally think of the doctor as an arrogant businessman who has insufficient respect for those on whom his income is dependent" (pp. 129–130).

We can hardly do justice here to the multifarious ways in which problems are created by the metaphors people use, for the subject is vast. The point, however, is not to avoid using metaphor; this would be nearly as impossible as speaking without using language itself. The point, rather, is this: "The abuse of language occurs when its metaphorical nature is hidden, if the representation is identified with the thing represented. Therefore the linguistically hygienic use of metaphor depends on the full recognition of its limitations, that is, on critical consciousness of the generalizations, analogies and abstractions involved" (Rapoport, 1953)

MIRROR ILLUSIONS: DECEPTIVE CIRCULARITY AND LEAPS IN THE DARK

It is inherent in our intellectual activity that we seek to imprison reality in our description of it. Soon, long before we realize it, it is we who become the prisoners of the description. From that point on, our ideas degenerate into a kind of folklore which we pass on to each other, fondly thinking we are still talking of the reality around us.—Aneurin Bevan

The old idea that words possess magical powers is false; but its falsity is the distortion of a very important truth. Words do have a magical effect—but not in the way that the magicians supposed, and not on the objects they were trying to influence. Words are magical in the way they effect the minds of those who use them. "A mere matter of words," we say contemptuously, forgetting that words have power to mould men's thinking, to canalize their feeling, to direct their willing and acting. Conduct and character are largely determined by the nature of the words we currently use to discuss ourselves and the world around us.—Aldous Huxley

Caught in the Tangled Web of Words

Once we are able to get beyond the naive view of language and clarify the relationship between language and reality (see Appendix II), it becomes all too apparent that, in a sense, we can never quite get out of the tangled web woven by our use and others' use of language. We may begin by speaking about "the facts," in our sense, about things "out there in the world," but sooner or later we end up spending much of our talking time responding to the words used themselves, addressing our remarks more to previous remarks than to the facts those remarks had addressed. We find ourselves in a Korzybskian hall of mirrors, a closed, self-reflexive system in which everything is reflected in everything else. We make remarks about remarks (as opposed to their content). We respond verbally and nonverbally to the form of those remarks; to the choice of words; to the way reality is construed by other persons; to what we interpret the significance to have been of their having chosen to say that to us in those words at this particular time (this interpretation itself being a linguistic process); to their tone of voice; to what we think it means to the nature of the relationship between us that they have made those remarks; to the timing and the circumstances; to the relationship of those remarks to previous remarks that they or we have made; and so on. Our remarks are thus not even always about other people's actual remarks or what we have taken their actual remarks to be, but often about our own idiosyncratic verbal classification of their remarks. And when we consider that other people are responding to our remarks in the same way, and that we take turns remarking about their remarks about our remarks about their remarks and so on, we can begin to have a real sense of this hall of mirrors.

This feature of language, which Postman (1976, pp. 158–166, passim) has called "semantic self-reflexiveness," has many important consequences for our present discussion. We begin with two of the simplest ones: First of all, people often say things they don't mean and "express feelings" they don't feel and never have felt. In the course of saying these things, they may well, as a result, start to feel them; however, this is simply an outcome of the self-reflexive spiral of talk between people. And it is not surprising, given this self-reflexive process, that, secondly, many things we say will turn out to be self-fulfilling prophecies that come true because and only because we have said them. For example, if someone has replied in a controlled but emphatic way to the remark of another person, who then raises her voice and says, "See—I can't say the simplest thing to you without you flying off the handle!" it is not unlikely that the first person will indeed at that point fly off the handle! The well-known phenomenon of the self-fulfilling prophecy is but another consequence of the way in which language "feeds on itself" (Postman, 1976), and it brings out clearly the way in which this self-reflexiveness is itself a consequence of the fact that language constitutes a major part of the environment in which we live and act.

The upshot of all this is, at the very least, that a therapist should take with a pinch of salt the content of the remarks of other people reported by a client, even if the report is in the form of a "video description." The same goes for the content of the client's own previous remarks as revealed in the client's report. It is not just that people get carried away in a self-reflexive spiral and say things they don't mean and later regret having said, but, worse still, that they don't just leave it at that but take their own and other's unconsidered remarks to heart (sometimes as revealing of "true" feelings), and adjust their own behavior and future remarks accordingly. This brings us to another consequence of the self-reflexiveness of language: the ecological principle of nonadditiveness—that "[e]very statement we make is limited and controlled by the context established by previous statements" (Postman, 1976, p. 235), just as "[if you put] a small drop of red ink into a beaker of clear water, you do not end up with a beaker of clear water plus a small drop of red ink. All of the water becomes colored. Telling a psychiatrist at a mental hospital that you hear strange voices works in exactly the same way. It changes the coloration of all the subsequent statements you are likely to make" (Postman, 1976, pp. 234–235). Although we have already made this point in other ways, this particular consequence of semantic self-reflexiveness is something the therapist ought to bear in mind with regard to her own statements, the client's statements, and the client's reports of statements made by the client or others.

Still another consequence of the self-reflexiveness of language, and in particular of the tendency of language to "feed upon itself," is that it is rather easy to bark a long way up entirely wrong trees. This is perhaps one of the more obvious ways in which language can bring about the most insidious kind of verbal closure in the problem-solving process, in that discourse tends to be a kind of a closed shop, allowing in as "relevant" only what is relevant against the background of what has already been admitted into the closed shop of discussion. And the longer discussion goes on in a particular direction, or the more detailed the discussion gets, often the more difficult it becomes to switch course and discuss the matter from a different angle altogether, and the more such a change seems an abrupt break requiring justification. It is like taking a wrong turn in the road: The farther we go, the more "progress" we make in that direction, the farther away we get from where we really want to be heading. Or, if we may change our metaphors, the self-reflexive, circular nature of language means that discussion, left to itself, tends to get bogged down, to get stranded in the shallows and doldrums, until a strong fresh gust of wind comes along to blow the discussion back onto a fresh course. In our view, long-term and even shorter-term psychotherapy often gets bogged down in the shallows and doldrums or makes splendid progress down a very long and winding road leading nowhere.

A particularly common form this takes is the pursuit of technique for technique's sake while forgetting or remaining oblivious to the effects of what the technique was supposed to achieve—what Postman has called "Eichmannism," after the reasonable and brilliantly efficient Nazi bureaucrat who without any personal malice (or, indeed, thought for the consequences) turned his administrative talents to solving the challenging logistical problems of getting millions of Jews to the gas chambers (Postman, 1976, pp. 178–185). Caught in the self-reflexive language process, it is easy to pursue ways and means while forgetting or, more importantly, not questioning the ends. Much thoughtful discussion in psychotherapy is devoted to "working on" something or other that is at best irrelevant to the client's solution of his problem, and at worst tends to reinforce problem-supporting assumptions about what must be done first before the problem can be solved, or sometimes to create new problems the client did not have before therapy.

Finally, one of the most pernicious of all the consequences of the self-reflexive circularity of language, for rational discourse in general and for the problem-solving process in particular, is adherence to a self-confirming and irrefutable closed system of beliefs. The process is one of devoting oneself exclusively to justifying one's beliefs, to seeking and accumulating evidence that they are true, rather than giving at least equal time to critically seeking reasons why one should not believe what one happens to believe. It is easy to build verbal houses of cards in which each card is supported merely by all the others—structures that, however magnificent, have no foundation and can bear no real burden of evidence placed upon them. They are thus incapable of providing support for rational action, and eventually (if challenged appropriately) come toppling down under their own weight or under the force of the gentlest skeptical breeze from outside. The opposite of adherence to a closed system of beliefs is what Postman and Weingartner (1969) have called "crap-detecting"—subjecting our beliefs to constant examination and criticism in the hope of reducing the extent of their error (see also Postman, 1976, p. 106). Many of the grander self-confirming systems or "-isms" have influenced the thought of clients and therapists alike. However, the more common way in which the pursuit of reasons to believe what one already believes can bring about verbal closure in therapy is through its occurrence on a much humbler scale, in much less evolved and much less involved self-confirming and irrefutable lines of thought—that is to say, lines of talk.

Here, what is important is the process: Seeking confirmation of what one already believes leads to verbal closure; holding one's views in a form in which one remains open to doubting what one holds to be so leads to the opening up of possibilities and the correction of one's views. Although there will probably be no shortage of those who would seek to turn it into yet another grand and self-confirming "-ism," *clinical epistemology is intended to be no more than a clinical methodology for opening up possibilities by introducing doubt wherever possible into those vast realms of belief—seeking certainty not in the weaving of elegant tautological systems, but in limiting ourselves to the simplest, most neutral presentations of what little we can know to be the case beyond any reasonable doubt.*

Wheels within Wheels

Of course, there is nothing wrong with tautological systems per se. It is a common error in everyday intellectual parlance to dismiss a particular proposition or theory on the grounds that it is a tautology. To say that something is tautological is merely to say that it is true simply in virtue of the meaning of the symbolic expressions employed in stating it; therefore it would be true irrespective of what may or may not "empirically" be the case in the world. It is to say that, therefore, it cannot be refuted through recourse to factual "evidence." But just because something is a tautology, however grand or humble, is not to say that it is not informative. Mathematics is itself but a grand tautology, and an extremely informative one without which science in recent years would doubtless have made little progress. No, the problem with circular, tautological systems of interpreting (reading meaning into) the facts is not that they go around in circles, but that those circles may fail to elucidate the facts in a way that is conducive to the problem-solving process. Equally disastrously, they may revolve around presuppositions that are not only misleading but simply *false*. The interpretative system being circular, the presuppositions—however false—implicitly receive continual recursive "confirmation." This contributes to their further "validation" and elaboration. Being presuppositions, they are not readily open to inspection and critical evaluation.

Many idiosyncratic circular systems of interpretation brought to bear on the facts by our clients are, whether our clients know it or not, wheels within larger wheels of some grander interpretative systems (such as psychoanalysis or learning theory) prevalent in our culture or in certain subcultures. Many of these grander systems of interpretation are indeed now taken for granted in our culture, informing our most commonplace metaphors. Within the smallest wheels of our clients' most personal interpretative systems are to be found the still smaller wheels that keep all the wheels turning—the presuppositions about how we can come to know how things are.

To continue to interpret (read meaning into) the facts within a particular (often implicit) system of interpretation is to accept the unstated assumptions—the presuppositions—on which the system is based; contrariwise, to make these presuppositions explicit and subject them to doubt and criticism is to step outside the system, to step outside the given framework by challenging the given-ness of the framework's "givens." Unless one challenges those "given" presuppositions or otherwise steps outside the implicit framework of meaning, it is too easy to become tyrannized by the way we have "framed" a situation, and to let our words and sentences define for us how we will view a matter and what we can or cannot do about it (Postman, 1976, p. 221). The most fundamental of all the presuppositions we can make, those that we refer to as epistemological presuppositions, can operate on many levels; on each of these levels, we can, if we are not careful, allow them to constrain our courses of action.

Knowing What Ain't So

There are many ways in which clients introduce verbal closure—not through ignorance, as Josh Billings pointed out a century ago, but through "knowing" all kinds of things that just
"ain't so." They make predictions about what will happen that
may simply be inaccurate and therefore misleading or constrain-
ing, or, worse still, that are of the nature of self-fulfilling prophecies. They make conjectures (assertions without evidence)
about anything and everything—conjectures that may be whol-
ly spurious, but that constrain their choice of options for taking
effective action. In particular, they often wrongly (and sometimes disastrously) conjecture about what someone else is
thinking or what that person's motivation or intention is. Or
they conjecture about how much another person knows what
they are thinking, or what they would like to have that other
person do, or what their own motivation is. Either way, such
mind reading can be the source of numerous imaginary obstacles to effective action. Among the most limiting kinds of conjectures, for reasons we have discussed earlier, are *causal
claims* about what causes what. Sometimes the entire link, the
supposed connection in the first place, is an utterly spurious
invention (as in "It's because I lost my mother as a small child,"
or "It's because he comes from a family of five brothers," or
"It's because there's a history of mental illness in the family," or
"It's because he suffers from a hyperkinetic syndrome," and so
on). Sometimes it is the identification of the link as being specifically causal that is quite spurious (as in "I scream at him because he winds me up," or "My getting depressed makes me
drink," or "My parents urging me to eat makes me worse—I only
starve myself more"). Not only can such causal claims lead
therapist and client on a wild chase after an irrelevant goose;
but moreover, as we have discussed, labeling an arbitrary link as
causal verbally creates limitations for the client that are either
self-imposed or suggested by the therapist.

   For the purposes of psychotherapy, at least, it is not usually
sufficient to dispute or cast doubt upon an individual predic-
tion, or causal claim, or instance of mind reading, or other
conjecture. It is preferable to avoid implicitly verbally reinforc-
ing such potentially limiting presuppositions by casting doubt

instead on the *possibility* of knowing for certain what will happen; on the *possibility* of knowing what caused what; on the *possibility* of one person's knowing (without inquiring) what another is thinking, or what the other desires from one, or what the other's intention or motivation is; and on the *desirability* of making assertions in the absence of evidence. Clients certainly limit themselves by the particular leaps they make in the dark, but the very process of making such leaps introduces a good deal of verbal closure into the problem-solving process. And it is a longer way around to deal with each leap on its own, than to question each time the wisdom of leaping blindly in general.

Interestingly, the more general kind of skepticism seems to meet with more acceptance from clients than the more particular kind, and perhaps this should not be surprising. Two people are more likely to agree that neither can ever really know for certain, than that one knows better and knows that the other is mistaken! The more general kind of doubt places both parties on the same level, and attributes the same level of uncertainty or undecidability to both of the preferred predictions and conjectures. This takes the discussion out of the frame of who is right and who is wrong, and therefore out of a frame in which the therapist claims to be right and in which the client might be proven wrong. Instead, since neither therapist nor client can ever know for certain about such things, they might as well assume no more than they have a right to and just get on with solving the problem. To go straight for questioning the epistemological presuppositions is thus to take the discussion into an entirely different and more constructive frame.

There is a further way, however, in which clients claim to know what ain't so, and where it is helpful for the therapist to introduce doubt: They claim to know what they think of something—that is, whether they ultimately approve or disapprove. Clients, like all the rest of us, do not always know without thoughtful consideration what fundamental values they actually hold, and how they would go about applying them in a given situation. And yet, in the heat of discussion, clients, like all of us, will at times uncritically and dogmatically declare their final aesthetic or moral judgment of a particular matter, slamming down their rhetorical gavel on a proposed course of action as if that were that. And yet, on reflection, they might consider the whole matter very differently. And, once again, to consider the whole matter differently may be a first step to taking the action they need to take to solve the problem.

PART TWO:
OPENING CLOSURE: THE PROBLEM MAP

If at the outset the patient and the doctor are both not sure what the problem is, there is an opportunity to shape the amorphous dough of discomfort in ways that will be most helpful to the patient. By selecting our cookie cutters with the utmost care, we can stamp out that dough in certain forms that have a strategic advantage to the patient and the therapy. Notably, we can pinpoint specific behavioral problems.—Richard Rabkin

Now your patients come to you and tell you their problems. But do they tell you their problems or do they tell you what they *think* are problems? And are they only problems because they *think* that the things are problems?—Milton H. Erickson

As I was going up the stair
I met a man who wasn't there.
He wasn't there again today.
I wish, I wish he'd stay away.

—Hughes Mearns

In Part One of this chapter and in Appendix II, we survey some of the general ways in which one can limit one's likelihood of solving a problem by limiting one's language resources—ways that are to be found wherever human beings are using language in their attempts to define and solve problems. Now, in Part Two, we approach the matter at a level at once more specific and more general. We are more specific here, insofar as we consider the particular semantic environment of the psychotherapy interview. We examine the varieties of limits that client and therapist can verbally introduce into this particular problem-solving process, and ways in which they can transcend those limits. We are more general here, however, insofar as we turn our attention to general categories of verbal closure, in the light of the actual linguistic (syntactic, semantic, and pragmatic) means of introducing such closure already surveyed in this chapter and in Appendix II.

WHAT'S THE PROBLEM?

Problems for Solution

Consider our proposed "map" of "the problem" (Figure 1). Our "problem map" is intended to be a map representing the whole of the client's problem, but it is not a map of anything

Figure 1. The Problem Map

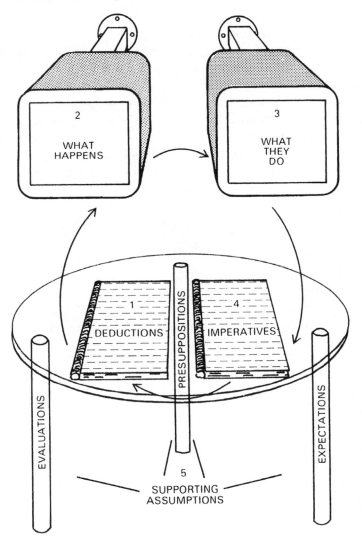

outside the therapist's office. The "therapy problem," as we have tried to convey throughout this book, does not have an objective existence outside that office. One person can set another a brainteaser or an algebraic equation to solve in the office, and the person for whom the problem was set can work on it alone or both people can work on it together. But what they are working on is the problem, and it would be rather odd for someone to ask what the problem is actually like (or how it "occurs") in the world outside office hours, or whether it gets worse during the evening. The same is true of "the problem" in psychotherapy. Steve de Shazer (1982) captures the sense of what we are trying to convey by speaking not of "the problem" but of "the puzzle," for one is not so readily tempted to wonder whether a puzzle is getting better or worse, or how it is doing when no one is considering how to solve it. One could also speak of the therapeutic problem in terms of a "quandary"— puzzlement as to what to do. Thus the "problem" is a practical dilemma that is propounded verbally and verbally puzzled out. *A psychotherapeutic problem is not an affliction, but a question that is proposed for solution and that is raised in discussion in the therapist's office.* Therefore, our "problem map" is a mapping out of discourse. It is a map of what is on the table for discussion and negotiation.

Since this is a map of the therapeutic discussion, it is more like the generalized minutes of a hypothetical meeting than a diagram of some portion of a damaged nervous system. *In no way does our map constitute, in diagrammatic form, a theory of how problems come about or how they are maintained.* Were we to state our view of how therapeutic problems come about, we would probably say it is because people wisely get together for purposes of problem-solving and reaching agreed-upon goals; hence they must draw up problems for solution. "The problem" is not the unembellished, uninterpreted facts of what the client actually does in her life and what actually happens in her life. In any given case, of course, those facts may be, for all that, undesired and undesirable. However, "the facts" are never problematic in and of themselves, for problems are only problems in the context of human purposes and perceived impediments to achieving those purposes. In psychotherapy, as we have emphasized earlier, there must be a clear demarcation of the negotiable and nonnegotiable areas. Now some of the impediments to achieving a particular goal are in the realm of fact, and, as there's no getting around those facts, one must find a way around those impediments. The existence of factual impediments is not a problem for psychotherapy. The therapist's job is to deal with those arbitrary additions, the impediments that exist only in that the client mistakenly takes them to be there and acts accordingly. The "problematic" areas are in the realm of verbal closure, introduced through a way of talking about the facts of the situation.

The Negotiation Table and the Video Monitors. In Figure 1, the screens of the video monitors represent the nonnegotiable realm of the facts of what the client does and experiences in her life, specified according to our frame of "getting the facts" (see Chapter Two)—that is, in terms of video descriptions. The negotiable realm is represented by what is either already on the negotiation table or else beneath it, supporting it from below. Let us go on to consider the other features of the map, one by one.

The Arrows. The curved arrows in Figure 1 indicate the general direction of negotiation in the approach to psychotherapy described in this book. That negotiation may start at any point, but would tend, in general, to follow the direction indicated by the arrows if described from the vantage point of an observer. Thus, this is not a direction the therapist attempts to pursue, for, as we shall see, the therapist wants the discussion to *stop* going around in this circle—that is, when the client finally runs out of self-imposed limitations and there is nowhere left to go but to the action needed to resolve the situation effectively. Likewise, this is not the direction the client is determined to go; rather, the diagram traces how the client tends to respond in discussion to the therapist's attempts to open up the verbal closure, at least up until the point at which the therapist's attempts break through to success.

The Table Legs. The three pillars of dubious wisdom supporting the negotiation table represent what is presupposed by the deductions and imperatives on top of the table. Thus both the client's deductions (1)[1] from her experience, and impera-

---

1. The numbers in parentheses refer to the numbered elements in Figure 1.

tives (4) about what she has to do, tend to presuppose certain unstated assumptions: "presuppositions" (5a) about how things are; ethical and aesthetic "evaluations" (5b) of actions, events, attitudes, states of affairs, and so on; and "expectations" (5c) of what will or ought to happen. These "supporting assumptions" (5) thus furnish necessary grounds for drawing such deductions (1) and making such imperatives (4). The deductions and imperatives would not even make sense, were it not for these underlying, unstated presuppositions, expectations, and evaluations, upon whose support these imperatives and deductions ultimately rest.

What is There to Discuss?

Deductions. Deductions (1) are statements conveying, in effect, what the individual makes of her experience (2), including (often) the failure of her actions (3) to bring about the desired state of affairs. Deductions include *explanations* (statements attempting to assign a reason or cause in order to account for some state of affairs); *interpretations* (statements construing or "reading" the facts in a particular way, setting forth a particular meaning by way of "paraphrase" or "translation"); *characterizations* (statements attributing relatively enduring qualities or characteristics to persons); *causal attributions* (statements identifying one thing as the "cause" of another); *assessments* (statements appraising or judging the value or character of some state of affairs); *generalizations* (statements attempting to infer a general principle or trend from the known facts); *conclusions* ("final" decisions regarding some state of affairs, reached by deduction and inference from the facts); *"inventories"* (statements or sets of statements implicitly or explicitly marking out certain facts but not others as relevant to the situation—i.e., implicitly defining what "the situation" shall be taken to include, and thus to be); *predictions* (statements purporting to forecast what will happen in the future, based on inference from the present facts of the situation and from past experience); *accusations* (statements imputing guilt, blame, or responsibility for some state of affairs to another person or to oneself); and so on.

What Happens. What happens (2) is the area of statements about what actually happens in the individual's life, the facts from which she makes her deductions (1). This area includes statements of both what happens to her as a result of events utterly beyond her control, and, more importantly (and typically to a more considerable extent), what happens as a result of what she does or does not do, or how she does what she does, in response to those and/or other events. Through close questioning using the "getting-the-facts" frame (see Chapter Two) and following the guidelines set out in Chapter Five, the therapist can get the client to specify the actual happenings (i.e., events, described at the level of video descriptions and uninterpreted descriptions of bodily sensations) on which her deductions (1) have been based. Thus, for example, if the client makes a characterization like "My child is disrespectful," the therapist can ask, "What actually happens, what does your child actually do, that leads you to describe her as 'disrespectful'?" Or if the client says "I'm just a bundle of nerves," the therapist can ask what actually happens in her life that leads her to describe herself as a "bundle of nerves," and get video descriptions of actual events, accompanied, if necessary, by uninterpreted descriptions of bodily sensations (such as "I get that butterfly feeling in my stomach whenever the professor asks me a question in class, and I start stammering when I begin to answer"). In this way the facts (2) of what actually happens in the client's life can be obtained, and the meanings or deductions (1) the client has added to them can be separated out for negotiation. The facts are not negotiable, and can only be "altered," as it were, through the client's subsequent actions.

What the Client Does. What the client does (3) is the area of statements about what the individual actually does or does not do, or how she does what she does, in the situation she finds problematic (i.e., the situation in which she claims to be unable to achieve her goal). This is the area of purely factual statements specifying the client's actual behavior in the world, in terms of video descriptions. It is an area of concrete actions taken and not taken, and is very much in the realm of "the facts." When the therapist questions the client about what she does in the situation under discussion, or about what she has actually tried to do (and has not tried to do) to resolve the difficulty and achieve her goal, the therapist can obtain the all-important details of what the client does and does not do. And, to a great extent, the direct outcome of what the client does and does not do (3) is the whole variety of unsatisfactory experiences (2) from which she makes all manner of spurious deductions (1).

Imperatives. Imperatives (4) are statements of what the individual claims she *must* do or what *must* happen, in accounting for why she does not simply take the action the therapist proposes in asking, "Well, why not just do this?" The client's "imperatives" tend to fall under three subclassifications:

1. *What the individual claims she needs to do or what needs to happen because of what has already happened* (causal imperatives). Examples of causal imperatives would be "I have to scream at my kids because they just wind me up," "I know that if I succumb to that first cigarette I'm back to 30 a day," "I simply can't go out of the house because I feel funny as soon as I open the front door," "I've got to be pretty permissive with my kids because I had very strict parents and I had a terrible childhood," "Whenever I get depressed I just get very short-tempered with people—I can't help it," "I act in that inhibited way with men because I was molested by my father from the time I was 8 until I left home at 17," "When my husband says that to me I just have to binge," "She comes late to all her appointments because she never had the experience as a child of being appropriately indulged by her parents," and so on.

2. *What the individual claims she first needs to do (or avoid doing), or what first must happen (or must not happen), if she is to be able to do the proposed action or if an undesirable outcome is to be avoided* (prerequisites). Some examples of prerequisites would be "I need to understand why my child is like he is, before I can do anything about his behavior," "I need therapy before I can do something about sorting out my life," "I can't start behaving more confidently until I can start to *feel* more self-confident," "I need to come to terms with my past before I can deal with the present situation," "I need to complete my mourning for my late husband before I can start eating properly again," "Dieting makes you fat—I have to stop dieting and get rid of my obsession with calories before I can

lose weight," "I keep poring over these thoughts in my mind because if I don't I'll repress them and it'll only make me worse," "I've got to be relaxed before I can go into a trance," "Until we can both agree on disciplining our son, there's nothing we can do about his behavior," "I can't go out unless I have someone with me who understands my problem," "He'll have to be cured of his drinking problem before he'll stop knocking me around," "I can't go out and look for a job until I can lick this depression," "I have to check whether the front door is locked 30, maybe 40 times before I can go to bed," and so on.

3. *What the individual claims she must (or must not) do, must (or mustn't) happen, simply as a matter of principle— that is, as an unqualified "ought"* (normative imperatives). Some examples of normative imperatives would be "I can't just throw food away!", "He's got to eat—no matter how bad he's been, I have to cook him dinner!", "I have to *at least try* to cheer her up," "I have to make it clear I won't tolerate that," "No way! That would be like giving in!", "I've just got to tell him," and so on.

Examples of imperatives are endless in psychotherapy, and, sadly, just as many are proffered by therapists as by clients. In sum, imperatives are statements of what people believe must happen or that they must do, either because of what has gone before, or as a prerequisite to something else, or "just because." The beliefs in question are consciously held views that compel action or inaction of a particular kind—"compel" in the sense that the individual considers the course of action in question to be the only reasonable, rational, or, indeed, possible option open to her. The individual may well, of course, fail to do what she "must" do according to her imperatives, in which case she might experience (2) regret or guilt or whatever, and may go on to draw certain deductions (1) to the effect that things would have worked out fine if only she had done what she needed to do (3). Such a deduction would be as spurious as the imperative in question.

Supporting Assumptions. Supporting assumptions (5) constitute the area of the fundamental, unstated premises presupposed by the individual's deductions (1) and imperatives (4). This area includes the following three categories:

1. *What the individual assumes to be the case about the world—how things are and how we can come to know how things are* (presuppositions). Examples: "Feelings (or thoughts) can cause behavior," "A person is necessarily constrained by the words or actions of others," "There is a process of healthy mourning through which a bereaved person must go," and so on.

2. *How the individual values things in the world and in her experience* (evaluations). Examples: "Nothing must be allowed to go to waste," "Sex is an important part of life," "It's important to have orgasms," "It is important to express whatever you feel," and so on.

3. *What the individual thinks will (or ought to) happen* (expectations). Examples: "Children ought to do as they're told without needing the threat of consequences," "This marriage will break up sooner or later no matter what happens," "Men are not to be trusted," "He'll probably wet the bed until he's 15, which is when I stopped wetting the bed," "Things will never get better," "I'll probably never meet someone and marry," and so on.

These supporting assumptions are simply taken for granted by the individual, and are accepted uncritically not as things she assumes but as "how things are." In the course of challenging the client's imperatives and deductions, the therapist can tease out the tacit statements they presuppose. Without these basic premises holding them up, the individual's deductions (1) and imperatives (4) would simply collapse.

WHAT'S THE SOLUTION?

When we as therapists ask, "What brings you here?", we initially get back the descriptions of what happens all tangled up with the deductions from what happens; the descriptions of what clients do tangled up with the imperatives allegedly "compelling" that behavior; behavior and imperatives tangled up with the events and deductions; and a whole load of implicit presuppositions, evaluations, and expectations. We steer through all this guided by our compass of "getting the facts," to move from

the *deductions* (1)—typically what clients first present in therapy—to the facts of the *events* (2) and *actions* (3) from which
these deductions were made. If we then ask why the clients do
such-and-such, or why they do not do such-and-such instead,
we can begin to tease out the *imperatives* (4) "behind" the
behavior, which emerge in the form of objections to simply
performing the actions we suggest that would eliminate the
difficulties. In challenging the imperatives and deductions, we
draw out the *supporting assumptions* (5), into which we can
then begin to introduce doubt. The specific means of introducing doubt constitute the subject of the next chapter.

CHAPTER FIVE

NEGOTIATING THE PRESENTING COMPLAINT
Assessment as Intervention

Every doctor, every psychiatrist knows that the way a medical condition is determined, the way the patient is asked a question, can and will alter the condition.—Lawrence LeShan and Henry Margenau

If therapy is to end properly, it must begin properly—by negotiating a solvable problem. . . . The act of therapy begins with the way the problem is examined.—Jay Haley

PREPARING FOR THE PASSAGE:
CLEARING THE DECKS

It is all the more surprising then that no treatise on the art and science of intellectual and emotional navigation has yet been written; for logic, which might appear to cover part of this field, in actuality hardly touches it.
—I. A. Richards

A story is told of a trainee of Jay Haley's who was badly stuck in a family therapy case. Haley asked the trainee what the problem was, and was told "the symbiotic relationship between mother and daughter." Haley replied, "I would never let that be the problem."

If a problem is by definition unsolvable or exceedingly difficult to solve, to attempt to solve it in psychotherapy is an exercise in frustration. We have already discussed in some detail the way in which "what the problem is" is the outcome of a negotiation process between client and therapist. Once we and the client have arrived at a consensus in our negotiation of the presenting complaint, once we have agreed upon how we are to mutually define the therapeutic problem to be worked on, the greater part of the therapeutic voyage is over, and, for our part, we are at that point within sight of shore. There is some truth to the notion that the reason clients are even in our offices is that they have framed their "problem" in a form in which it is insoluble, and once we have negotiated a form in which the "problem" is eminently soluble, all that then remains is to implement the solution (and that implementation, on occasion, requires no further therapeutic assistance). In the course of this negotiation process, "problems" that had previously been crystallized tend to go into solution.

It is our view that the length and success of treatment and the manner in which therapy is conducted is predicated on the definition of the "problem" that is negotiated between therapist and client. Many therapists (including the two of us, when we look back on many of our failures) "buy into" the client's frame of reference in spite of themselves, inadvertently taking on board many of the client's presuppositions and attributions that are essential to the continuance of the difficulties. As Rabkin (1977) says "[M]ost of our therapeutic successes can be attributed to the opening phases of psychotherapy. . . . Like chess, the game is won or lost in the beginning" (p. 11).

In this chapter, we look more closely at some of the specifics of the process of negotiating a soluble problem. As we set sail equipped with our "problem map" by which to chart our course through these (each time) uncharted waters, and with our compass of "getting the facts" providing a needle pointing to a "magnetic north" to steer by, it is as well to double-check that we have all the other essential items on board before we leave port. Once having assured ourselves of this, we then have to direct our attention to the question of what to steer clear of—the icebergs and coral reefs, snags and sunken rocks, shoals and shallows, eddies and maelstroms, squalls and doldrums, horrible sea monsters and dangerously tantalizing mermaids, Scylla and Charybdis.

LADING THE ESSENTIALS: THE CONDITIONS FOR WORKABLE PSYCHOTHERAPY

The client is in the therapist's office because she has a complaint with which she wants help, but she will not typically just come in and tell the therapist what that is. She will tell him many other things in addition. The complaint with which she arrives can nonetheless invariably be reduced to one of the following three forms, to which we have already alluded: (1) There is something she does in her life that she does not want to do; or (2) there is something she does not do in her life that she wants to do; or (3) there is something she does in her life in one way and wants to do differently. This does not constitute any kind of selection criterion. What we assert is that at the heart of every psychotherapeutic problem is to be found a presenting complaint in (at least) one of these three "canonical" forms—a complaint that is the reason for the client's appearance in the therapist's office. If the complaint is not reducible to one of these three forms, the ensuing discussion may be interesting, but it is not, in our view, psychotherapy.

To take a common example, "feeling bad" in any particular way is not, in and of itself, a problem in the context of psychotherapy. Feelings are not problems unless they interfere with the client's actions in a way that she finds bothersome. "How is 'feeling bad' a problem for you?" "What do you do that you don't want to do, or don't do that you want to do, or do and want to do differently?" The presenting complaint is to be found in the factual realms of (3) what the client does and (4) what follows naturally from what the client does.[1] If the therapist does not know what the presenting complaint is (i.e., if he does not know how it can be stated in one of these three forms), he is in no position to do effective psychotherapy to resolve that complaint.

A presenting complaint is not enough, however, to ensure that therapy will be workable. Here are the five conditions that we assert must be met if psychotherapy is to be workable at all:

1. There must be a *therapist*. There are many ways to influence people, even people who do not particularly wish to be influenced. But if therapy is to be workable, on the whole there must be a therapist—someone to whom someone else comes explicitly for help. We say "explicitly" because a so-called suicide gesture (for example) is often taken to be a cry for help.

1. The numbers in this sentence refer to the numbers on our "problem map" (see Figure 1, Chapter Four).

Getting these two confused and attempting to be helpful is the source of many ethical and clinical difficulties. A suicide gesture is not a cry for help; it is a suicide gesture. A cry for help, on the other hand, is a cry for help. And the therapist had better make certain even with a cry for help that it is his help that is wanted, or at least, when it arrives, explicitly welcomed. As mentioned above, this is not only an ethical point, but a point essential to clinical effectiveness, which is in turn an ethical matter if effective therapy is what a therapist is purporting to offer.

2. There must be a *complainant*—not just any old "client." The person in the office (or wherever the therapist might see her) had better be the person with the complaint, or at least with the complaint on which the therapist is going to agree to work. There is a world of difference, for example, between a "troubled" teenager and a "troublesome" teenager. Only the "troubled" teenager qualifies as a complainant, and not every troublesome teenager is troubled. So the therapist had better get the troubled parents or school personnel in his office as complainants with whom he can agree to work to sort out the difficulties, or, failing that, work with the troublesome teenager on another complaint—such as getting the parents and school authorities off her back. The work of Fisch, Weakland, and Segal (1982) at the Mental Research Institute has much that is useful to say on this subject of "customership." More colloquially, they sometimes ask themselves, "Who's got the beef?"

3. There must be a *complaint* in one of the three "canonical" forms discussed above, and the therapist needs to find out what this complaint is in the form of video descriptions. What does the client want to do, not do, or do differently?

4. There must be a *request*; that is, given this complaint, what does the complainant want the therapist to do about it? What sort of help is being requested? "How can I help with that?" The request must be explicitly obtained, and, if therapy is to be effective, the request must be (a) a request that the therapist knows how to meet (e.g., there is no point in accepting a request to do hypnotic pain control if a therapist does not have the skills to do hypnotic pain control), and (b) a request which, if successfully met, will actually eliminate the complaint. For example, the request may be to help the client under-

stand why she does what she does, but unless the therapist is sure he knows a way not only to get that understanding but to resolve the problem in the getting of it, then he is setting off on a wild goose chase if he accedes to this request.

5. Finally, if therapy is to be effective, there must be, from the start, *criteria for successful results*, so that the therapist and the client can agree on the video descriptions that would constitute successful resolution of the presenting complaint. If therapist and client cannot agree at the beginning where they intend to end up and how they will know when they have arrived there, they might overshoot or fall short of the mark and never know. They might get off on an irrelevant tangent and waste time and money (as well as inadvertently create new "problems" at times) if they don't have a clear, agreed-upon outcome. Without such agreement before leaving port, it is likely that they will go off course, and they may not even know whether or not the voyage has been completed.

To sum up, then, the conditions that must be met for psychotherapy to be workable, are that each of the following must be available then and there: (1) a therapist who is being asked for help, by (2) a complainant telling the therapist what she wants to do, not do, or do differently—in other words, bringing (3) a complaint; (4) a request regarding that complaint that the therapist knows how to meet, and meeting which will eliminate the complaint; and (5) criteria for successful results in the form of sensory-based descriptions of how both therapist and client will know therapy is over. When we get stuck with a case, we often find that we have set sail without one of these essential elements on board.

STEERING CLEAR: NEGOTIATING THE OBSTACLES—THE "INDEX"

To label a child as "delinquent" or as suffering from "minimal brain dysfunction," or to label an adult as an "alcoholic" or a "schizophrenic," means that one is participating in the creation of a problem in such a way that change may be made more difficult. A therapist who describes a family situation as characterized by "a dominating mother and a passive father," or "a symbiotic relationship between mother and daughter," has created problems, although the therapist might think he is merely identifying the problems put before him. The way in which one labels a human dilemma can crystallize a problem and make it chronic.—Jay Haley

Therefore it seemeth to me, that the truest way to understand conversation, is to know the faults and errors to which it is subject, and from thence every man to form maxims to himself whereby it may be regulated. . . . —Jonathan Swift

George Orwell, in *Nineteen Eighty-Four*, pointed out that "the purpose of Newspeak was not only to provide a medium of expression for the world-view and mental habits proper to the devotees of Ingsoc, but to make all other modes of thought impossible." In a similar fashion, the personal "Newspeak" of clients—in ways surveyed in the last chapter—serves to make impossible any of the modes of thought that would enable the problem to be "solvably" formulated and then solved. Looked at another way, of course, the therapist's own newspeak—a kind of anti-Newspeak newspeak—serves, if all goes well, to make impossible all other modes of thought, including, in particular, the client's previous modes of thought that were necessary to maintaining the "problematical-ness" of the problem situation.

The therapist, in navigating the high seas of the client's words, is aided, we believe, by knowing what specifically to steer clear of, and how specifically to negotiate the obstacles that he will inevitably encounter. Perhaps the easiest way to present a large part of this material is in the form of an *Index expurgatorius*, as it were, proscribing certain forms of expression and specifying how to render those expressions in more felicitous forms of language (forms, however, making impossible the modes of thought implicit in the former modes of expression), or how otherwise to deal with them. Our proposed "Index," which makes no claims to being definitive, would thus (to change the metaphor) be a list of contraband forms of language that clients often wittingly or unwittingly smuggle in, along with some rules of thumb for detecting the smuggled items, and guidelines suggesting how they might be handled.

Despite our rather different epistemology and very different approach to psychotherapy, our "Index" is in much the same tradition as the justly celebrated Chapter Four of *The*

Structure of Magic, Volume 1, by R. Bandler and J. Grinder (1975), a chapter we consider to have been one of the few great landmarks in the literature of psychotherapy. Although we feel their analysis is needlessly complicated, relying as it does on Chomskian theory, we believe there is much that remains valuable in it even if one rejects the theory and terminology of Chomsky's transformational grammar in which it is couched. The distinctions the authors introduce have certainly played an important part in our development as therapists, without our having accepted either Chomskian theory or their own theory (about people having "maps" and representations that the therapist discovers), and the influence of that chapter is apparent over the next few pages. Above all else, it was that landmark chapter that first explicitly recognized the word "specifically" as one of the most important words a therapist can include in his questions.

Our "Index," then, proscribes the following:

1. *Vague statements*. Obviously, since video descriptions are what we are seeking, we do not accept statements or sets of statements too vague to pick out particular events, particular performances of what our clients are referring to. We request specific examples and continue to ask questions of detail until we are fairly certain we have relatively complete, blow-by-blow video descriptions into which we have not interpolated any significant details. Any details that we may have inadvertently supplied from our own imagination, we make sure to verify with our clients.

2. *Unspecified verbs*. Content can be subtly left out of descriptions through the speaker's failure to specify a verb's subject (the actor), as in "The brakes have been adjusted" (who adjusted them?), some aspect or mode of the verb itself (the action), as in "She's spoiled the relationship" (how? in what sense?), or the verb's (direct or indirect) object (what is acted upon), as in "I'm scared" (of what?) or "I find it hard to communicate" (communicate what? to whom?). Paul Watzlawick has pointed out (1982) that in everyday life if someone says "I'm depressed," we tend naturally to ask, "About what?", whereas a psychotherapist's first question is more likely to be,

"Since when?" Basically, in this approach to interviewing, we do not let half a verb go by—we want the rest.

3. *Unspecified adjectives.* Again as we have discussed earlier, adjectives may be left unspecified, either in ways analogous to unspecified verbs ("the frightened child" [frightened of what?], "an inconvenient time" [who would have been inconvenienced? in what way?]), or in quite different ways, commonly by failing to specify the standard being used ("tall," "intelligent," "overweight," "lazy" [compared to whom or what?]). Wherever we encounter such incomplete adjectives, we seek out the missing parts of the corresponding verb form (actor, action, or what is acted upon), just as when dealing with incomplete verbs; or, if it is simply the standard being used that has not been specified, we get our clients to specify that standard.

4. *Superlatives and comparatives.* Failure to specify the standard being used (what we call the "compared-to-what") is equally a problem where superlatives and comparatives are stated baldly in assertions: "It would be best" ("most honest," "quicker," "more practical," "cheaper") to . . . ". Once again, we get our clients to specify the standard by asking questions like these: "In what way?", "Compared to what?", "In what respect?", "Why do you say that?", and "How do you know?"

5. *Empty nouns.* These are "thing" words that may have content for the speaker but not for the listener (unless the listener supplies his own). Abstract nouns such as "respect," "love," "hurt," "aggression," "caring," "stability," "behavior," "depression," "support," and so on are not accepted without specification. We get the clients to specify the content of such nouns in the form of video descriptions. Sometimes, where the abstract noun ("cooperation," "respect") is a nominalization of a verb form ("to cooperate with," "to respect"), we ask our questions by converting the abstract noun back into its verb form and treating it as an unspecified verb ("Who doesn't cooperate? Who does he not cooperate with? In what way? Can you give me an example of that?"), once again ultimately specifying down to video descriptions of particular performances.

6. *Unspecified specifiers.* A common way in which clients may fail to specify vital content is by failing to indicate what

they are using referring expressions to refer to, or "pointing expressions" (so-called "indexicals" such as "here," "now," and "those," which depend for their meaning on where the speaker is literally or metaphorically standing—or pointing her index finger—when she utters them) to point to. (One person can be speaking to another on the telephone and, as a kind of joke, can say, "It was about so big," or "It was in that direction.") If the client fails satisfactorily to do so, the therapist must get the client to clearly specify which one (or ones) she has in mind, so that her expressions indicate specific items in the world—persons, things, locations, directions, times, or whatever. Otherwise, the client will not have succeeded in communicating to the therapist the identity of what she was, as it were, using words to point to.

Plural nouns are common culprits ("people," "punishments," "specifics"), as are, though perhaps not so commonly, nouns preceded by the indefinite article ("I was told by *a therapist*," "I get into *a state*," "I missed out on *an opportunity* for *a job*"). Other common culprits include pronouns without explicitly specified antecedents ("he," "she," "they say," "this," "that," "one," "something else"); indexical adjectives ("this person," "these problems") and "template" adjectives that fail to add specific information ("certain ones," "some people," "that sort of person," "Don't you ever feel that way?"); and indexical adverbs ("here," "there," "that much") and "template" adverbs ("sometimes," "somehow"). "Where," "when," "how," and "which one(s)" may be important pieces of information for the listener to get specific hold of.

7. *Generalizations*. Generalizations such as "all," "none," "every," "always," "never," "everything," "nothing," "everyone," "no one," or "invariably" serve to infer an often quite spurious general principle or trend from the few known facts. These generalizations are always challenged. ("Always?" "Well, usually.") "Nothing?" we ask. "No one?" "All the time?" "Even when she's asleep?" We doggedly ferret out the exceptions, suggesting possible exceptions ourselves and checking them out, employing absurdity if necessary. Where possible, we pre-empt the generalizations in the first place by asking such questions as "Where (or when) do you *always* have the symptom, and where (when) do you *never* have it?" Finding these

exceptions is one of the most important parts of the therapeutic process. This particular line of questioning is discussed in more detail in Chapter Eight, because of its intimate connection with pattern intervention.

8. *Syntactic presuppositions.* Where any statements made by our clients presuppose other statements through the syntax of the sentences themselves, we tease out the presupposed statements before we do anything else. We make them explicit and then subject them to the same editing process as any other statements. If we do not make this our first move, we will be implicitly affirming what is presupposed. For example, a client might say, "Johnny's innate aggressiveness can be very annoying and can sometimes be quite dangerous." We would be implicitly affirming the presupposition that Johnny is innately aggressive if we asked such questions as "Who gets annoyed by it?" or "Who is endangered?"

In Appendix B of *The Structure of Magic*, Volume 1 (1975), Bandler and Grinder list 29 syntactic environments in English in which presuppositions are commonly to be found, and these are certainly worth studying. However, we can reiterate here the simple rules of thumb for identifying syntactic presuppositions (whatever one must assume the speaker regards as being true for the speaker's statement even to make sense): Simply consider what would have to be true for either the statement in question *or its negation* to even have a *possibility* of being true. For example, for either "The present King of France is bald" or its negation, "The present King of France is not bald," to have a chance of being true, there must at least be a present King of France, so "There is a present King of France" is the syntactic presupposition we have teased out.

9. *Claims of necessity, impossibility, or inability.* Statements employing "necessity words" ("has to," "must," "necessarily," "needs to," etc.) are challenged in terms of "What would happen if not?" Those employing "impossibility words" or "inability words" ("cannot possibly," "is unable to," "would be impossible," "couldn't," etc.) are typically challenged with inquiries such as "What prevents you (them, one)?" or "How so?" So what we get our clients to specify are precisely "What would happen if not?" (for necessity claims) and the impediment (for impossibility or inability claims), the

latter by asking "What prevents you (them, one)?" or "What would stop you (them, one)?" or "How so?"

10. *"Cannot" and "will not."* We substitute the more descriptive "do not" or "does not" (for the present tense) or "have not" or "has not" (for the past tense) when clients assert that either they themselves or some third party "cannot" or "will not" do a certain thing. "Cannot" presupposes inability and hence a causal explanation; "will not" presupposes intention and hence a motivational explanation. We get the clients to agree that we just don't know whether they cannot or simply will not, but that we do at least know that they *do* not, or so far *have* not.

11. *Characterizations.* Statements that attribute any relatively enduring characteristics ("aggressive," "domineering," "lazy," "disrespectful," "weak," "too easygoing," "unassertive," etc.) to the clients themselves or to others are challenged. We want the clients to make explicit the standards according to which these attributions are made and to supply evidence (in descriptive terms) for the attributions. We then get agreement on replacing the characterizations with the relevant video descriptions, and on the fact that we don't know what these facts mean. Often, we directly ask for the content of the characterizations: for example, "What does he actually say or do that you call being 'lazy'?"

12. *Attributions or self-attributions of emotion.* These are challenged in terms of "How do you know?" (e.g., "How do you know you feel guilty?"), and in this way are progressively reduced to the more certain level of sensory-based descriptions of actions and (in addition, for first-person reports) more neutral descriptions of bodily sensations. "Neutral" in this sense means describing any sensations without going on to attribute any particular meaning, significance, or cause to them. Thus, for instance, "Then I suddenly felt depressed" might in a particular instance end up re-edited as "Then I suddenly had a sort of sinking sensation just here in my chest." As discussed in Chapter Two, it is not that we regard emotion statements as equivalent to descriptions of sensations and behavior; rather, we believe that emotion statements are rarely descriptive at all.

13. *Predictions.* Predictions are ruled out of order, and we obtain the clients' agreement that we and they really don't

know what will happen. The past is not permitted to be a guide to the future; otherwise, with the best of intentions, the map tracing where a client wandered when she was getting lost will be taken implicitly as a valid map for marking out her future route.

14. *Conjectures: assertions without evidence.* We want the evidence in the form of video descriptions. "How do you know?" is a question we frequently ask. We also challenge the conclusions our clients make from the evidence. The etymology of "conjecture" concerns the notion of "throwing together" or putting together the facts—"putting two and two together," as we say. Conclusions or suppositions drawn from evidence insufficient to ensure reliability (i.e., going well beyond the facts) are prime candidates for negotiation and the introduction of doubt, and are obviously frequent sources of verbal closure. We don't necessarily insist on the incorrectness of the conjectures (for, again, sufficient evidence for our counterassertion is usually lacking!); we just take the position that we don't know what the facts add up to, and we get our clients to join us in suspending judgment.

15. *Mind reading.* We do not accept any assertion that our client knows what another person feels or thinks or what his motivation or intention is; we seek evidence and argue the case for uncertainty. Likewise, we question any attempt to attribute a particular meaning or meanings to another's actions. Even when the third party's own words are quoted as evidence for the assertion, we may dispute that one can necessarily tell what a person feels or thinks even from what he reports. (As we have discussed in Chapter Four, people often, in the heat of the moment, are led into saying things they don't mean and into claiming to "feel" things they don't feel; to make things worse, they themselves and those to whom they've said those things tend afterwards to take those things to heart and to [incorrectly] regard them as indicative of "true" feelings or what they "really" think.)

16. *Causal claims.* Any and all statements by our clients asserting cause–effect relationships ("makes," "causes," "because," etc.) or implying them ("I would, but . . . ," "if it weren't for . . . ," "if only . . . ," etc.) are subjected to skeptical challenges. In the case of implied causal factors, we ask ques-

tions along the lines of "How does that prevent you?"; with explicit causal attributions, once again, the key question is "How do you know?" We aim eventually to reduce a causal claim ("*A* causes *B*") to the weaker claim of constant conjunction (i.e., "Whenever *A* happens, then *B* happens"), ending up with video descriptions of recurring sequences or patterns minus any implications about anything causing anything else. While we would not accept "He upsets me when he says that," we equally would reject "When he says that, I upset myself over it," in favor of the more factually acceptable "When he said that, I got upset," or "Whenever he says that, I get upset." Implied causal relationships ("I would, but . . . ," etc.) are first made explicit ("How does that stop you?") and then challenged.

In all of this negotiation, it is important to keep one's priorities straight. The top priority must always be, as indicated above, to tease out the syntactic presuppositions before anything else is done—not because such presupposition has any pre-eminent importance in itself, but because not doing this first may result in the therapist's lending credence to some of the client's more dubious assumptions and hence missing out on valuable opportunities for negotiation. Moreover, it is easier than one supposes for the therapist herself to unwittingly accept the syntactic presuppositions in the course of negotiating the rest, and thus (to borrow Postman's [1976] phrase) to end up in never-never land without quite knowing how she got there. So if one of our clients said, "His being so obstinate makes me give up before I start," were we to challenge the causal claim (paragraph 16 above) by asking, "How does that make you give up?" we would be accepting the syntactically presupposed characterization, "He is obstinate." Instead we would begin by making explicit (paragraph 8) and questioning the characterization (paragraph 11), and would ultimately end up with something like "So there have been so many occasions in the past when the ways you have tried so far to influence your husband on this point failed to do the trick, that now you sometimes don't even bother trying." Needless to say, the original version—"His being so obstinate makes me give up before I start"—verbally closes off ("before I start") many possibilities not excluded by the latter rendering.

Second, the time allotted for the therapy session is not infinite. It is not possible to challenge and negotiate everything that is negotiable. The therapist's clinical judgment must play a large part in determining what avenues of negotiation to pursue at the (time) expense of others. Certain considerations, however, can be specified in general terms:

1. The therapist should, above all, pursue video descriptions of the pattern of behavior involved in the problem situation. (The details of the kind of information about patterns that should be most relentlessly pursued will become clearer in Chapter Eight.)

2. The therapist should avoid getting into an argument or philosophical discussion with the client. To avoid losing rapport and credibility, the therapist should not dawdle over matters that the client starts to make an issue out of, but should move on to something else, following the principle—known to all good negotiators—of negotiating when and where the other side shows itself to be most prepared to negotiate.

3. As in all negotiations, psychotherapy involves a degree of give and take. The therapist has to be willing to "win a few, lose a few," to make trade-offs and concessions. We are reminded of the story of Moses coming down from Mount Sinai with the stone tablets, telling the waiting Hebrews, "I've got good news and bad news. The good news is . . . I've got them down to 10. The bad news is . . . adultery is in." The therapist does not have to challenge and successfully cast doubt upon every dubious and potentially negotiable presupposition, characterization, causal attribution, and so on. Simply to cast a good deal of doubt upon only one of them, or a small measure of doubt upon first one and then another, may be sufficient to dissolve the problem.

4. The therapist should remember that one of the most powerful interventions she can make is, without being rude, to *deliberately ignore* certain communications by simply not taking them up. Freudian therapists hear a lot more about dreams than behavior therapists. We doubt whether their clients in gen-

eral experience a different number of dreams. We find that a lot of what our clients say we deal with by ignoring; our very behavior presupposes that a particular matter is not worth discussing or is not relevant to the solution of a problem.

5. In terms of the presuppositions to pursue, the therapist should pursue, where possible, the "lowest common denominator" or "greatest common factor," or follow Isaac Asimov's dictum (in *The End of Eternity*) of effecting "the minimum necessary change to produce the maximum desired response." In other words, if there seem to be one or two "keystone" presuppositions without which the whole problem edifice would collapse, one or two logs that if pulled out would be sufficient to break up the logjam, those are the presuppositions to go for.

TACKING INTO THE WIND: RESOLVING THE PROBLEM BEFORE IT GETS TO YOU

Deal with a thing while it is still nothing; keep a thing in order before disorder sets in.—Lao Tzu

What is concluded that we should conclude anything about it?—Benjamin Paul Blood

Do not pull the knot tight before you are sure that you have got hold of the right end.—Ludwig Wittgenstein

How do I know what I think till I see what I say?

Just as we contend that there is not some objective "problem" of which a client comes in and gives a descriptive account, there is likewise no such thing as a client's "position" on the problem (contrary to Fisch *et al.*, 1982). The client does not "have" any fixed and determinate position on the problem. It is not as if, in answer to the therapist's questioning, the client goes inside, has a peek at his "position" on the matter in question, and then reports back to the therapist on what he has found there. Clients are in therapists' offices not only because they don't know what to do, *but because they don't know what to think*. And like all of us (therapists included), they often don't know what they even do think until they see what they say. In the negotiation process of continually "censoring," editing, and transforming what a client says about his problem, the therapist is all the while intervening to help in transforming what the client thinks. The client's "position" on the presenting complaint, like the presenting complaint itself, is inevitably going to be the outcome of the negotiation process between therapist and client.

We never do find out what the client's presenting complaint or position would have been had we just kept quiet, not interrupted, and not started intervening from the moment the client began to speak. We never do find out what the client would have thought about the problem had we just listened politely and reflectively. But we assert that what we thus undeniably "miss out on" is not the client's "real problem" or "real" views. There just ain't any such animal. The therapist cannot not intervene in both the definition of a presenting complaint and in the determination of a client's position. To say nothing, or to nod wisely and understandingly as a client paints herself into a corner, are as much interventions as our own preferred moves to prevent a client from painting herself (and us with her) into a corner. If the client doesn't know what she thinks till she sees what she says, why on earth allow the client to crystallize an untenable position? If the betting could still go either way, why let the client put her money down on a losing horse? Why not stop her before she commits herself to losing her shirt? Why nail her to a position she's only just now starting to assume?

Not infrequently, our clients leave their first sessions with us declaring that they had thought they had a problem when they came in, but now realize they haven't got a problem or that they now know exactly what action they need to take to resolve the difficulties. And perhaps it had all seemed, from our point of view, relatively easy. In those instances, the only way we get to find out the extent of the difference our negotiation has made is by learning afterwards of a long previous history of failed psychotherapeutic and psychiatric treatment, or by getting a referrer's heavy report (which sometimes arrives after the client in question has left "without his problem").

Our approach has, with some justification, been referred to as "pickpocket therapy" (Roe, 1983) after the "stage pickpocket" of variety shows, who goes through the audience chatting amiably and shaking hands before the TV camera, each time momentarily distracting the attention of his mark and of the audience and making his move unobserved even by the camera; he then comes back on stage and produces his spoils. A client comes in to the first session loaded down with his "problems," and by the end of the session nothing very noteworthy seems to him to have transpired. But it is as if, as he gets up to leave, he were to go to check his watch and find it missing, and so begin to frisk himself frantically to find his wallet also gone, and his comb, and checkbooks, and credit cards, and handkerchief, and tie, and keys, and glasses! Operating in subtle ways quite outside the client's awareness, snatching away his presuppositions "while he isn't looking"—presuppositions that by their very nature are outside awareness from the start—we may not appear to the client to be doing anything more than asking for some basic information, telling a few anecdotes, making a few jokes. But by the end of the session, the client may have been robbed of the presuppositions necessary for there to be a problem, and, to the client's relief and satisfaction, the problem may simply have disappeared, so that he leaves the session much lighter.

While watching other therapists at work and noting how we would operate very differently, we are able to see too how the negotiation process can—if conducted according to "rules" different from ours—land a heavy, intractable, severe problem, whereas in our own approach the same presenting complaint might have been resolved in a single interview. So we don't believe for a millisecond that the people whose problems are resolved in relatively few sessions with us have less serious problems than those who spend years in other forms of psychotherapy with little improvement to show for it.

In our approach of working at the level of the presuppositions themselves, we can undermine presuppositions that underlie a whole host of other difficulties our clients experience in life, with the frequent result that not only the presenting complaints under discussion but a whole variety of other difficulties (many of which we do not learn about until follow-up) disappear as well. It is to this feature of our approach—our working at the level of the clients' presuppositions and altering these most fundamental assumptions as we go along (often preempting and dissolving them before the clients even have a chance to reveal them to us)—that we attribute the success of our approach in bringing about *generative* change, far-reaching improvements (the so-called "character change" of other epistemologies of psychotherapy) throughout areas of the clients' lives that were never directly addressed in the therapy sessions.

So, rather than letting our boat be blown 50 miles westward off course before correcting our course by sailing 50 miles eastward, we are continually making adjustments, in a zigzag pattern, tacking into the wind. If the wind is coming out of the north, and north is the direction we want to go, we sheet the sail in hard, set the craft's helm on a northerly heading; every inch of the way, hard on the wind, we use that very force to empower us on a zigzag tack, now to starboard, now to port, clawing to windward.

Our more experienced sailing friends (Butler, 1983) tell us that "close-hauled sailing" (i.e., sailing "close" or "hard" on the wind) is by far the easiest way to sail, and though it may give you a wet and bouncy ride, the boat is well under your control. Also, in "close-hauled" sailing the boat may appear to be moving more slowly than when sailing with the sheets free, but it gets to its destination more quickly by traveling a more direct course.

THERAPEUTIC PRESUPPOSITION

In all of this negotiation, we do not in any way argue with our clients, or get into philosophical discussions, or teach them (in any explicit fashion) our model of sifting facts and meanings. We don't do rational–emotive or cognitive therapy, trying to convince the clients to recognize and discard their irrational beliefs. We challenge gently and persuasively rather than confrontively, in an attitude of benevolent skepticism.

Whenever possible, we prefer to challenge indirectly rather than directly, through our own use of presupposition and through the "pre-emptive" use of anecdotes and metaphor. For example, rather than directly challenging a client's generalization about her having the "symptom" "all the time," we prefer to ask, "When does it always occur and when does it never occur?'' before there is even a chance for the generalization to be made. Not that we would hesitate, if necessary, to challenge a ''contraband'' statement; but we prefer whenever possible to get clients to join us in weaving a context in which such contraband statements become fewer and fewer. Paramount in all of this will be the subtle and pervasive influence of the presuppositions we ourselves happen to hold.

For example, our presupposition of positive outcomes does not go unrecognized by the client, for this presupposition is continually being communicated both verbally and nonverbally; it could not be otherwise. And this provides in itself a challenge to the client's presuppositions. For example, a client with a long-standing difficulty that he regards as fairly intractable cannot but be challenged (and perhaps heartened) by our presupposition—however dimly perceived by him—that there will be a positive outcome without much ado. A case in point is our nonverbal response to his description of the chronicity of his symptom and of how it has resisted all previous therapeutic efforts. Since these sorts of features don't unsettle us in the least any more, what is communicated nonverbally is that these features of his history do not necessarily offer any grounds for pessimism.

A client who sought hypnotherapy to give up smoking was questioned thoroughly in the session along the lines of negotiation we have been discussing. Numerous times in the first part of the session, there were opportunities to ask such questions as ''What brand of cigarettes have you been smoking?'', ''Once you'd given up completely for, say, 3 months, what could possibly stop you having a cigarette 13 weeks or so from today, and if you had that first cigarette, what makes you think it wouldn't also be your last for, say, another 13 weeks?'', ''How many cigarettes did you smoke each day?'', ''How will you politely tell people you've given up smoking, say, if someone (who hadn't seen you for a month and so didn't know that) were to offer you a cigarette?'', ''I know you travel a good deal—how many flights do you think it will take before it becomes *automatic* to ask for a nonsmoking seat?'', ''What other habits have you succeeded in giving up?'', and so on. (Cf. also Zeig, 1982b, pp. 259 ff., for good discussion and further examples relevant to smoking.) About 10 minutes into the session, the client (a long-time chain-smoker) remarked, "You know, when I used to smoke, it often occurred to me that—hey, did you hear what I just said? I said 'when I used to smoke'; that must be a good sign!" Compare this to the more common situation in which a client who has resolutely smoked his last cigarette before coming to the therapist's office, is asked, "How many cigarettes *do you smoke?*", which presupposes continued smoking! Syntactic presupposition can, of course, work either way, and so the therapist must use language as a precision instrument, not as a blunt one.

Since (as we discuss further in Appendix II) people tend to respond to assertions by agreeing or disagreeing, and since to answer a question is often implicitly to accept the presuppositions contained in that question, we can structure our assertions and questions in therapy so that whether clients agree or disagree with the assertions, or however they respond to the questions, in doing so they are implicitly affirming what we wish to presuppose. In this manner, we can avoid allowing the client to commit herself to an untenable position that she then feels she needs to defend, or one that she backs down from, feeling she's been wrong or even foolish. More than this, we encourage the client to build a position from which the problem can be solved, or, better, from which it doesn't exist any more.

Sometimes it is sufficient merely to say "Yeah, me too" (provided, of course, that it's true), if a client says, for example, "Things have been getting me down lately." An ounce of pre-emption is worth a pound of cure. And while syntactic and behavioral presuppositions don't automatically bring about the desired results, they are major components in the creation of a context in which successful results are more likely to appear.

One of the subtlest and most elegant ways of negotiating the problem and challenging presuppositions, evaluations, and expectations (without ever even getting within sight of an argument or philosophical discussion) is through relating anecdotes and jokes that gently and indirectly pre-empt the relevant generalization, characterization, causal claim, or whatever. These are matters we discuss in more detail in our chapter on working methods (Chapter Seven).

FURTHER NEGOTIATION: SPLITTING AND LINKING

THE STORY SO FAR

Just because meanings are variable and uncertain, it does not mean that one should always only confine oneself to the facts. It means that one *need not* confine oneself to one *particular* set of meanings for those facts. As long as the therapist distinguishes clearly for himself what is negotiable from what is not, he can feel free to introduce perfectly negotiable (and hence ultimately arbitrary) meanings, provided he and the client can agree to "do business" on these new terms.

One way of conceptualizing the negotiation of the presenting complaint might go something like this: The client comes in and gives the therapist a summary of "the story so far." What is related is not only the *facts* of the story so far, but those facts strung together or arranged in a particular way. The way in which the facts of the story so far have been put together, there is no way for the story to have a happy ending. Sometimes, indeed, the resulting construction is a story that keeps returning to its starting point and so is destined to repeat itself over and over again without a satisfactory resolution. The therapist extracts the actual facts from the story and strings them together differently. The way in which the therapist puts the facts together, however, leaves open the possibility of a happy ending. The new story often makes it obvious what further facts (i.e., actions from the client) need to be added to bring about a successful resolution.

SPLITTING AND LINKING:
MAKING AND BLURRING DISTINCTIONS

The processes of splitting (making new distinctions, breaking old associations) and linking (making new associations, blurring old distinctions) are central to the therapeutic process (O'Hanlon, 1982a), and much of the negotiation of the problem can usefully be described in these terms. Through the "languaging" process of punctuating or ordering experience in particular ways (see Appendix II and Chapter Four, Part One), abstracting particular patterns of interest to us, naming these abstracted patterns, attributing these newly created "entities" to persons (or places or things or times, etc.), and characterizing them in terms of these attributes or qualities that are regarded as being somehow representative, we distinguish (split) aspects of our experience and associate (link) aspects of our experience. The naming process involves an implicit classifying process, obscuring distinctions between different things with the same name and obscuring resemblances to other things with different names. These classifications, labels, and distinctions are not fixed, immutable discoveries, but are merely ways of ordering our experience through splitting and linking.

At every juncture in the negotiation process, the therapist is offered limitless opportunities for splitting and linking in alternative ways. The therapist can proffer alternative punctuations, an almost infinite variety of alternative names (and hence implicit classifications), and alternative metaphors for everything under the sun in the client's "story so far." In taking inventory of the client's "situation," the therapist can include various facts or features not considered relevant by the client, and can suggest that some of what the client has included as part of the situation be excluded as not really relevant. The secret is to include as relevant (linking), matters whose pertinence the client cannot dispute, and to make apt distinctions (splitting) in the matters raised by the client, the validity of which distinctions, likewise, it would be difficult to deny. Similarly, when proffering alternative names, metaphors, and so on, it is important to present one's case in such a way that it is self-evident and fits perfectly with the facts of the client's situation so far.

REFORMULATING THE PROBLEM: PUTTING MEANING BACK IN

Into each life some confusion should come; also some enlightenment.
—Milton H. Erickson

The alternative name or punctuation or metaphor can be proffered in the first instance as an *interim reformulation* of the problem, or of part of the problem, as a way of merely introducing doubt—"depotentiating conscious sets," in Rossi's terminology (Erickson, Rossi, & Rossi, 1976). The interim reformulation may not actually be pursued or necessarily followed up later, but it can often serve very quickly to make negotiable matters appear more obviously negotiable, and, as it were, to loosen the hold of the names, punctuations, and metaphors the client has initially proffered in the session. For example, one client began by saying she had been having very bad headaches lately for which the doctors had been unable to find any medical cause, and said that she knew she'd been very tense and under a lot of stress recently, and that she'd been letting the littlest things get to her. Before she could go any further and proffer her own punctuation (for, from what she'd been saying, an obvious punctuation she might make could be anticipated), she was interrupted with the following: "You know how when you have a bad hangover, even the tiniest noise or annoyance gets blown out of all proportion into a source of intense irritation and suffering? And how, when you're not feeling well, or you've got a headache, you seem to have a lot less patience for dealing with the most minor frustrations? Well, do you think these headaches might be the cause of a lot of the tension you've been feeling and the stress you're under lately? And perhaps that because you've been suffering with these headaches, the smallest things have been able to get you down? I mean, particularly since, unlike with a hangover, there's the added worry of what's causing the headaches, isn't there?" The client responded with a look of astonishment, saying, "Yeah, that makes a lot of sense, but I'd never thought of that before—I just assumed it was the other way around." The response to that was simply that it was difficult to know.

At some point in the negotiation process—having tried out numerous small interim reformulations; having "seeded" numerous ideas and gauged the client's response to each of these; having gathered, for his own purposes, sufficiently detailed information in the form of video descriptions of the relevant patterns; and having adequately secured the conditions for workable psychotherapy—the therapist may begin an *overall reformulation* of the problem. The ground, of course, has already been well prepared for this. By this point, much of the negotiation has already been carried out, and the territory represented by "the problem map" has already been covered numerous times. Likewise, by this point, the therapist has already obtained a consistently affirmative response to the various components of the impending overall reformulation when these ideas have been floated in the conversation ("seeded"). It is as if the negotiator has already confirmed the other side's agreement to the component parts of the package, and is preparing to wrap them up into his overall proposal for a negotiated settlement— "the deal."

As a precaution, to avoid difficulties later, we often say at this point, "I've got a few pretty good ideas about all this, but before I share them with you, is there anything else that you think I ought to know?" We await the response and negotiate anything that comes up, and then repeat the process to ensure that the clients have said everything they feel it is important to say. This simple precaution is to avoid the situation of presenting a perfectly good overall reformulation of a problem, only to have a client say, "Ah, but what you don't know is . . . "—like the situation in court when the other side suddenly produces the surprise witness or crucial piece of evidence. A client may find a therapist's overall formulation of the problem to be quite acceptable and a thoroughly satisfactory account of the situation, but there will be considerable room for doubt if the client (rightly or wrongly) believes that she has not yet told the therapist everything the therapist needs to take into account in any considered formulation of the problem. Often, the new information is extremely valuable and will significantly alter the final form of the therapist's overall reformulation, but even where the client proffers what turns out to be a red herring, the therapist will be far more credible after hearing the new information than before. This is related to a point we have made earlier— that for the therapist to ignore a communication (by not pursuing the topic) after making clear that he has heard it can communicate infinitely more to the client than simply acting as if it had never been said. We prefer to ensure that we have cleared the ground before we begin any new construction.

In reformulating the problem—which essentially involves "adding meaning back in"—what we do is to "reframe" it, which means "to change the conceptual and/or emotional setting or viewpoint in relation to which a situation is experienced and to place it in another frame which fits the 'facts' of the same concrete situation equally well or even better, and thereby changes its entire meaning" (Watzlawick, Weakland, & Fisch, 1974, p. 95). The reformulation of the problem should make it clear what action (if any) needs to be taken to solve the problem. This needs to be clear to the therapist, even though it may not be immediately clear to the client, and it may require further elucidation on the therapist's part as he prepares to propose the action required or to begin negotiating the design of a possible therapeutic task. (This is a matter that is addressed in a later chapter.) The solution proposed, of course, may not be very different (if at all) from the solution proposed right at the start when the therapist opened the negotiations by saying, "Well, why not just do this . . . ?" However, a great deal of negotiation will have taken place since then, and the proposed solution will appear in an entirely different light.

For example, an elderly gentleman, brought by his son, complained of "depression," for which he had received extensive chemical and psychological treatment and had even been hospitalized twice. He had first complained of being depressed 2 years before, when his housekeeper/companion died tragically, and he had moved into a hotel because he could not physically look after himself on his own. Now out of the hospital, he was spending the entire day in his hotel, mostly in his room, sometimes not even bothering to get dressed; he was bored to tears and thoroughly fed up. He badly wanted to go out and call on friends, but feared what they would say, since they undoubtedly knew through local gossip "that I'd been a loony in the hospital." So he would get worked up into an anxious state, thinking the worst of what the consequences of going out would be, and would not go out. The reformulation eventually offered was that he was not "suffering from depression," but was understandably miserable, bored, and lonely, spending the day isolated in his hotel room, very much "a fish out of water." His problem was one of "thinking scary thoughts about going out, and then acting on those thoughts by staying in." Moreover, he would repeat this frustrating pattern day after day with the same outcome, and so now, understandably, he sometimes couldn't even be bothered to get dressed. What he needed to do, we said, was not to try not to think scary thoughts, but to think the scary thoughts and then go out, or go out while thinking those thoughts. We went on to negotiate a therapeutic task with him. Now much earlier in the session we had asked, "Well, why not just go out and see your friends?", but by the end of the session this proposal could be presented in a rather different context.

CAVEAT ON METHOD

In this chapter, we have endeavored to provide some specific guidelines for negotiating the presenting complaint, particularly in the form of the "Index" and "the conditions for workable psychotherapy," thus filling out our account presented in Part Two of Chapter Four, which attempts to describe the overall structure of the therapeutic negotiation process. In Chapter Seven, we fill out our account still further with some specific "tools" or methods that we have found useful in carrying out the negotiation. However, with respect to the guidelines we have offered, we would like to stress that, in I. A. Richard's words, "[c]ritical principles, in fact, need wary handling. They can never be a substitute for discernment though they may assist us to avoid unnecessary blunders. . . . Everything turns upon how the principles are applied. It is to be feared that critical formulas, even the best, are responsible for more bad judgement than good, because it is easier to forget their subtle sense and apply them crudely than to remember it and apply them finely" (1929, p. 12).

The aim of all psychotherapy is, if all goes well, "to talk clients out of their problems." It is easier, unfortunately, for therapists and their clients to talk themselves into problems; our guidelines in this chapter (the "Index" in particular) are intended more to serve the negative aim of assisting them to avoid doing so, by bringing to therapists' attention some of the verbal obstacles to steer clear of, to negotiate, so that their craft will not run aground. But if psychotherapy is not to degenerate from an ordinary conversation into a grilling session, research interview, grammar lesson, philosophy tutorial, or rhetoric competition—not to say a contest or battle—then the principles must not be adhered to blindly but followed subtly and finely, always fine-tuned to a client's observable moment-by-moment responses. And, as in the pursuit of any method, it is important to keep the end in sight from the beginning.

CHAPTER SIX

WORKING ASSUMPTIONS
Furnishing Premises for Effective Practice

Examination of our epistemological assumptions will enable us to more fully understand how a clinician perceives, thinks and acts in the course of therapy.—Bradford P. Keeney

Our primary and ultimate loyalty as clinicians must be to our patients and their needs, not to our colleagues and their theories.—Alan Gurman

Don't let your mind be cluttered up with prevailing doctrine.—Alexander Fleming

By now it should be clear that a therapist cannot avoid operating from certain presuppositions or implicit assumptions about the nature of human beings, human problems, the human mind, and, of course, psychotherapy. In this chapter, we consider the matter of furnishing premises for effective practice. Since one must operate (if only implicitly) from some working assumptions, one might as well operate from assumptions that work to facilitate successful results in therapy in the briefest time. We find most of prevailing psychotherapeutic doctrine objectionable, not only because it often presents pure speculation as if it were fact, but because its conceptions seem to us to introduce arbitrary and unfounded limitations to what clients can achieve right now.

In our view, these assumptions tend to lead to protracted treatment, to create barriers to results, and to create the context for an adversarial relationship between therapists and clients, in which therapist and client are pitted against one another. In our observations of other therapists' work, it has been our impression that these assumptions often contribute to therapists' unwitting disrespect toward and suspicion of their clients. In our experience, operating from any, several, or all of these principles leads to frustration for both client and clinician. Since we know of no substantial evidence that these assumptions are true, and since in our estimation they are hindrances to successful results in therapy, we advise therapists to challenge and discard them, or at least, when they get stuck and realize that they would not be stuck *if* a particular valued assumption they hold turned out not to be a valid assumption, simply to see what happens when they act *as if* that assumption were erroneous or irrelevant.

In place of these dubious assumptions, we offer an alternative set of minimal assumptions (indicated in italic print) arising naturally from the facts–meanings frame. This minimal set of assumptions, we believe, contributes to creating a context with the maximum therapeutic possibilities both for ourselves and for our clients. We offer this alternative set of assumptions not merely as an aesthetic preference, but as a paradigm for briefer, more effective, and more respectful psychotherapy.

THE NEGOTIATION TABLE

We have already devoted considerable discussion in this book to the most essential piece of furniture in the psychotherapist's office—the negotiation table. Although, as it happens, we don't have a real, physical table in either of our offices, this metaphorical table (see Figure 1, Chapter Four) is at the center of our thoughts about therapy. The psychotherapeutic "problem," in our view, is *not an affliction, but a problem only in the sense of a statement of what is to be solved,* and what exactly the problem is to be is decided by the process of negotiation between therapist and client. This negotiation of the definition of the problem (see Chapter Four) is for us the essence of psychotherapy.

THE COUCH

Second only in importance to the negotiation table is the couch.
We believe it is essential for every therapist's office to have a
couch, and we have found that many of our trainees are more
than somewhat surprised to hear us say this, as they sometimes
fear that we have regressed to psychoanalytic styles of therapy.
However, in our offices, the couch is intended not for the client's use but for the therapist's. The reason for this is that *every
now and then, in the course of a session, a hypothesis might
accidentally enter the therapist's head, and the best remedy for
it is to lie down until it goes away.* We believe that any and all
hypotheses about the meaning (plain or hidden), function, purpose, or cause of symptoms, or about supposed underlying
problems or issues, limit both therapist and client and serve
only to introduce premature closure.

We approach therapy without any notion that the reason
people have psychological, emotional, behavioral, or somatic
"symptoms" is that the symptoms serve a function or purpose
for individuals or for the systems of which they are part, or that
there are hidden underlying causes, reasons, and/or motivations
(conscious or unconscious) for symptoms. We do not believe
that rigid, automatic functioning and behavior produce symptoms, or that symptoms result from faulty past conditioning, or
that they are a response to present contingencies of reinforcement. We do not believe that symptoms represent solutions to
problems, or that they serve to ward off some avoided or undesired state for either individuals or their families. Nor do we
accept the theory that symptoms are the result of conflict. Likewise (outside the realm of physical medicine), we reject the
notion that symptoms are "signals" alerting one to conflict,
stress, imbalance, or other dysfunction, or indeed that they are
"signs" of any kind pointing to anything whatsoever beyond
themselves. Nor do we believe that children's problems indicate
or reflect the presence of a marital conflict or a structural/or-
ganizational dysfunction in the family. Not only do we believe
all of these notions to be pure speculation and contrary to what
we ourselves actually find in psychotherapy; we also believe
that the therapist's hypotheses involving such notions often

provide a major obstacle to the client's reaching the desired therapeutic outcome. To hold such hypotheses, however lightly, is to introduce unwarranted deductions and imperatives into the negotiation process, and (most importantly) to introduce prerequisites about what has to happen first before the therapeutic outcome can be reached. *We do not accept any claim that something has to change for people to behave differently.*

Instead, we propose the following working assumptions:

- *There are no such "things" as the presenting problem or the client's personality.*
- *It is not necessary to know the cause, function, or meaning of the presenting complaint in order to resolve it.*
- *Nothing special needs to happen or be resolved before the person does what they say they want to do, so long as it is* physically *possible for them to do that.*

THE CHAIRS

Where the therapist sits in relation to the client is a matter of considerable importance. In other words, how the therapist regards and approaches the client plays an important part in influencing how the therapist conducts the therapy. For example, whether the therapist regards her relationship with the client as a "real" one or as an "as-if" one will influence how she behaves in that relationship. Clearly, we do not believe that the client's relationship with the therapist exhibits "transference," or that it is to be seen as a recapitulation of some earlier relationship, or as representative of how the client conducts himself in relationships outside therapy; rather, we approach the relationship with the client as if the interaction in the session is relevant only to the interaction in the session. Moreover, people are human, and it is not unreasonable for clients to enter therapy with a certain amount of healthy skepticism about what they are getting into. This does not mean that they are "resistant" or "ambivalent." Rather than seeking ulterior motives or attributing diagnostic significance to clients' hesitancy, dissatisfaction, or objections to the way the therapy is being conducted, we seek commonplace explanations first, and are willing to alter our approach to better meet the requirements of our clients as they express them.

Since we do not believe that people "have" emotional/psychological "disorders," we do not regard the people who come to psychotherapy as psychologically/emotionally flawed, disturbed, damaged, or ill. We do not believe that people (or posited "parts" of people) who seek therapy don't want, are fundamentally ambivalent about, or are resistant to obtaining the results they say they want. Nor do we believe that people wouldn't continue to have the symptom if they (or their families or "the system") did not get something out of it. And although we regard clients as sincere in their requests for help and in their desire to be rid of the presenting complaints, we do not believe that individuals (including those who seek therapy) are necessarily doing the best they can with what they have and know at the moment. We do not view clients as resistant and in need of confrontation, as ill and in need of treatment or healing or curing, as weak or unstable and in need of support, as damaged and in need of repair, as underdeveloped and in need of nurturing, as fragile and in need of careful handling, or as misguided and in need of educating. Nor do we regard therapists as being experts in how to deal with life and as knowing best how to resolve life's difficulties.

As far as the relative heights of the chairs is concerned, some therapists believe it is imperative for the therapist to sit higher than the client ("one up"), while others believe it is strategically important for the therapist to be seated "one down." We, however, prefer to be "on the level."

Our preference, in the selection of seats at the start of each session, is simply to have the clients sit where they find it most comfortable. We do not read any meaning into who sits next to whom, "how" clients select their seats, and so on, nor do we deliberately place an extra chair in the room to represent some member of the family who is not attending the session. And we only have our clients *talk* to chairs when there are real people sitting in them.

Instead, we offer the following principles concerning how we regard our clients, which give people the benefit of the doubt throughout therapy (and, we should add, they rarely disappoint us):

- *People who come to therapy sincerely want results.*
- *The client's communications are to be taken at face value.*
- *The simplest, most common-sense, or most commonplace explanation is to be preferred in the first instance.*
- *Nothing needs to be added to, removed from, or changed about the person or persons who seek treatment to obtain successful results.*

THE CARPETING

It is essential to this approach that *we do not take clients on the carpet.*

We do not argue with our clients, and we do not subject them to "therapeutic" cross-examination, still less to grilling or badgering. Psychotherapy is not an inquisition. It isn't a trial or a debate. It is not a contest or a competition. It is not a lesson in logic or philosophy, or an exercise in the arts of rhetoric and persuasion. We do not browbeat our clients until they relinquish their "irrational ideas." Psychotherapy is not brainwashing.

When our clients do not do the task assignments we have given them, we do not take it personally or as if they are letting us down or letting themselves down, and we do not keep reminding them of this "failure." In short, here as elsewhere, we just do not take clients on the carpet.

It should also be said that we do not sweep anything *under* the carpet. We do not minimize the discomfort or the seriousness of clients' situations. We do not sweep the facts under the carpet, or attempt to distract clients from the (nonnegotiable) "realities" of their situations. Neither do we sweep objections under the carpet. We seek to draw out clients' objections and deal with them as we would any imperatives in therapy. We welcome "Yes, but . . . ". (When one of our trainees asked, "How do you deal with the 'yes-but'-er?", we replied, "The yes-butter is the lubricant that keeps the wheels of therapy turning.'')

THE WASTEBASKET

The wastebasket is, of course, a vital accessory in the furnishing of any therapist's office. It needs to be possible for the therapist to dispose of irrelevant rubbish that would otherwise clutter up the therapist's mind and litter the therapy with so much misleading stuff that it becomes harder for the therapist and client to find what they are actually looking for. When such waste material is not quickly disposed of, it is time that ends up being wasted instead. Into the wastebasket go all the epistemological presuppositions that create imaginary obstacles to the client's simply doing something different. Thus the wastebasket will be filled with characterizations, prerequisites, causal claims, predictions, and so on, including the whole gamut of epistemological prejudices about the nature of human beings and their functioning.

Here are some specific classes of items that we regard as false or unknowable, and as irrelevant to therapy and harmful to its progress:

• That an individual's behavior and experience is determined by her past experience, her genetic material, her "unconscious," her feelings, her thoughts, her family (or the interaction around her), and/or her environment, and that an individual's behavior has to be controlled by these factors, either singly or in combination.

• That past experiences limit present or future behavior.

• That people have fixed characters or personalities, or fixed psychological/emotional characteristics (e.g., "personality traits").

• That people can know about other people's internal experience (feelings, thoughts, perceptions, sensations), motivations, and intentions, without being explicitly and candidly informed.

• That the "cause" of a symptom, or indeed of any item of human behavior, can be known with certainty.

• That rigid, automatic functioning and behavior is inherently undesirable.

• That emotions are fixed entities or quantities, or even internal psychological states, and that they can be discovered (e.g., "He has a lot of unexpressed anger") or "worked through."

• That unexpressed or "unexperienced" emotions or thoughts can build up and express themselves in some way.

• That feelings can cause behavior (without the "help" of people's belief that they can indeed wield such causal power).

• That thoughts can cause behavior, or that behavior is determined by how a person views a situation, (which implies that that person could not simply keep his present view but behave differently).

• That it is possible for one person to interpersonally control another.

• That a person can be psychologically or emotionally damaged by unpleasant or traumatic experiences.

• That bereaved individuals need to go through a process of mourning involving a particular progression of stages, and that this takes a fairly predictable amount of time; or that mourning can be delayed or interrupted or unfinished.

• That there is such a thing as "psychological development"—that is, that not only do individuals develop physically and, as they get older, learn new things and new skills and adopt different views at different times, but that there is a process of psychological "development" that they go through (perhaps conceived of as involving stages or steps), and hence that it is possible to speak of such "development" as being actually or potentially "delayed" or "arrested" or "distorted" or as having "gaps."

• That what one has learned from experience cannot be mistaken.

This "itemization" of classes of assumptions that we consign to the wastebasket is not exhaustive, but should serve nonetheless to give an idea of the sort of assumptions that we believe should be disposed of if therapy is to be as effective as possible. In place of these assumptions that we do *not* hold, we suggest the following as forming a firmer foundation for effective psychotherapy:

- *Meanings (interpretations) are distinct from facts (sensory-based observations and descriptions), and speculations about human beings should not be regarded as facts.*
- *No one can know the cause of human behavior and experience.*
- *People's future actions and experience cannot be predicted with certainty, and what they have done in the past provides no reliable guide to what they will do in the future.*
- *The only way to behave differently is to behave differently.*
- *At any moment, an individual can do something different, irrespective of any feelings, thoughts, or circumstances.*
- *Individuals are accountable for their behavior.*

THE WINDOWS AND CURTAINS

Some people draw conclusions like curtains.
Don't they draw them tight!

—John Martyn

We prefer our offices to have large windows with the curtains drawn open, so as to have at all times as unobscured a view as possible of the world outside. Throughout therapy, and indeed throughout each therapy session, we keep our sights set on the outside world, where the action is. The therapist's office is not, for us, "where it all happens." All that matters is the client's actual behavior outside therapy, in his everyday life. We are not in this business to talk with people but to make a contribution to their lives, and the extent of that contribution can only be judged by the observable results in the client's daily life. In sharp contrast to some psychotherapists, we do not believe that some mystical transformation, a decisive moment when the scales fall from the client's eyes, is necessary. "Transformation," if it occurs, is all very well, but transformation and 60 cents will get you a cup of coffee. We are simply not interested in any "progress" that occurs in therapy; all we are interested in is the client doing something different in his life. And as we have emphasized throughout this book, there is no therapeutic change or transformation or breakthrough that needs to take place first.

THE LIGHTING

The atmosphere of the therapist's office should be light rather than gloomy. No matter how heavy and serious the client's "problem" may appear to the client, psychotherapy to resolve that problem need never be heavy and "serious." Part of the therapist's task is to get the client to "lighten up," and jokes, humor, a light-hearted attitude, and an informal, casual manner are important means of carrying out this task. On entering some psychotherapists' offices, one has the impression of entering a church, or indeed a *sanctum sanctorum*. In our view, psychotherapy should never have even the slightest hint of preciousness about it. The telephone rings during a session and is answered. The therapist is not a mysterious being cloaked in secrecy, but a transparent, fallible person doing an interesting but very ordinary job. The lightness of the atmosphere should convey this message: "We're here to go about an ordinary business of solving problems and figuring out what to do, not to participate in some mystical rite of passage."

It is as well that our offices have large windows with a view to the outside and the curtains well drawn, because *we prefer natural lighting whenever possible*. If our rapid therapeutic results appear out of the ordinary, we believe that it is largely because that is precisely where our solutions come from: *out of the ordinary*, the mundane, the commonplace, the everyday. We prefer to give a task assignment that does not depend on the psychotherapy context, but that would be an ordinary, natural solution to an ordinary problem, a solution that can be applied if necessary long after therapy has been forgotten. We attempt to avoid anything that smacks of "technique" or of esoteric therapeutic expertise. We prefer interventions that are obvious in retrospect, and that can be seen by the clients not really to have required therapy in the first place. Any illumination the clients receive thus turns out to be the natural illumination available to everyone under the sun, and not the arcane province of specially "enlightened" psychotherapists.

Where we require some additional lighting, however, at times when we would otherwise be operating in the dark, we prefer *indirect lighting*. While always keeping our spotlight on the facts and on the action the client is to take, the general source of illumination supplementing natural lighting is indirect rather than direct. We do not believe that conscious insight provides an essential source of illumination in psychotherapy. We do not hold the assumption that insight, conscious understanding, or awareness is desirable or a prerequisite for therapeutic results, and we believe it is neither necessary nor sufficient for successful psychotherapy. Nor do we hold, as a general assumption about people, that conscious awareness and functioning is better or more effective than unconscious, automatic functioning (and we doubt that it is even always possible!). Thus we often prefer indirect suggestion to direct suggestion or rational discussion; we prefer unconscious learning to conscious learning; and we prefer to illumine our subject obliquely, through stories, metaphors, and other forms of parallel communication.

THE CLOCK AND CALENDAR

We reject a common notion in psychotherapy that the longer the therapy, the better, deeper, or more enduring the results. Moreover, we do not believe that one can predict with certainty how much time will be required for the treatment of a given complaint. There is nothing in the description of a complaint that would give any indication at all of how much time would be required to resolve it; there are, in our view, no "diagnostic categories" or other descriptive categories of symptoms or complaints that on the whole take longer to resolve than others. And we assert that they can all at least potentially be resolved in a single session, or without any psychotherapy at all. The chronicity of a given symptom only tells us one thing: that so far no one has solved the problem. A "problem" that has gone on for 30 years need take no longer to solve than one that has gone on for 30 days. Plugging in a clock left unplugged for 10 years will work as well as plugging in a clock left unplugged for 10 minutes.

In the same way, there is no telling in advance how much time will be required for a given session, and so decisions about scheduling of appointments on a given day will have to be dictated to a great extent by purely practical or administrative considerations. If in a given session we feel we need 2 hours and have 2 hours available, we take it; but if we are finished in 15 minutes, we don't hang on for the sake of filling up the hour, or if we do, we chat socially rather than "doing more therapy." Likewise, there can be no fixed "standard" interval between sessions, and this interval must be adjusted to fit the needs of each individual case. It cannot even be presupposed from the start of the first or subsequent sessions that a further session will be necessary or desirable. Time-based contracts (or contracts specifying a set number of sessions), from our point of view, seem rather arbitrary and pointless, and add unnecessary presuppositions about the length of time that might be required to solve the problem. Although, in our approach, problems are typically resolved within a few sessions and at times in one session, there is no telling in advance how many sessions will be needed. The one thing we do hold is this:

- *The briefer successful therapy can be, the better.*

THE DOOR

In our approach, we are willing to see whoever comes in through our door. We have no selection criteria, or indications and contraindications. Our psychotherapeutic approach is, we believe, an effective approach for dealing with all presenting complaints that can be dealt with in therapy. We also are willing to see whichever members of the family come in through our door, and we do not struggle to get "missing" members, let alone the whole family, into our office.

Because we do not believe that everyone needs and can benefit from therapy, we do not try to get people in through our door. That does not mean that we minimize problems; rather, it means that we do not see psychotherapy as always supplying the most effective solution.

If an individual who consults us has a number of other complaints for which she is not seeking help because she does not believe that anything can be done about them, we may offer to deal with these other complaints if we know a way to resolve them. And so sometimes we may open up possibilities by pointing to "problems" where the client has just resigned herself to putting up with an undesired and undesirable situation, but unless the client then requests our help with these further difficulties, we do not go any further with them. And so if therapy is resolved to the client's satisfaction, and the original criteria for successful results (see Chapter Five) have been fulfilled, we do not press the client to go on with therapy just because we happen to see a lot of difficulties we think we could do something about. So, though we may show the client to the door at this point, we always leave the door open for her to return.

If someone has a headache and takes an aspirin for it and then no longer has a headache, that person doesn't usually keep on taking aspirin to prevent the next headache from coming on (Segal, 1980). Even more important, if the person gets another headache a year later, he does not take the view that the original headache has come back or that it had never really gone away or been properly dealt with, but had merely been covered up superficially and had gone underground only to re-emerge later. And he certainly doesn't say it has re-emerged in another form—"symptom substitution"—if the ache he gets a year later is an earache or a stomachache!

Since we do not believe that "problems" are maladies or afflictions, we do not believe they can be "cured." There is not even any guarantee that the client won't go back to a previous unsatisfactory pattern of behavior and so have similar difficulties in the future. But this does *not* mean that "the problem has come back," or that the original therapy was not "really" successful. There are no entities we are surgically removing or otherwise treating. A nonworking (i.e., "problematic") pattern of behavior will fail to produce a client's desired results now, next year, or in 10 years. And the solution required then may be the same as that required now. We certainly do not believe that if the symptom is resolved without resolving the "underlying cause," "symptom substitution" will result. We do not believe there ever really is an underlying cause (or at least one that can ever be known about and resolved), and we do not know how one could ever substantiate an hypothesis to the effect that one symptom has replaced another.

But a lot will depend on how broadly the problem is originally defined in the negotiation process. For example, we may successfully help someone who has trouble asking for a date because he is looking for the perfect opening line, and have him reappear in our office a year later unable to finish his dissertation because he can't write a chapter until he finds the perfect chapter title. One does not need to hypothesize "symptom substitution," nor is there any need for an hypothesized Freudian "compulsion to repeat." Rather, the pattern of the problem we have already dealt with and the pattern of the problem a year later are both instances of a more general pattern (e.g., "not getting started until he's devised a 'perfect' beginning"), and had we negotiated this broader definition of the problem in the first place, we might have dealt with a wider class of potential and actual presenting complaints. But "life is just one damn thing after another," and the end of therapy is not put off until all of life's present and future problems have been resolved, even if this were possible.

Finally, we do not believe that the therapist's agenda takes precedence over the client's agenda in determining when it is time to show the client the door. Therapy is over when the agreed outcome has been reached, not when certain hypothetical "therapeutic issues" have been dealt with. We submit:

- *Successful therapeutic results are equivalent to observable behavior that the client says is the kind he wants in the area of the presenting complaint, and/or the client's saying that he no longer has the complaint.*

And so, inevitably, clients go out the same door through which they came in.

CHAPTER SEVEN

SKILLFUL MEANS
Working Methods

The thing to do is to get your patient, any way you wish, any way you can, to do something.—Milton H. Erickson

In this chapter, we offer some general descriptions of the ways in which we put clinical epistemolgy into practice in our own work. This chapter should supplement what we have written in previous chapters about our ways of working, both by drawing attention to certain aspects of "technique" that may not have been apparent, and by summarizing in one place some of the general approaches to interviewing that seem to arise naturally from this approach. These "working methods" are offered not as rigid procedures and rules, but as guidelines for therapists wishing to put these ideas into practice, who might wish to benefit from what our inevitably limited experience has so far shown to be most useful. We regard these working methods as merely "skillful means" (from the Sanskrit *upaya*) that might be used to achieve the ends of clinical epistemology, in assisting the client to reach "the other shore" (cf. Watts, 1961, p. 132). The "skillful means" are all, in every sense of the word, options.

We expect this to be the most "parochial" chapter and the chapter most likely to become obsolete, influenced as it is by our history, background, and training. Our ways of working in psychotherapy are continually being refined, and just as we find that what we were doing a few years ago in psychotherapy now seems hopelessly crude and primitive from our present perspective, we operate always with the earnest hope that in a few years' time we will look back on our present working methods and find them to be but the first, faltering steps in a promising direction.

We are aware that this chapter—indeed, this book—provides far from an adequate description of what we do in therapy. We are continually seeking further and updated *descriptive generalizations* for identifying what it is we do that seems to be effective. And so these descriptions are evolving all the time, particularly in our work as psychotherapy trainers as we try to teach our trainees how to master these ways of working and to achieve similar results. It is from this teaching and supervision process that we have learned most about how to describe what we do. However, we are only too keenly aware of areas that for the moment must remain, in Bateson's analogy, as knots tied in our mental hankerchief to remind us that we have left some matters unformulated for the time being. Rather than constructing limiting, artificial, temporary fences "hiding the unknown from future investigators," we prefer to put up signposts instead that read, "UNEXPLORED BEYOND THIS POINT" (Bateson, 1978, p. 61).

PART ONE:
NEGOTIATING OPERATIONS

As discussed in Chapters Four and Five, one of the main goals we have in therapy is to negotiate a "presentable" problem—that is, one that doesn't have built-in barriers to its own solution. To this end, we usually make use of a number of operations, many of which have already been discussed in various connections. All of these operations are performed throughout therapy, and our list is not intended to be sequential.

CREATING THE THERAPEUTIC REALITY

Sometimes even before we ask clients what brings them into therapy, we endeavor to create a therapeutic reality, setting out the nature of the interview and/or the therapeutic process as we see it. Often, we provide a brief account of how we see our role as therapists. For example, when we interview parents who we know have come to consult us about a child, we may begin by saying, "Our job is to be consultants to you as parents, to help you to deal differently with whatever situation you may be dealing with, in order that you might get more of the kind of results you've been wanting to get." This explains our role as that of consultants rather than that of necessarily the ones who are going to "fix" the child; it acknowledges that the parents' intentions are to have good results (whatever those might be defined to be) and that they have already been trying in various ways to deal with "the situation"; and it emphasizes that they are going to do the work and that this will involve doing something different or differently in order to achieve the desired results. Everything we say and do in psychotherapy contributes to creating the therapeutic reality, but at the outset we sometimes pre-empt any possible misconceptions in order to get therapy off on the right foot.

OPERATIONS FOR BUILDING RAPPORT

From the beginning of therapy and throughout, it is important, we believe, for the therapist to build rapport with the client. The most important means of doing this is "speaking the client's language"—making use of the client's preferred terminology, ways of phrasing things, and so on. Thus the character of the psychotherapy interview will differ dramatically according to whether the client is, for example, a Harvard professor with a PhD in psychology or a semiliterate farm laborer. The therapist's behavior must continually be flexible enough to adjust to each client's unique style. Even though the therapist is aiming eventually to alter the client's word choices in the direction of sensory-based descriptions, this is most rapidly and easily done by initially "appropriating" the client's word choices and then gently steering these away and/or redefining them in terms of video descriptions.

Likewise, although the therapist is aiming to get the client to lighten up, this can most easily be accomplished by initially matching the client's degree of seriousness and then gradually shifting, but only so fast as the client actually follows along by altering her own demeanor accordingly.

Another important means of building rapport is for the therapist to offer metaphors, anecdotes, similes, or examples to show that she understands what the client is saying. While building rapport, this can be used at the same time to reformulate what the client is talking about, or at least to alter the connotations. For example, a client who complained of "tension headaches" complained also that he couldn't "take anything in" when people talked to him, and that is was "as if I'm not really there." He continued to describe this experience in abstract, "psychology" terms that suggested "alienation" and similar existentialist notions. We interrupted to say that we imagined he felt the way someone would feel if his trousers had ripped and he was trying precariously to hold them up while trying to conduct a conversation: It's pretty hard to pay attention to the subject of the conversation and to what's going on around you if you're preoccupied with trying to hold your trousers up. A series of similar anecdotes and examples from our own experience were then offered, on this theme of not being able to pay adequate attention and so "not really being there" because one is preoccupied instead with some other activity (such as negotiating a difficult intersection while driving with a talkative passenger) or preoccupied with a distracting bodily sensation (such as a stone in one's shoe or a cut finger). Thus while building rapport through descriptive matching of the client's experience, we were able to take the experience out of the existential/phenomenological realm and back into the realm of everyday human experience.

"NEUTRAL" QUESTIONS (RELATIVELY FREE OF PRESUPPOSITIONS)

We most often begin the first session by asking "What brings you here?" rather than, for example, "What's the problem?," since the latter presupposes that a problem exists and, moreover, that the client ought to be able to report to us what that (reified) problem is. This initial neutral question—"What brings you here?"—is often virtually the *last* neutral question we ask. We want to begin by getting back the client's initial report so that we have something to which we can respond, in order to tease out any presuppositions, query any generalizations, and so on. From this point onward, our questions are seldom neutral, or designed primarily to elicit data; rather, they are designed to open up possibilities and to steer the client in particular directions. For example, we might open a second or subsequent session with, "Well, what did you do and how did it go?" if a homework task was assigned, or with "What would you like to accomplish here today?" In either case, our question is no longer neutral, but is designed to structure the negotiation process along particular lines.

INTRODUCING DOUBT

Throughout the process of therapy, we continually call into question anything that is not verified fact—and we always remain open to the possibility that even those "facts" can change at any moment. We are continually "suspending judgment" and encouraging our clients to do the same, sometimes in a very offhand way and sometimes in a very direct way. If, for example, a client conjectures that his complaint may be related to such-and-such, we are likely to reply, "Well, it could be that, could be something else—we can't be sure, but tell us . . . " and go on to ask about something else. We introduce doubt especially about knowing with certainty the causes of situations, symptoms, and so on; about the prerequisites for desired results; and about the future course of things. This process of introducing doubt, which has already been discussed in some detail, pervades our approach, and may be considered under three subheadings.

Challenging Attributions and Deductions

When the client makes verbal deductions or attributions (including characterizations of himself or others—the attribution of relatively enduring characteristics), the questions we most often ask are "How do you know?" and "What do (you/they) actually say or do that leads you to say (you/they) are *X*?" The point of this and other questions is either to challenge these attributions or deductions by calling them into question, or to specify the actions (the facts) that constitute the client's "evidence" for the attributions or deductions. Once the client's evidence or *descriptive content* for the attributions or deductions has been adequately specified in sensory-based terms, we may later go back to using the client's word as shorthand for the descriptions, speaking, for example, of "what you call being obstinate."

Where a causal attribution, for example, is contextually implied (cf. also Appendix I) by the mere fact that a client mentions it ("I have low self-esteem," "Well, he comes from a family of five brothers"), we frequently make the attribution explicit (so that it can be challenged) by asking, "How's that relevant or related?"

We often deal with attributions or deductions by *introducing new possibilities*—that is, by suggesting alternative possible deductions or attributions, or by *renaming* the behavior (or whatever) in question. Not uncommonly we will offer an alternative deduction in the form of a reversal of a client's punctuation; in other words, we turn the causal arrows around the other way. For example, a client might claim he avoids women because he is shy, and we might just as easily claim that he is shy because he avoids women and doesn't have much experience with them. Neither explanation is necessarily "accurate," but our suggestion may serve to challenge the deduction the client has been making about his situation (and possibly his prerequisites for reaching the desired results as well). Likewise, a client with a number of "obsessional" behaviors and habits, who experienced episodes of panic and who was typically very worked up and "highly strung," described his obsessions as caused by his anxiety; we presented an equally good case that perhaps, with all of these habits taking up so much time and attention, it wasn't surprising he was so wound up so much of the time as a result (cf. also the stress–headache example discussed in Chapter Five). Our reversal of causal arrows is offered as a "throwaway," so to speak, and we conclude only that it's difficult or impossible to know what is responsible for causing what, rather than insisting on "our" version.

Challenging Evaluations

We challenge implicit and explicit evaluations by asking some variation on the question, "So what?" "You might not get the job you applied for . . . so what?" A client usually responds to such a question either by dropping his evaluation (in which case the problem might be gone) and/or by giving us a report that will contain other claims we can challenge, or further information we can use to specify the facts. We might also suggest some other evaluation of the experience—either a "positive" one if the client is evaluating the experience only as negative; a "negative" one if the client is viewing the situation as inherently positive; or a more "neutral" evaluation of the situation. Parents who characterize their child as "immature" (with a negative evaluation implied) might be told a story about one of us who seemed as a child to be immature, but really was a "late bloomer" who turned out more mature and successful in the end than some of his more "mature" peers.

Clients often implicitly ascribe an inherently negative value to their reports, usually based on their prerequisites and causal attributions, which we challenge. For example, a client with a weight "problem" might report that she is hungry "all the time." We usually respond by asking, "How is this a problem for you?" This either challenges the evaluation or elicits the causal attributions or prerequisites (e.g., that hunger causes overeating or that the hungry feeling will have to be dealt with before she can lose the weight she wants to lose), thereby developing the negotiation process further in some way.

Challenging Prerequisites

When a client implies that there is some prerequisite to reaching some desired outcome of doing or not doing something, we may initially intervene with some variation of "Don't do that" (for something the client wants not to do) or "So, do that" (for something the client wants to do). (Alternatively, we may reply with a gentle "Well, why not just do this . . . ?") If the client replies in turn that they "can't," we ask "What stops you?" (or "What would stop you?"). We then attempt to unhook the client from this limiting prerequisite. For example, if parents are hamstrung because they are hooked on the prerequisite that before they can get their children to behave, they must first agree about everything regarding rules for their children and the sanctions for breaking those rules, we may tell them that there's no law that says they've got to agree. We might add that their kids need to learn to adapt to different people with different standards, rules, and tolerances, and so why deprive the kids of one of the benefits of having two parents?

One of the most powerful ways of unhooking the client from limiting prerequisites is to provide counterexamples or exceptions from the client's own experience. A client who thought she had to feel different before she could behave differently (e.g. to eliminate the desire to smoke before she could stop smoking cigarettes, or to stop feeling depressed before she could start taking constructive action) might be asked whether she has ever felt like going back to sleep when the alarm rings in the morning, and, still feeling that way, has gotten out of bed because she had to get to work on time.

Anecdotes from our own or other clients' or acquaintances' experience are offered as counterexamples too, particularly to assist the client in finding similar counterexamples from his own life. For instance, a client hooked on the prerequisite that he had to have different thoughts before he could take different action might be told about a friend of ours who took up jogging and only had time to jog before work in the morning. In the first few weeks, our friend would wake up to the alarm at 5:30 and start telling himself, "Well, I can start jogging tomorrow," or "I don't need to jog every day," or "I need to conserve my energy for work—I've got a big day ahead," or "I got to sleep late last night—I really need the sleep this morning," and so on. And he would turn over and go back to sleep, setting his alarm in time to get up for work. He was committed to taking up jogging, however, and finally dealt with these thoughts by just "listening" to them but not acting on them. So he would think, "Well, I can start jogging tomorrow," and swing his feet over the side of the bed and put on his tracksuit; and then think, "I don't need to jog every day," and go to brush his teeth; and then think, "I need to conserve my energy for work—I've got a big day ahead," and put on his trackshoes and go out the front door; and then think such thoughts as "I got to sleep late last night—I really need the sleep this morning" while jogging along the road.

We might negate the client's prerequisite much more directly and explicitly by giving permission or providing validation to keep the alleged "impediment" and nevertheless do the desired behavior: "You can feel like yelling and not yell," "You can want to have a cigarette, and not have one," "You can think all the thoughts you like about food and calories and getting fat, and still eat appropriate amounts," "It's all right to be scared about asking a girl out for a date, and then go ahead and ask a girl out for a date while still being scared," and so forth.

"CHANNELING" QUESTIONS, STATEMENTS, AND ACTIONS

Many of the questions we ask, statements we make, and actions we perform in therapy are designed to channel our clients' communications in certain directions. It is inevitable, of course, that a therapist's communications will channel a client's communications, and this occurs in all forms of psychotherapy. However, we deliberately use certain verbal and nonverbal means to channel the negotiations in a constructive direction.

The Road Not Taken

> If your train's on the wrong track, every station you come to is the wrong station.—Bernard Malamud

We have already discussed (see Chapter Five) how we "ignore" certain of the client's remarks—acknowledging the remarks so that the clients know we have "gotten" them, making it clear that we have heard and understood, but essentially letting them pass by. The client may bring up the same theme, or implied prerequisite, or implied causal attribution, or whatever, numerous times, finally dropping it when our behavior suggests that it is not relevant. Acknowledging such communications is as important, though, as letting them pass by.

We have tried to give guidelines throughout this book for how to decide which roads are worth taking and which are best to pass by, and this matter will become clearer in the course of the present chapter. As a reminder, however, we can offer the following summary of hints:

• *Things to avoid*: anything unverified or unverifiable; conjectures; characterizations and other attributions; hypotheses; predictions; the area of subjective experience; anything not yet described in terms of the client's actual actions; any attempt to alter thoughts or feelings before altering behavior; discussion of the past apart from past successes; solutions dependent on factors outside the client's control (e.g., cooperation in initiating new behavior on the part of people who are not involved in the therapy session); arguments; utopian goals; and pursuing a preconceived "game plan" for the session.

• *Things to pursue*: video descriptions; the facts; details of the client's actual actions; the search for invariant pattern (see Chapter Eight); the limits of the symptom context (see Chapter Eight); simple, obvious solutions; solutions successfully applied in other areas of the client's life; the client's goals or ambitions in life, particularly those that have been (through a prerequisite) postponed until the solution of the problem; utilizing existing resources; *small* shifts; getting the client to do something; the *normal* aspects of the complaint; exceptions to the occurrence of the complaint; the introduction of doubt; the "path of least resistance"; whatever can be done right now; win–win situations; and responding to the responses elicited.

Minimally Structured Unspecified Questions

One of our most commonly used means of channeling the client's communications is the asking of minimally structured unspecified questions—questions that can potentially call forth a wide range of responses in terms of content, but that restrict the responses to a particular range. For example, we often ask, "If I followed you around with a video camera, how would I know you were experiencing this difficulty?" or, when establishing criteria for results, "If I followed you around with a video camera, how would you and I both know for certain, from watching the video, that we were finished with therapy—that you had achieved the desired results?'' These questions sound quite general and open-ended, but they considerably narrow down the range of likely responses.

Multiple-Choice Questioning

Another form of channeling is the asking of multiple-choice questions ("Is it A or B or C or D or E?"), or, while the client is deciding how to answer a more open-ended question, suggesting specific possible answers ("such as A, B, C, D, E, . . . "), if only to identify for the client the class of items from which we want her to select a response. This not only saves time by making clear to the client the sort of information we are looking for, but gently steers the client in the direction we are wanting to go.

Therapeutic Interrupting

In creating the therapeutic reality, we sometimes call attention to the fact that we will be interrupting a lot in the session, and that this is not because we are being rude, but because we need to understand, and also because "You know your situation so well that you may take for granted that I'll know what you're talking about when in fact I may not, so whenever I don't understand something, I think it's better to stop and check it out rather than nodding wisely and pretend to understand." And indeed, we do interrupt our clients a great deal. (A poster in one of our offices reads, "If there's anything I can't stand it's someone who talks when I'm interrupting.") Rather than letting clients verbally paint themselves into an unhelpful corner, we prefer to cut them off and divert the conversation, challenge a deduction or imperative, or pre-empt what they are about to say. (It seems extraordinary to us that some therapists, even when there is something they are especially eager to say, act from the prerequisite that they must wait for their clients to stop talking, even in instances where they would not do so if they were in everyday conversations with friends or respected colleagues!)

Pre-empting, Roadblocks, and Detours

As we have discussed in Chapter Five, we prefer to deal with clients' imperatives, deductions, presuppositions, evaluations, and expectations, whenever possible, by pre-empting them before the clients even have a chance properly to proffer them. When we can "see one coming," or gather from what a client is starting to say that a particular (familiar) one may be on its way, we might interrupt with a pre-emptive remark or anecdote or joke. This approach involves, as it were, placing a roadblock in the road and detouring the traffic away from the potentially problematic route before the expected traffic even arrives. So if a client with a weight problem begins to say, "Whenever I get hungry, I . . . ", we may interrupt with " 'Hungry' is an interesting word, you know . . . " and begin relating half a dozen short anecdotes and interesting medical facts on the theme of people not knowing how to know whether or not they're hungry. This roadblock and 5-minute detour, all the more powerful because the client has not yet said anything she might otherwise have had to back down from (i.e., if we had told the stories after she'd finished what she'd started to say), may save us from having to get the client to make a U-turn and double back after going a long way down a road leading nowhere.

Giving the Punch Line

On occasion, we will channel the negotiations by "giving the punch line," indicating where we are heading, so that this statement of the ultimate objective can influence the course of the discussion. For example, "What we're looking for is the pattern of the temper tantrums, because there is always a pattern even though it's not usually apparent at first," or "We're trying to find a situation in which you probably wouldn't have a panic attack, but which is otherwise as near as possible to some situation in which you probably would."

Normalizing Moves

One of the main general directions in which we channel the client's communications is toward viewing things as normal, everyday phenomena rather than as instances of "psychopathology" or as anomalous, exceptional, or mysterious experiences. This "normalizing" of the behavior and experiences reported by the client, can be done very straightforwardly by saying, "That sounds pretty normal," and then placing the behavior or experience in its normal context. We often say, "Well, that's understandable," and go on to give an account of how what they've presented as unusual is really quite understandable, given the circumstances. For example, a young man who added to his list of complaints that he had a "social problem," insofar as he had no friends and had never had a girlfriend, was simply told, "Well that's pretty understandable, considering you rarely go out of the house; if you don't go out, there's little opportunity to make any friends or meet any women." We tend to offer commonplace explanations at every opportunity, and shrug off a great many of the client's "news items" as simply "not newsworthy." This is also of course an approach well known to physicians in general practice, who reassure their patients less by what they say than by what they don't seem to regard as even worth remarking upon. In children's problems we draw attention to the range of appropriateness for specific behaviors, particularly with regard to what seems, in fact, quite "age-appropriate."

But there are other, more indirect ways of normalizing experiences and behavior. We may tell anecdotes that place the behavior or experience in question in a normal context, particularly anecdotes from our own or friends' experience. Particularly useful are stories by which we can suggest, "Yeah, me too."

Another (not incompatible) approach to normalizing we use is to (pre-emptively) interject, "I sure know what you mean" and proceed to give examples to demonstrate that we do indeed know what the client is talking about, thereby by implication taking matters out of the realm of the anomalous or exceptional. To anticipate the pattern the client is about to describe or to accurately anticipate the client's report (e.g., "Don't tell me—the more you try to get it out of your mind, the harder it gets not to think about it") can, again, implicitly normalize the subject of that report. Anticipating the facts of the client's situation such that the client immediately recognizes himself—"That's it exactly"—has the added advantage of normalizing without any indication that this is what we as the therapists are trying to do. One way we anticipate the client's situations is through the multiple-choice questions we ask, clearly revealing knowledge of a familiar kind of pattern. It can be quite a powerful and reassuring intervention to ask the parents of a child with temper tantrums, "Does he ever do this?" and then proceed to give a pretty good video description of that child's behavior. If parents somberly report, for example, that their child in temper says, "I want to be unhappy," or "I wish I was dead!", we usually ask, "Have you had *any of these* yet?: 'I don't love you any more,' 'You don't love me anymore,' 'I hate you,' 'I wish you weren't my parents,' . . . " and so on, running through a whole list of the kinds of things kids say in anger. When we correctly identify one after the other, the context changes to one in which we and the parents can smile or laugh with recognition at each one, and often the parents add further ones to the list that we can all laugh about too.

However it is accomplished, the effect of normalizing is to return the situation to the realm of the client's potential competence, where the client can get moving in doing something about it. In this way the negotiations are kept channeled toward what the client can actually do (if indeed anything needs to be done), and away from the mystified and mystifying realms of psychological characterization and pseudoexplanations.

Suggesting Way-Out Alternatives

Finally, one of the ways we channel the negotiations is by putting forward way-out alternatives to widen the range of possibilities, followed by suggesting comparatively mild or conservative alternatives that previously would have been unacceptable to the client but that now, by contrast, seem fairly innocuous. For example, parents who are reluctant to take firm action with regard to disciplining their child, and who, at the same time, cannot see that anything they might do could make a difference, might be told, "Well, you could starve him for a week. You know, just give him water and vitamins, and three crackers a day—he could survive on that for several weeks; but you'd probably only have to do it for a week." And then we would go on to discuss how they could go about this and how it would indeed influence their child's behavior. After pursuing this line for a while (and the longer we discuss it, the more "real" it becomes in a way), we might then suggest that, of course, it would probably be sufficient just to give him his meals but let him go without desserts or special treats. What would have seemed unthinkable a few minutes before now seems perfectly acceptable. By stretching the client's frame of reference wide enough, like stretching a stretch cotton waistband too far, when it returns to its shape it may be somewhat looser than it was before.

"LOADED" QUESTIONS, STATEMENTS, AND ACTIONS

Whereas "channeling interventions" are meant to lead the client and the negotiations in a certain, more or less broad direction, "loaded" questions, statements, and actions on the part of the therapist are intended to put a much more specific slant on things. There is naturally a certain degree of overlap between these two classes of intervention, but we regard an intervention as "channeling" if it is designed merely to steer the client (or the negotiations) away from particular avenues ("the roads not taken"), and as "loaded" if it is designed to steer the client toward or even down particular avenues.

Blocking Unhelpful or Destructive Remarks

A borderline case between "channeling" and "loaded" interventions (and there are many such borderline cases) is that of blocking unhelpful or destructive remarks in a very direct or forceful fashion, by directly interrupting clients. This is of particular importance in conjoint marital interviews or in interviews with parents and teenagers, where it is sometimes necessary to shut people up before they say something that it will later be difficult to unsay. Sometimes we need to stop someone very directly from responding to a provocation by insisting, "Don't answer that, don't answer that!" Here we are steering the person away from a road that is not to be taken, but we are going beyond a general channeling and are limiting the available choices much more strictly.

"Loaded" interventions, however, are not necessarily less subtle or less gentle than channeling interventions.

Presuppositional Questions and Statements

We have already discussed in some detail (especially in Chapter Five) the deliberate use of syntactic presupposition in our own questions and statements in order to presuppose certain matters, irrespective of how clients answer the questions or irrespective of whether they respond to the assertions by agreeing or disagreeing. In this manner, we can very subtly make heavily loaded interventions. To ask a client, for instance, "What will you be able to do when you get over this symptom that you don't do now?" presupposes that the client will get over the symptom; the suggestion is dropped into the conversation very casually and is usually accepted by the client with equal casualness.

The Suggestive Use of Verb Tenses

A closely related operation involves selecting our verb tenses carefully in order to avoid unwanted presuppositions and to introduce more desirable ones. This is another matter we have already discussed in Chapter Five, where we give the example of not asking a person who seeks therapy to give up smoking "How many cigarettes do you smoke?", which presupposes continued smoking, but asking instead, "How many cigarettes did you smoke per day?" The choice of verb tenses, like many of our choices of words in the negotiation process, follows naturally from our own expectation that the client can reach her goal right now, and that there is no reason why there should still "be" a problem by the end of the session.

"Have You Got One of These?"

A form of "loaded" intervention we use frequently in various aspects of the negotiation process is one that, for shorthand, we think of in terms of the questions "Have you got one of these?" and "Got anything like this?" Either we describe a general type of experience and ask whether the client can think of an experience of her own that would fit this description, or we relate one or more experiences of our own and ask the client whether she has ever had similar experiences. In this manner, we get the client to sift through her own experiences to find one or more fitting the bill we have in mind. For example, if we are trying to unhook the client from a prerequisite about having to feel like doing X before they can do X, we might ask, "Can you recall some of the times in your life when you didn't feel like doing something, and did it nonetheless because it simply had to get done?" ("Have you got one of these?") If no recollections are forthcoming, we might then offer some fairly common examples, such as getting out of bed when one doesn't feel like getting out of bed, going to work when one feels like staying home, and so on. Or we might simply begin by relating a few personal anecdotes about times when we did something directly contrary to what we felt like doing, and invite the client to offer some similar examples from her own life. ("Got anything like this?")

Summarizing with a Twist (or on the Rocks)

Frequently we "summarize" what a client has been saying ("Let me see if I understand this so far . . . "), but in the summarizing we introduce a significant twist of some kind. Our summary includes all of the significant facts of the client's story so far and perhaps some aspects of the story the client has woven around those facts, but introduces a twist in the story—to which we do not draw attention, but which is offered merely as part of the summing up. We get the client to "ratify" our summary and to add "anything we've missed," and then we proceed on the basis of the version of the story so far represented in our summary.

Taking the (Wise) Words Right Out of the Client's Mouth

A related operation involves interrupting a client after he has said something significant but before he can go on to specify what he thinks the significance of his statement is or what the implications are for solving the problem. We interrupt to agree with the point made and sometimes stress its importance or insightfulness, and go on to attach a rather different significance to it from that which the client might have intended to attach to it. The form the interruption takes will usually be something like this: "Boy, I agree! That's a very important point. What you're saying is . . . " and then we go on to put forward our version.

For example, after we have spelled out what action a client needs to take, the client might begin, "You know, I can't even imagine myself doing anything like that, not in my wildest dreams . . ." and the therapist can come in at that point with " . . . *not in your wildest dreams* . . . you know, I agree, and that's so important. You can't imagine yourself doing anything like that, and I'm impressed that you're aware you won't be able to imagine it before you've actually done it. A lot of clients naively think that they have to be able to imagine themselves doing it before they can do it, and it's a vicious circle. But then when you've done it, as you say, it's bound to be so surprising— like you couldn't imagine yourself doing it even in your wildest dreams, and yet there! you've done it . . . like the first astronauts landing on the moon not being able to even imagine doing it until they were actually on lunar soil. So what you're saying is very important, and will help you get over this difficulty quickly: You've just got to do it, because unless and until you've actually done it, it will always just seem like a pipe dream."

Converting to an Action Description What Is Presented as Involuntary Experience

Wherever possible, we paraphrase any statements by the client describing something as involuntary experience (and himself as the passive recipient of the experience) in terms of the client's actual or potential actions. If a client says, "These headaches prevent me from concentrating," we may paraphrase this as "So with these headaches you've got, one thing you do is that you keep attending to them instead of paying attention to whatever you're supposed to be attending to." If a client says, "But as soon as I see the food in front of me, all my self-control goes out the window," we may paraphrase this as "When you've actually got the food in front of you, you do the very thing that earlier you had decided not to do." If a client says, "When he does that, my anger just gets the better of me, in spite of having agreed to give your suggestion a try," we might paraphrase this as "So when he does that, you just go through your usual routine of speaking and acting angrily—almost out of habit, I hear you saying—instead of doing the task you'd decided to try as an experiment." Where the experience described by the client can be paraphrased in terms of what the client does or does not do, has done or failed to do, we make the relevant translation. This takes us out of the realm of mysterious, fortuitous experience that befalls the client, and into the realm of what the client does and can do to make a difference in his experience.

Giving Recipes for the Complaint

An approach we sometimes use to emphasize the role of the client's actions in the undesired experience, and to recontextualize it in a powerful way, is to offer a "recipe" for the experience in question. The recipe will be customized according to the facts we have obtained about the pattern of what this particular client actually does. For example, we may say to a "depressed" client: "I'll tell you what. I'll give you a recipe for how to 'do' depression. If you should ever want to 'do' a really deep depression, here's all you or anyone has to do: (1) Go over and over in your mind all the things you didn't do in your life that you should have done. (2) Keep comparing yourself to other people, and losing by the comparison. (3) Let anything pile up that can pile up, and neglect it—dishes, laundry, bills, housekeeping, personal business, work, studies, personal appearance, hygiene—continually put off dealing with it. (4) Stay in bed as long as you can, particularly if you are not sleepy. (5) Stay in your pajamas or bathrobe and don't get dressed. (6) Move about slowly, preferably hanging your head, breathing shallowly, shuffling your feet. (7) Spend as much time as possible clearly doing nothing, preferably sitting or lying down; staring off into space or at the floor for prolonged periods is always to be preferred to looking alert. (8) Tell yourself things will never get better, never be any different. (9) Blame yourself, but don't do

anything about what you're blaming yourself for, and if someone suggests you do something about it, then turn to blaming
others for a while. (10) Reduce the amount of physical activity
and stimuli you have; spend a lot of time watching the television or sleeping, but definitely avoid seeing friends or doing
anything new." The list, of course, can go on. The details of
this, although there a few familiar patterns that tend toward
being universal for any given complaint, need to be based on
what the client actually does, and the recipe is offered as a
general recipe that if followed by *anyone* would ensure her
being, for example, depressed.

Likewise, an "insomniac" can be offered a recipe for insomnia such as this "(1) Take as many precautions as you can
think of to 'help' yourself sleep. (2) Worry before and after
getting into bed about whether you'll be able to sleep tonight.
(3) Look at the clock as often as possible to see if you're asleep
yet, and how much sleep you have already lost. (4) Try to force
yourself to sleep. (5) Get frustrated with yourself and the universe for your failure—a few expletives and sighs are often helpful. (6) Toss and turn as much as possible." And so on. The
person troubled by compulsive thoughts can be told, "Try as
hard as you can to get those thoughts out of your mind, and
keep checking to see if they are gone yet. As practice you might
try to keep the thought of a polka-dot elephant out of your
mind for a 60-second timed period." These recipes, tailor-made
for each client, can be offered in a humorous manner, and we
sometimes even write them down for clients, "in case you ever
want to see if you can get depressed (have insomnia, have compulsive thoughts) again."

Sometimes, on the basis of more minimal information,
some educated guesses, and a careful moment-by-moment ad-
justing of the recipe to a client's verbal and nonverbal responses, a more abbreviated "recipe" can be put forward pre-
emptively. With some complaints (insomnia and compulsive
thinking are good examples), the "headlines" to the recipe can
be offered pre-emptively very early on, before hardly any details have been obtained. In this way, "giving the punch line" at the
beginning, the negotiations can be over almost before they've
begun.

PART TWO:
INTERVENTIONS AFTER INITIAL NEGOTIATION

SEEKING OBVIOUS, SIMPLE SOLUTIONS

"Why Not Just Do This?"

Although we have tried to emphasize (in previous chapters and particularly in chapter eight) the extraordinary variety of options for intervention open to therapists, our overwhelming preference, it should be clear, is for simple, obvious solutions. We particularly favor those tasks that (unlike certain "therapeutic tasks") do not rely on a continued "therapy" context, and that clearly could have been arrived at without professional help. A question we might ask very near the beginning of therapy—indeed, to start the negotiations off (see "Benevolent Skepticism: Beginning at the End," in Chapter Three)—is also one with which we may begin the process of wrapping things up: "Why not just do *this*?" Or we might say, at various stages of the negotiation process, "You've probably already tried this, but . . . ," or "You've probably thought of this, but . . . ," and go on to propose some obvious, simple solution.

Garbage Bag Therapy, Laundry Basket Therapy, and Plastic Lenses Therapy

Here are a couple of clinical examples illustrating the level at which we prefer to do psychotherapy.

In one of our cases, a boy of 10 had been throwing tantrums for years and getting into ugly battles with his mother, and our process of "getting the facts" (in a session with mother and son) revealed that the majority of the battles and tantrums were over the boy's refusal to take out the garbage. He was supposed to take it out every other day, though he invariably either forgot or refused. We asked the mother why it was "every other day" instead of "every day," and she said it was because she couldn't face a battle every day. "And why not then every third day or once a week?" "Because the garbage bag is full to overflowing by the end of the second day." The boy kept remarking throughout that he wouldn't "do that job because it stinks." So we finally asked him whether he meant he wouldn't do it because the garbage stinks or because he didn't like the job, and he said, "Both. The garbage stinks and that's why I hate that job." We pointed out that it was better to take the garbage out every day because it stinks less after only one day, and because it's easier to remember to do because you can get into a routine. We asked about what sort of garbage can the mother had, and it turned out to be only a brown paper grocery bag under the kitchen sink. We asked the boy, "Would you take the garbage out every day if it was sealed in plastic and didn't stink?" He said, "Sure I would . . . IF!" We suggested that the mother use plastic garbage bags with wire twist ties, and when she said there wasn't room for a garbage can under the sink, we negotiated the use of the brown paper bag as the garbage can, with the plastic bag as a sealable inner liner. This was acceptable to both mother and son. Moreover, the boy liked his dinner, and the rule was to be that the mother would only start preparing dinner each night once the boy had thrown out the garbage and replaced the plastic liner.

In another case, a boy of 13 was messing in his pants. He would hide the dirty underpants where they would be found weeks or months later. He was one of four children, and he was ashamed of his problem and bothered by the others' teasing him about it. Whenever he put rinsed-out dirty pants in the laundry basket, he'd be in for a rough time from the others. His mother kept him supplied with large numbers of underpants because so many pairs would regularly disappear. The mother was sure (and so were we) that if she could actually keep tabs on how often he soiled and made him responsible for using the toilet regularly and so keeping himself clean, he would be clean. But linking not being clean to loss of privileges meant knowing exactly how many days in a given week he was clean, and she had no way of knowing. The intervention was simply for the mother to buy four plastic shopping bags in different colors, to serve as personal laundry bags for each child. As she did the laundry once a week, the boy was to have a total supply of seven pairs of underpants and she was to store the rest away. She expected (and, incidentally, got) seven unsoiled pairs of pants in his laundry bag each week.

Finally, in a case brought to a peer supervision group, a man sought therapy because in certain situations he would get angry at either his mother or his wife (the symptoms never occurred when he got angry with anyone else); at a certain point he would take off his glasses, put them face down on the table or desk, and smash the lenses with his fist. This was a "compulsive" pattern that had gone on for years, and the man was forever having to get his glasses replaced. The intervention selected (suggested by a member of the group, Frank Franklyn) was for the man to get glasses with plastic lenses.

UTILIZATION

A major guiding principle that we make use of in the design and delivery of our therapeutic interventions is that of "utilization"; it derives from the work of Milton H. Erickson (Erickson, 1980; Erickson & Rossi, 1979, 1981; Erickson *et al.*, 1976). The principle is one of utilizing clients' existing resources, skills, knowledge, beliefs, motivation, behavior, symptoms, social network, circumstances, and personal idiosyncrasies to lead them to their desired outcomes. We have found two frames to be particularly useful for thinking about utilization in psychotherapy.

The First Frame: "What's It Useful For?"

First, for any given item of a client's behavior, beliefs, or whatever, we can consider its various "class memberships"—the classes (of items) of which the item can be considered to be a member—and select the class or classes that might be useful to us in some way in reaching the goal. For example, if we were locked out of the house and were trying to break in, and our only tool was a screwdriver, we could consider the screwdriver as a member of each of (at least) four potentially useful classes of items: items for removing screws from hinges; items that can pry open windows by force; items that can dig putty out and free glass panes; and items that can break glass. If a client's typical behavior tends to be "obsessional," the relevant class of useful items might be "He is conscientious in carrying out tasks," or "The smallest differences make a big difference to him." A psychiatric inpatient who claimed to be Jesus and went around in a bedsheet preaching to patients and staff was approached by Erickson, who said, "I understand you have some experience as a carpenter." Erickson got him involved building some bookshelves and shifted him to productive work (Haley, 1973, p. 28). There are an almost infinite number of class memberships for any given item, and the utilization approach involves selecting the item's membership in those classes that can be considered useful in reaching the goal.

The Second Frame: Building a Bridge

Second, we can think of the utilization approach as involving building a bridge from where the client is now to the eventual goal. So with our eyes on the goal of therapy, we find those of the client's beliefs, patterns of behavior, and so forth from which we could conceivably build a bridge to the goal. We "bridge backward" from the goal and "bridge forward" from our client's existing beliefs, behavior patterns, and abilities, "aiming" our bridges so that they meet somewhere in the middle.

Utilizing Everything

There is nothing, we assert, in the client's behavior, "symptomatology," beliefs, motivations, and so on that is not potentially a useful means to the client's (and our) desired therapeutic end. Therefore, we are prepared to use anything that is available— "whatever the client brings"—as a potential therapeutic aid. Once the initial negotiations have been completed and we begin the process of "wrapping up," putting meaning back in, and getting the client to go out and do something, we are keen to find ways of using the client's existing motivation, beliefs, and behavior to lead to the action that will dissolve the difficulty.

Responding to the Response

We have learned from Erickson the importance of responding to the response we get rather than sticking to the game plan, for every response can be utilized in some way to lead the client nearer to the goal. Every response to our communications and interventions can be utilized positively, and so every response is an important guide to how we are to respond in turn.

REFORMULATING THE PROBLEM

Once the ground has been prepared, an overall reformulation of the problem can be offered. The reformulation takes into account the facts of a client's story so far, but weaves them together with a different story, different meanings—a story that now makes it obvious what simple action or actions the client needs to perform to solve the problem.

E Pluribus Unum: Selecting the Pattern that Connects

As much as possible, the reformulation we offer to a client ties all of the relevant facts together in a single story. We define all of the client's complaints as but facets of a single complaint, or as so many variations on a single unifying theme. In terms of our own process in arriving at this unifying reformulation, we find that it simply "gels" at a certain point in our search for the pattern that connects the many aspects of the client's reported difficulties. As far as we have been able to articulate it, this search for "the pattern that connects" is essentially a search for the class of problems and class of solutions of which each of the client's individual "problems" and potential solutions can be considered to be members. Bateson (1979, pp. 84, 142–144), borrowing a concept from C.S. Pierce, refers to this process as "abduction," which he defines as the "lateral extension of abstract components of description." He talks about this process as one of describing some event or thing and then looking around in the world for other instances of the same abstract relations occurring in our description, other cases fitting the same "rules" we have devised for our description. It is a matter of finding some generalization, some abstraction fitting one "matched pair" of (1) a "component" complaint plus (2) the action necessary to resolve it, which also fits each of the other problem–solution pairs. This notion will become clearer with the aid of our discussion of the "template," in our section on "Therapeutic Metaphor" later in this chapter.

Seeking Contexts of Competence: Building on Exceptions

Either before or after reformulating the problem we seek contexts of competence, contexts in which a client has handled this kind of difficulty competently. So we might ask, simply, "Have you ever handled this kind of situation successfully?"

We often seek to discover instances where there has been an exception to the general rule of the problem—that is, times when the conditions were ripe for the symptom to occur and yet it did not occur. For example, a "bulimic" client who claims that she binges when she gets anxious may be able to recall some time when she was anxious and did not binge. Merely reminding her of that instance may emphasize her ability to stop bingeing. Or the instance can be examined to discover what it was about the situation that was different. For example, one bulimic who invariably induced vomiting whenever she overate and claimed she couldn't help it was asked about occasions when she overate and did not vomit. She admitted that if her husband was home she could overeat and not vomit because he would know about it. After a discussion about one-way mirrors, bugging devices, and satellite espionage techniques, we suggested she could never really know for certain, even when alone, that her husband was not spying on her. She agreed that she could imagine her bathroom mirrors to be spy mirrors, and the house to be bugged, in order to overeat without vomiting while alone.

Naturalist William Bateson, Gregory Bateson's father, once wrote: "If I may throw out a word of counsel to beginners, it is: Treasure your exceptions! When there are none, the work gets so dull that no one cares to carry it further. Keep them always uncovered and in sights. Exceptions are like the rough brickwork of a growing building which tells that there's more to come and shews where the next construction is to be" (C. B. Bateson, 1928, p. 324).

TRANSFERRING KNOW-HOW ACROSS CONTEXTS

Part of our frame for psychotherapeutic intervention involves assisting the client to transfer his know-how across contexts, so that the relevant skill or behavior that the client has already applied, or regularly applies, in one area of life can be applied in the area of the complaint in order to solve the problem.

Widening the Contexts in Which Clients Can Already do *X*

This transferring of know-how from one context to another might simply involve getting the client to widen, by degrees, the contexts in which they can already perform the relevant action successfully, or solve a particular class of problem, or do the behavior in question. Task assignments might simply be directed toward utilizing the successful behavior and building a bridge—perhaps in the form of a series of stepping-stones— from where the client already does the behavior to where they need to do it in order for there not to be a problem any more.

Reframing

Perhaps more commonly, as part of the further negotiation process and often either as part of or following reformulation of the problem, we will reframe the problem context and the context in which a client already applies the required know-how as being two versions of the same thing, and thus facilitate the transfer of know-how from the latter context to the former. The reframing thus involves finding some wider frame that includes both contexts so that they now come under the same umbrella. The problem context (P_1) and the "native" context of the know-how (P_2) are thus defined as specific instances within the wider category: We find a "pod" into which we can put both "P's." Or to put the matter less metaphorically, *in reframing, we find a descriptive abstraction that applies equally to the problem context and the "native" context, and so provides a more general description of both, so that they can be described as two versions of the same thing*.

The bulimic woman described above, who was to imagine

that her husband was spying on her and would always know if she was vomiting, was not sure she could carry this off. We asked if she hadn't ever imagined she was being observed in some situation in order to be on her best behavior. A series of "Got one of these?" questions succeeded in eliciting such an example from her own experience: When she was first out of teacher training college, she used to imagine that the principal was listening in on her classes by reversing the intercom circuit, and that this had helped her make the transition from teaching with her supervisor in the classroom to teaching on her own. The wider frame that made that experience and imagining her husband spying on her appear as two versions of the same thing enabled her to use that "pretending" experiment to stop her "compulsive" vomiting.

Such reframing interventions differ most significantly from context interventions (to be discussed in Chapter Eight) in that a therapeutic reframing can only achieve its effect of enabling the transfer of know-how to the problem context if a client comes to accept the reframing at a conscious level, though he need not be conscious of having done so. In other words, for a "reframing" to make any difference at all, the client must "buy" it or "take it on board." The client must come to view the problem context in terms of the new, wider frame, and thus see the problem context and the "native" context of the know-how as being comparable in some important way or ways. Context interventions, on the other hand, achieve their effect irrespective of how the client chooses to view the relevant context. As we discuss in Chapter Eight, contextual interventions, on the one hand, and interventions (including reframing) aimed at assisting individuals to do something different in the problem context, on the other hand, involve intervening in (as it were) opposite directions. In the former, we aim to abolish the context or pattern (or system) and throw the individuals back on their own devices (know-how), while in the latter we assist the individuals to exercise the relevant know-how (often by getting them to see the problem context differently) and so abolish the context or pattern (or system) through their own subsequent actions.

Here is an example of facilitating the transfer of know-how by getting clients to see two contexts as comparable. Parents were beside themselves with despair over the soiling and smearing of their 9-year-old and felt they could not cope with his smearing feces all over the bathroom towels and walls. They did, however, know how to cope with his being messy at the dinner table. They had made him responsible for keeping the tablecloth clean, and had set penalties for any untidiness. And how great a difference is there between dealing with untidiness in the dining room and untidiness in the bathroom? The parents were told that, whether the child was smearing in the dining room or in the bathroom, he could be made responsible for his cleanliness; whatever the cause of his soiling, there was no excuse for untidiness. The mother carefully showed him how to clean himself up and keep the bathroom clean, and the parents laid down strict penalties for any lapses. They also made him responsible for making sure to use the toilet, and they set penalties for the results of any lapses. The smearing stopped immediately, and the soiling stopped within a week. The parents knew nothing about encopresis, but they knew how to deal with untidiness.

Another example of the use of reframing to transfer know-how across contexts can be seen in a case of Erickson's. An enuretic girl of 11 whose sphincter had been very stretched through hundreds of cystoscopies for a bladder infection years before, wet her pants whenever she laughed. Erickson asked her, "If you were sitting in the bathroom, urinating, and a strange man poked his head in the doorway, what would you do?" She replied, "I'd freeze!" Erickson said, "That's right. You'd freeze—and stop urinating. Now, you know what you already knew, but didn't know that you already knew it. Namely, that you can stop urinating at any time for any stimulus you choose. You really don't need a strange man poking his head in the bathroom. Just the idea of it is enough. You'll stop. You'll freeze. And when he goes away you will start urinating" (Rosen, 1982, pp. 113–117).

First Providing a Context for the Acquisition of Know-How

Where we cannot readily find a context in which a client already applies the relevant know-how, or has done so at some time in the past, we can as a preliminary step provide the client with a context in which the know-how can be readily acquired. Such a context may be provided either in the therapy room or outside in the world by means of a behavioral prescription (task assignment), so long as the context arranged is related at most tangentially to the problem context and is, above all, a context in which acquiring this know-how is the natural response that this individual would have to being in this context (given what we know about his patterns of responsiveness). Often we need only rely on the fact that the client is a human being and on what we know about the natural patterns of responsiveness universal among human beings.

In one of our cases, a 9-year-old boy was continually provoked into fights at school when the other kids baited him by calling him names. He felt he "couldn't help it" because he just got so angry. In our office, he quickly acquired the know-how he needed through the simple expedient of our calling him every name in the book: He supplied the names, and we called him those. In our office he had to control himself, and he soon "couldn't help" giggling uncontrollably. At school he was no longer provoked by name-calling, and so the other kids of course gave up.

Again, the client can often be sent out on an assignment to get the know-how required. In one of Erickson's cases, a father who was being rather overprotective of his 6-year-old son was sent with his son up Squaw Peak, a nearby hill that was a popular climb. The father found he could hardly keep up with the boy, and learned how to let him look after himself; he was afterwards able to apply this know-how in other contexts.

A prim and proper young woman, who was told by us that she needed to learn how to feel good about learning from her "own stupid mistakes," was given the assignment to go out and make five stupid mistakes in public in the next 2 weeks and to be curious about what she might learn. She completed the assignment as perfectly as she had always done everything. For example, she stood in a major street asking passers-by directions to that street; she "accidentally" went swimming without changing out of her clothes; she asked at a London Underground ticket counter for a ticket to a nonexistent station, insisted the ticket seller was mistaken, and went on to have an argument with the station master, still insisting on her station.

She reported she had felt freer and happier than she had ever felt in her life and learned she was "happier not trying to be so perfect all the time." She was soon feeling free to make and learn from mistakes in many areas of her life and so began to overcome some of her self-imposed limitations.

Therapeutic Metaphor

In therapy, what emerges are stories and stories about stories. Stories reveal how people punctuate their world and therefore provide a clue for discovering their epistemological premises. In general, therapy is a process of weaving stories between therapist and client systems.—Bradford P. Keeney

Reframing can also be accomplished at a metaphorical level. Therapeutic metaphor is simply another means of reframing, accomplished through the metaphoric use of stories (which is but one of a great many therapeutic uses of stories and anecdotes, as we discuss later in this chapter) or through assigning a metaphoric task. Here we briefly outline the structure or process of therapeutic metaphor, which, once mastered by the therapist at a conscious level and consciously practiced repeatedly, eventually can be followed quite automatically and without deliberately keeping the format in mind.

1. *The therapist extracts for herself the facts of the client's "story so far."* This is accomplished in the course of the negotiation process.

2. *The therapist selects for herself a way of representing the facts of the problem in solved form.* Here, selecting a relevant combination of facts of the story so far, together with an action the client could take in relation to those facts so that the problem would be solved, the therapist formulates for herself a summary of one way in which the client could take action to solve the problem effectively.

3. *This summary of the problem, together with its solution, is then generalized and represented in more abstract form.* The therapist thus moves from the specific solved problem to the more general class of solved problems of which this specific one is an example. Dropping out all the episodic features or incidental details, the therapist abstracts to the general form of—a "template" for—the solved problem.

4. The therapist then generates a succession of stories or tasks also fitting this template. Drawing on her store of anecdotes, or designing relevant metaphoric tasks, the therapist offers a succession of stories or tasks that have the same abstract form as the solved problem (i.e., fit the same general template).

5. The process is then repeated from step 2 using an alternative selection of facts, together with a different way of solving the problem. Further stories (or, much more rarely, tasks) are then run through this process, which can be repeated any number of times, each time with a different set of stories metaphorically suggesting a solution. The stories of the different groups can also be mixed up, in order to be more indirect and to keep the person from grasping the point on a conscious level, if it seems more effective on a particular occasion to communicate the point at a purely unconscious or "subliminal" level.

Figure 2 illustrates this process diagrammatically. The left-hand box in the diagram represents the literal level; the right-hand box represents the metaphorical level; and the box in the center below represents the generalized, abstract form or *template* that the client's literal problem and each story or task offered share in common. The horizontal dotted line across each box represents the time of the intervention: Everything above the dotted line in the left-hand ("literal") box is what has already occurred ("the story so far"), and everything below the dotted line is still in the future, including the action the client might take to solve the problem. The x's in the left-hand box represent one selection of extracted facts of the story so far (above the line), together with (below the line) one action the client needs to take to solve the problem (the x enclosed by a circle). The therapist, in her own mind, then generalizes to the more abstract form of that constellation of facts-plus-solution, which forms a kind of generalized template represented by the lower box, with circles in place of the x's. When the therapist then selects a story or task, Y, also fitting this general form or template, this is represented in the upper right-hand box by filling the circles in with little y's. The eventual aim, after telling further stories or giving further tasks ($Z, A, B, C, D, E, \ldots$) is for the client, on the literal, practical level (upper left), to make the leap below the line to perform the action represented by the x

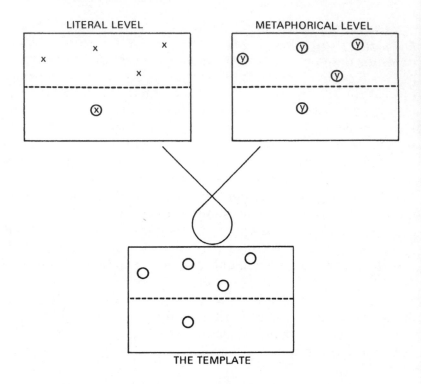

Figure 2. Therapeutic Metaphor: Selecting a Story or Task *Y*

in the circle. The process is then repeated, selecting a different constellation of facts plus solution; shown in Figure 3.

As an example of how this model of therapeutic metaphor operates, we can briefly consider a case of Erickson's in which he simultaneously treated the husband for phantom limb pain and the wife for tinnitus (ringing in the ear) (Erickson & Rossi, 1979, pp. 102–123). Erickson made quite a number of different kinds of therapeutic interventions simultaneously in this case, as elsewhere, but here we simply select a sample of some of the two dozen or so anecdotes that he told, and use them to illustrate the application of the model. The interested reader can follow the case up further to see how the model helps to make more understandable Erickson's metaphor in the husband's and

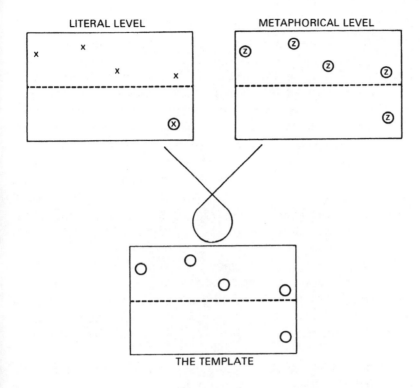

Figure 3. Therapeutic Metaphor: Selecting a Story or Task Z

wife's therapy, as well as to test it against other examples of Erickson's use of metaphor. The reader can also use the model to generate his own selection of anecdotes to use metaphorically in therapy.

Both the phantom limb pain and the tinnitus could be represented in *generalized solved form* (see paragraph 3 above) as follows: "Noxious stimuli that are there all the time, you can accommodate to and learn to tune out so that you don't perceive them." Thus Erickson told a story from when he was a premedical student, about doing an experiment of sleeping on the floor of a boiler factory where 12 pneumatic hammers were pounding away. When he arrived at the factory he could see the workmen talking to each other but he couldn't hear them; the

foreman could hear Erickson, but Erickson had to step outside
to hear the foreman. But when he woke up in the morning, he
could hear the men's voices, because he had tuned out the
pounding of the hammers during the night. He told a story
about the nomadic tribesmen in Iran wearing many layers of
undergarments on the hot desert plains; about getting so used
to sleeping comfortably on the hard ground or in the canoe
during a canoe trip that afterwards he found a soft bed to be
torture; about how we all get used to being cooped-up in rooms
where "everywhere you look, your looks come to an end," and
how he only noticed this when coming back from a 3-month
canoe trip on the Mississippi, as in the stories of sailors' claus-
trophobic reactions on shore; about people living on the farm
and getting so used to the barn smell on their hands that they
don't smell it until they've been away from the farm for a while,
and how they soon lose it again after being back on the farm for
half a day; about Hebbie making his roommate Lester take a
bath, because Lester (who was accustomed to living in dry conditions and only taking a bath three times a year) couldn't smell
himself.

Both the phantom limb pain and the tinnitus could also be
represented in generalized solved form as "If you can have
phantom unpleasant sensations due to no real outside source,
you can have phantom pleasant sensations as well." And so
Erickson told the story of watching a psychiatrist friend scratch-
ing his ankle, and asking him, "John, that really itches, doesn't
it?" and John agreeing, and both of them knowing all the while
it was a wooden leg. Erickson later told a story about a patient
with tinnitus who had worked at a war plant where there was
music all day long and who "wished she could have that music
instead of the ringing," who learned to use the ringing in her
ears "to play those tunes softly and gently," and thus replaced
the ringing with music. (Each of these two stories could relate
to both complaints via the relevant abstraction.)

The same principles apply when designing a metaphoric
task. The task is designed to fit the same template as the problem in solved form, including both an analogue of the problem
and an analogue of the solution.

"Read What You Wrote"

Finally, another means of assisting clients in transferring know-how across contexts, comes in handy when a client says in a session, "This is great, sitting here in your office—I feel I really know what I need to do—but if only I can remember all this and keep my head when I'm actually in the situation!", or if a client says in a subsequent session, "It all seemed so clear to me last time, but when I was faced with the problem I just couldn't put it all together—I just couldn't recollect what had only the day before been so clear to me." We suggest to such clients that they take notes either in the session or after the session, or at moments when they are really clear about how to handle the situation, and then, when the need arises, to read what they wrote. Thus they can transfer the know-how from when and where it's immediately at their fingertips to when and where it's needed.

DESIGNING AND DELIVERING TASK ASSIGNMENTS

Requisitions, Errands, and Incantations

Not all task assignments are designed to be carried out, and not all need to be carried out to achieve their therapeutic effect. Some task assignments are behavioral prescriptions that, to achieve their therapeutic effect, must actually be carried out by the client; we call assignments that must be performed if they are to work *requisitions*. Some task assignments need not be carried out to achieve their effect, but if the assignment is to be effective the client must somehow be induced to keep it in mind at some level, and she must leave the session intending or at least prepared to carry it out; we send some clients on such task assignments, which we call *errands*. Finally, some task assignments need not even be accepted by the client to achieve their effect—they may have the form of a behavioral prescription, but the giving of the prescription is itself the intervention; Such "spells that need only be uttered and taken in" we call *incantations* (Wilk, 1980, 1982). (Among task assignments that are contextual interventions [see Chapter Eight], context interventions often have the form of errands or incantations, whereas most, but not all, pattern interventions are given in the form of requisitions.) Most types of task assignments, such as those involving simple, straightforward solutions, for example, or those directly involving the transfer of know-how from one context to another, are usually prescribed as requisitions.

It is not uncommon, however, for a task intended by a therapist as a requisition—actually to be carried out— to have its effect in the end as an errand, insofar as the client's problem is resolved through the task without the task ever being carried out. This is frequently the case with pattern interventions (see Chapter Eight). But although a task may be intended in one way and succeed in another, it is important for the therapist to know how she intends the task to function, because different considerations apply in the final design and in the delivery of the task according to whether the task is to be carried out or not.

Incantations. Incantations constitute an important, if less frequently used, category of task assignments, particularly in making context interventions (see Chapter Eight). Some incantations ("spells that need only be uttered and taken in") do not have the form of a task at all, but consist only of a statement or statements making a direct or implied attribution of meaning. Incantations must be highly "redundant" as a protection against interfering noise—that is, they must stand out clearly against the background of other communications in and outside of the session, and this is usually achieved through tiresome repetition or a highly dramatic build-up or both. The intervention must be so memorable that it cannot simply be missed or disregarded or forgotten.

An extreme example of such repetition is the case of the concert pianist (Haley, 1985, pp. 277–286; Haley & Weakland, 1983) who flew from out of state to see Erickson (the journey itself, of course, provided some insurance against disregarding Erickson's intervention!). The man's problem was that he got in a terrible panic whenever he had to perform, and overcome with an attack of anxiety, he would be "unable" to play. He had a particularly important concert coming up, upon which his job as a music teacher depended, and which he had so far been unable to successfully approach without being paralyzed by panic. Erickson began by pointing out that he personally was tone-deaf, and then promptly proceeded to lecture the man on the proper way to go about playing a piano! Then for 2 solid days he boringly droned on and on, lecturing the man about "the importance of being fluid," belaboring the point with endless anecdotes and minor or trivial illustrations of the importance throughout nature, in music and in human life of "fluidity." The man grew increasingly bored, impatient, irritated, and angry, as Erickson went on about being fluid, fluid, fluid. He wasted the man's time (and journey) for 2 days. At the end of 3 days, he sent the man home, thoroughly irritated and disgusted. But just as the man left, Erickson said to him, with dramatic emphasis, "For years you have rigidly refused to play a concert in the concert hall, and you know that music is fluid, and that it should stream and flow in fluid fashion through the windows. The artist is always a part of his music, and his fluid movements of his hands. There's no room for rigidities." The man went home and began to perform in public on a regular basis.

Erickson's work is a fertile source of examples of incantations. A nice transcript illustrating the extent to which one can carry repetition and drama in delivering an incantation can be found in the case of the young couple in conflict over whether or not to have an abortion. Their parents were pressuring them to have an abortion, but the couple were not certain they wanted this. Erickson told them that no matter what they did, they should not under any circumstances think of a name for their unborn child, for if they did, they would surely decide to keep it. They, of course, did just that and kept the baby. (Erickson, 1980, Vol. 4, pp. 370–373; Erickson & Rossi, 1979, pp. 360–363). In making this intervention, Erickson repetitiously labored the point, to an almost absurd extent. Incantations can, of course, also be carried off without excessive repetition, so long as the context is carefully arranged in other ways to ensure that the recontextualization or decontextualization (see Chapter Eight) will be "irresistible."

Errands. With errands, the essential thing is to obtain the clients' commitment to carrying them out, whether the commission is actually necessary or not. On the whole, the design and delivery of errands follow the same rules as for requisitions—and always with a view to the possibility that the client may actually carry them out, irrespective of what the therapist may have intended! The main difference in design and delivery is that errands are designed to work even if they are not actually accomplished, and that, since it is not so vital that they be carried out, less time and effort need to be expended in mutual negotiation of the details of the task to ensure its viability.

We used to refer to errands as "spoiling interventions" (Wilk, 1982), insofar as their main thrust is usually to "spoil" the context in which the problem is performed, similar to the way in which the wife can spoil things for her husband and herself by saying, "I wish you'd sometimes bring me flowers the way you used to."

Some errands (of which symptom-contingent and non-compliance-contingent tasks are good examples; (see Chapter Eight) seem to have their effect through clients' *avoidance* of carrying them out. In other instances, the errands seem to work through supplying the client with a way of dealing with the situation that they need never actually resort to, because, knowing they can now deal differently with a previously threatening situation they simply interact differently.

A colleague of ours (Herr, 1982) provided the classic example of an errand working in such an "empowering" way—like providing the client with a loaded gun she need never remove from its holster. A California wife sought counseling because her husband (who would not come in for marital therapy) spent all of his spare time on his own in his garage, tinkering with his car, listening to his stereo and watching TV, enjoying a beer, and so on; he refused to help out around the house accomplishing essential chores, and spent little time with his wife. She complained about the fact that they never went out together any more, that she hardly saw him, and that she couldn't get him to do such chores as (and this was a particularly sore point) fertilizing the lawn. The therapist, to make a long story short, told her that she was to order the required amount of manure from the garden supplies store; she was to have the store deliver it on Friday and instruct the driver to dump it in a pile in the driveway, immediately in front of the garage door. When her husband complained about it, she should tell him that since he had to shift it anyway, he might as well shift it onto the lawn. As the session was on a Friday, it was too late to do anything about the task until the following week. But she reported in the next session that she never needed to do it at all, because when she got home from the session she found her husband, that weekend, "had become a totally different person." He offered to do various chores, ordered fertilizer so he could attend to the lawn, and accepted her suggestion that they go out to dinner. They were now spending plenty of time together, and she was quite pleased with the relationship.

A case reported in *Change* (Watzlawick, *et al.*, 1974, pp. 130–131) furnishes an example of an errand that may have worked both in this "empowering" way (i.e., on the principle that "if you know you've got it you don't have to use it") and through the avoidance of having to carry out the task assignment. An experienced executive assistant was getting into tangles with her boss, who often offended her deeply by belittling her and putting her down in front of others, to which she responded with an even more distant and condescending attitude that provoked further belittling. Matters were so bad that, at the time she sought counseling, the big question at work was who would act first: Would she resign, or would he dismiss or transfer her? She was given the assignment to wait for the next incident "and then to utilize the first opportunity of taking her boss aside and telling him with an obvious show of embarrassment something to the effect that 'I have wanted to tell you this for a long time, but I don't know how to tell you—it's a crazy thing, but when you treat me as you just did, it really turns me on; I don't know why—maybe it has something to do with my father,' and then to leave the room quickly before he could say anything." After some discussion she at last could hardly wait to try it out, but reported in the next session that she hadn't needed to because "that very next morning her boss's behavior had somehow changed overnight, and that he had been polite and easy to get along with ever since" (p. 131).

The response to the intervention in both of these cases is, in our experience, a typical response to errands. On countless occasions of prescribing an errand, particularly in situations involving relationship difficulties, we have had clients come back reporting, "I didn't need to do the task, because I found when I got home that he had (in the meantime) become a com-

pletely different person." In fact, it sometimes strikes us as
uncanny how predictably a client will come back with these
exact words.

In the case of pattern interventions (see Chapter Eight), it
can be seen how they can come to function as errands in perhaps yet another way: The "choice element" is made so unde-
niable, and so the tasks are carried out only once or twice—sometimes a plan to carry out an eminently "do-able" task obviates
the need to carry it out at all. If a task is at all arduous or
inconvenient or a nuisance to carry out, this only makes it all
the more tempting for the client to omit it and just overcome
the self-imposed limitations; hence the overlap with the afore-
mentioned element of the errand working through the avoidance of carrying it out. (There is a feature that applies not only
to symptom-contingent tasks but to many pattern interventions,
particularly when functioning as errands; this was summed up
by Erickson when he admonished therapists to "make it awfully
difficult for your patient to go on having the symptom.")

In a case seen by one of our trainees, a man who had a
natural pallor sought therapy. What emerged in the negotiation
of the presented problem of "depression, social anxiety, and
obsessive thinking" was simply this: He had previously been
quite enjoying life, but in recent years he had become stuck in a
seemingly compulsive pattern in which, more often than not,
he would be getting ready to go down to his local pub for a beer
with "the regulars" there—an evening activity that was an important and fulfilling part of his social life—and while combing
his hair (or whatever) he would look in the mirror and start
becoming "obsessed" with his pallor, fearing he looked particularly pale this evening, and becoming increasingly worried
that if he went down to the pub tonight his friends would start
asking, "Are you all right? You don't look well," and generally
making a fuss over him. He would then fret about, "feeling
torn," and finally decide to stay in and watch TV, and become
very morose. And life was getting lonelier and emptier by the
day. A detailed video description of the pattern was obtained,
and he was given this task assignment: At a particular point in
the sequence, when looking in the mirror and deciding he was
"too pale" to go to his local bar, he was to go out of the house
and go to a specific bar across town. He was to have one beer at

the bar where he wasn't known, and then travel to his local bar and spend the rest of the evening there. The journey in each direction involved a long bus ride and a transfer to another long bus ride—four buses in all. After successfully completing the task twice, on the third attempt he made the decision that he was too pale, went out of the house, and then decided he couldn't face all the bus travel and just went straight to his local pub. He had no problems since and has made satisfactory adjustments in all respects following this single session.

Requisitions: Negotiating Tasks in the Open. Although we sometimes make use of errands and incantations and are intrigued by the unexplored possibilities in these areas, most of the task assignments we prescribe are task assignments that we intend the client to carry out. Since we actually want the client to perform the task, we try to ensure that the task is easily performed, nonobjectionable, neither potentially hazardous nor expensive, and, above all, custom-tailored to the client's own situation. In order to ensure "do-able" tasks, we often spend a lot of time in the session negotiating something that the client can successfully carry out and that we can be fairly certain will genuinely be "on target" and have the desired effect.

In sharp distinction to some therapists, if we want the task to be carried out by the client we do not simply pull it out of the air (i.e., it doesn't spring full-blown from the head of either Zeus or the therapist) nor do we "spring it on" the client. Some therapists deliver a task the way they would deliver a hand grenade: They reappear from behind the one-way screen, toss in the task, and make a run for it before the client or family can question it. Our approach could not be more different. It is not atypical for us to begin negotiating the form of the so-called "final intervention" (the task assignment) as early as 15 or 20 minutes into the interview. Sometimes we spend rather longer getting video descriptions of the complaint and negotiating the problem, and relatively less time negotiating the details of an intervention; and sometimes we spend rather less time getting the video-descriptive details, and get those in the process of negotiating the details of a "do-able" task. Indeed, it is possible in principle for the mutual negotiation of the task assignment to be the form the very negotiation of the problem takes, and hence the form of the entire interview; sometimes an interview comes quite

near to this in practice. The main point is that a task is negotiated *mutually*, with the client, *in the open*, and not imposed
on the client from without. Much of the work involves negotiating objections and honing the details of the task to the details
(including the most mundane details) of a client's daily life.

The Experimental Frame

A frame we frequently use in prescribing the task assignment is
that of inviting the client to do the task simply as an experiment, and to report to us on what happens. This defines any
outcome of the task as useful and worth pursuing until the next
session, because (and how could it be otherwise?) any response
to the doing of the task provides both the client and us with
useful information. Postman and Weingartner (1969) write: "An
astrophysicist is rarely frustrated when he is confronted by
something he didn't expect to see, and he knows that what he
sees at any one point in space-time may not be 'true' at any
future moment. Anything different from what was expected is
admitted into the system, leading the scientist to change his
perception and actions as a consequence" (p. 116). The experimental frame avoids implicitly promising a client too much in
the way of benefits from doing the task. This is particularly
important when a task is designed merely to introduce an interim shift to a new position—as undesirable, perhaps, as the original situation—from which it may nonetheless be easier to get
the client to see his way to doing something that will eliminate
the problem. Moreover, the experimental frame fits in well with
the idea of modifying the task in subsequent sessions and trying
it out again with the appropriate modifications, and avoids
creating a context for the client to be disheartened in the course
of this often necessary process.

"What Did You Do, and How Did It Go?"

We almost invariably open a session following the assigning of a
task with the question, "What did you do, and how did it go?"
We almost never begin a session by asking "How are things?" or
by asking how the "symptom" or "problem" "is" or "has
been," because this introduces all kinds of unwanted reifying

presuppositions, invites discussion outside the realm of a client's actions, and carries a connotation that we expect to hear of some improvement or alteration. Even if a therapist actually holds such an expectation, it may not be helpful to convey it to a client in case it turns out that no improvement or even any difference has been experienced.

Honing Tasks through Reports

When getting a report back in response to "What did you do and how did it go?", we can begin honing the task down with a view to represcribing it in a modified form that is more likely to have the desired effect. If a task has not been carried out, or was prematurely abandoned without the problem being solved, or was modified in an unacceptable way (in terms of what the task was designed to "do"), we can elicit the client's alleged "barriers" to performing the task as prescribed and negotiate these. The prerequisites and other imperatives proffered by the client, objections that only arose in the course of doing the task, and so on all provide invaluable grist for the negotiation mill. If a client has forgotten all or part of the task, we can write it down for the client so that it cannot be forgotten the next time. If a client has simply not done the task, and offers no objections or whatever but simply "didn't get around to it," we might choose to end the session (even if after only 10 minutes) and represcribe the task if the client is still prepared to carry it out in the agreed form. This is done for the very real reason that we may at this stage have nothing further to contribute to the process of solving the problem until the client does the task prescribed.

DEALING WITH RELATIONSHIP PROBLEMS

Negotiating Relationships

Although we do therapy that might be called "marriage therapy" or "family therapy," we think of such therapy as "relationship counseling," and we mainly do "relationship counseling" when people are not getting along with one another. The focus of such counseling is on specific relationship problems, and its orientation is primarily a future orientation, geared to negotiating how couples or family members are going to get along with one another more effectively from here on; the farthest back we go in time is to the here and now, or, at most, the recent past. We seek from the start to find out who the complainants are (each party may be a complainant, each with different complaints), and what their specific complaints are. "What's the beef," specifically? And from there, in all essential respects, the negotiation process is the same as that described throughout this book—with the main difference, perhaps, that the negotiation involves a degree of mediation between or among complainants who can make mutually acceptable trade-offs with one another. Here, however, are a few guidelines about some of the specific emphases in our application of clinical epistemology to relationship counseling.

Getting Specific

We ignore or challenge irrelevant reports, we silence accusations, and we generally block unhelpful or destructive remarks, very directively if necessary. We challenge the various items in the "Index" (see Chapter Five)—in particular, causal claims, mind-reading claims, predictions, conjectures, and characterizations. We challenge in all of the usual ways, but in particular by persistently pursuing video descriptions, and accepting video descriptions as the only "legal tender" for the therapeutic transactions. We are continually moving from characterizations and other attributions to video descriptions of complaints. We frequently ask such questions as "How do you know?", "What does she do?", "What don't you like about it?", and "How is that a problem for you?"

Getting Content and Getting Action

We get each complainant to specify her descriptive content (in the form of video descriptions) for the desired behavior from the other person (i.e., the "opposite" of the complaint), and then we negotiate with the other person and get him to do that—to produce the goods. Where "producing the goods" means simply not doing some particular behavior, or not saying particular things that the other person finds provocative or unpleasant, we may directly tell the relevant party, "Don't do that!"

The *Quid Pro Quo*

We attempt to identify and utilize each person's self-interests or "selfish" motives and/or desired end-states in the negotiating and bargaining process, and to use them as a basis for getting the person to do the behavior desired by the other person. Frequently, we arrange a *quid pro quo* (a term we borrowed from Don Jackson [1961], although we use it in a different sense) in which we strike a bargain between the parties, trading off "concessions" of a specific type of behavior desired by the other party.

Breaking the Stereotype

We challenge generalizations and characterizations, as we have said, and seek counterexamples or counterevidence from the present and/or past, as much as possible. However, if one person has a fairly unshakable (and usually "well-documented"!) characterization of or generalized attribution about the other person, we get the other person (i.e., the one characterized, the noncomplainant on this particular issue) to do a specific type of behavior from time to time to break the generalization or violate the characterization. Again, this involves seeking the invariant pattern in the person's behavior (the one the other person is complaining about) and getting the person to introduce variance into his behavior, doing behavior falling clearly outside the defined (characterized) range (see also Chapter Eight).

Pattern Intervention

For the most part, if further intervention beyond the basic negotiation seems to be required, we do pattern intervention. In other words, we identify invariant patterns of interaction and introduce variance according to the 15 modalities of pattern intervention that we distinguish (in Chapter Eight). In addition, however, to such pattern interventions accomplished through task assignments, we make in-session pattern interventions, getting the partners to try out a different type of behavior with each other in the office as well as outside the session.

Context Intervention

Occasionally we make use of the therapy context to recontextualize or decontextualize (see Chapter Eight) undesirable or undesired behavior, for example by prescribing it in some form. The paradigm case here might be Haley's *ejaculatio praecox* example (described in Chapter Eight).

Introducing the Responsiveness Frame

We introduce the couple or family members to the notion—and to the practice—of observing what response they get when they do and say specific things, or do and say them in a specific way, and to adjust their own behavior until they get the response they want to get, or at least until they stop getting the response they definitly *don't* want to get. In addition, when we observe a "signal reaction" in the session (see Appendix II) and it's not clear what aspect of the communication the "receiver" is responding to, we may get that person to specifically identify what he is responding to: tone of voice, facial expression, choice of words, mismatch between words and deeds, symbolic value—in other words, some "typical" communication that for the receiver epitomizes a whole area of complaint. We then stop and point out to the person in the session who is sending out such "signals" the undesired response she gets from the receiver each time it occurs; remind her that this is not a response she wants to get; remind her what it is that "pushes the other person's buttons"; and urge her, "So don't do that!"

"Family Therapy"

If we work with a family, either conjointly or seeing each member of the family individually, or in varying combinations, we do this simply as "relationship counseling" with the aim of helping the family members to get along with one another better, and emphatically not to indirectly affect one family member's "symptom." We are not interested in such hypothetical exercises as restructuring the family organization or hierarchy, altering contingencies of reinforcement within the family, working with family myths, or whatever; nor do we believe in the "inventities" in question anyway. Instead, we confine ourselves to the matters of who isn't getting along with whom, and then make the same kinds of interventions as we make with couples—either with the whole family in the room or with each family member individually, negotiating and mediating.

Consequences and Clear Limits

Particularly where struggles between parents and teenagers are concerned, we ensure that the parents establish clear (video-descriptive) rules and specify, in advance, clear (video-descriptive) consequences or penalties for infringing those rules. We get the parents off the bandwagon of "punishment" (the deliberate inflicting of pain and suffering on someone deemed to have done morally wrong), and encourage them instead to work on the basis of "penalties" (the prearranged consequences of infringing an established regulation) (Bruggen, 1984). We get parents to stop characterizing and predicting, and to stop getting "involved" in the "purely private matter" of the teenager's infringement of regulations and accompanying consequences: The parents just lay down the rules and let the "legal system" run its course automatically, without arguing about each infraction or seeking to protect the teenager from voluntarily (i.e., knowingly) incurred consequences. Where possible, we try to arrange for parents to make use of natural consequences; indeed, even in the case of parents who seem to be particularly strict or severe, the main intervention in practice is simply to get the parents to stop protecting the teenagers from the natural consequences of their behavior. This might mean, for example, not keeping a son's dinner warm if he comes in late for the meal, or not helping a daughter to get up for school in the morning if she comes in at 2:00 A.M. In addition, we get parents to keep their rules to a minimum, not fussing about minor issues or things that really are not all that important to them. We counsel teenagers in terms of the responsiveness frame, and utilize "selfish" motives and goals in a context in which they are now no longer protected from the natural consequences of their own behavior.

PART THREE:
THERAPIST STANCE AND STYLE

THE THERAPIST'S OPERATING STANCES

Future Orientation: The Action after Words

Much of traditional psychotherapy has had an orientation toward the individual's past, while much of more recent psychotherapy—particularly family therapy—has tended to have a here-and-now orientation, concerned with the present situation. Our own orientation, it should by now be clear, is very much a future orientation. From the moment clients come into our offices, what we are interested in is what they would like, from now on, to do differently in their lives, and what we need to do to get them to see their way to doing that. As one client said to us (at the end of the second of three sessions), "I'm beginning to see what you do—you turn 'problems' into goals and set about reaching them." As Erickson said, "Psychotherapy is sought not primarily for enlightenment about the unchangeable past but because of dissatisfaction with the present and a desire to better the future" (in Watzlawick *et al.*, 1974, p. ix). And as he said elsewhere, "[T]here is nothing you can change about the past. You live tomorrow, next week, next month, hopefully next year and so you go ahead wondering what is round the next corner. And enjoy life as you go along" (in Gordon & Meyers-Anderson, 1981, p. 27). The past, for us, is simply irrelevant. The future, the client's future outside of therapy—that's where the action is. As for "the problem," for us that is simply something the client and the therapist construct within the therapy session through a process of negotiation, and the end of that negotiation is the client's going out and taking action to create a better future.

Observation and Not Thinking

In doing psychotherapy, we endeavor to remain externally fo-cused—focused on observing the clients and their responses at all times—for only in this way can we attune our own therapeutic communications to the clients' moment-by-moment responses. We don't "think" while we are doing psychotherapy, except to the extent that we act thoughtfully and do our thinking out loud, not knowing what we think until we see what we say. What we do *not* do is conduct an internal dialogue or "briefing session" in our heads while we are supposed to be "out there" doing therapy. We don't make hypotheses about "what's going on." In spite of the aftereffects of our previous training, an hypothesis very rarely crosses our minds nowadays, and should one accidentally intrude, we shrug it off as we would a prejudice. And, indeed, hypotheses in psychotherapy have the same effect prejudices have in everyday life—of blinding one to the reality before one's eyes.

The Transparent Therapist

As we are not thinking behind the literal or metaphorical screen, our therapeutic mirror is always a two-way, not a one-way mirror. A far cry from the neutral, opaque psychotherapist common to the most diverse schools of psychotherapy, we present ourselves honestly, candidly, and transparently, sharing our views, our experiences, and the experiences of our friends and families, our past foibles and present interests, just as one would with friends, except that we do this whenever and how-ever this relating would best further clients' progress toward their goals. Our clients tend to get to know us much better than most clients tend to get to know their psychotherapists, and probably learn more in one session about what we are like as people than most clients get to learn about their therapists in years of daily or weekly sessions. We do not adopt a different or special "persona" for doing therapy; the way we are in therapy is just the way we are in everyday life. We are ordinary, fallible human beings engaged in an ordinary, fallible business, and we make no bones about it. The therapeutic conversation is an ordinary professional conversation—only the goal is different. In doing psychotherapy, we are just "being ourselves"; and, just as in everyday life we relate in different ways to different people with different "styles" and different kinds of relationships with us (and we adopt a degree of intimacy appropriate to whom we are with and to the degree of intimacy the others seem to be comfortable with at any given moment), we do not adopt any special "tone" when we do psychotherapy.

Running Commentary

Along with the idea of being nonmysterious, ordinarily transparent persons, we do not add any unnecessary mystery to the proceedings. In contradistinction to many therapists' seemingly (to their clients) inexplicable leaps from one subject or line of thought to another (e.g., suddenly "bringing in" a client's "mother"), we tend to provide somewhat of a running commentary on what we are doing. We explain what we are "going for" in pursuing a particular line of inquiry, and how this relates to the subject at hand (cf. "giving the punch line"). We are also quite prepared to decline to give an explanation, particularly for a task ("You can make up your own reason for it if you want to, but you don't get to know *my* reason"), but if we are keeping something from a client in this way, we are prepared to make this "not telling" explicit (more a lighthearted attitude of "I know, but I'm not tellin'!" or "You better just guess" or "I'd rather not go into all that—just do this as an experiment and see what happens," as opposed to the more typical "denied cover-up" or "standing on the superiority of the expert").

Not Lying

It somewhat saddens us that this even needs to be said at all, but in the present climate in the psychotherapy field—in which one has the impression that "anything goes" if a therapeutic "expert" decrees it—it perhaps needs to be emphasized that we do not tell lies in therapy. We hope that there are still a few innocent readers to whom all this will come as a shock, but by now most therapists are aware of how widespread are some of the dubious practices to which we refer, particularly among many (but not all) of the therapists and schools of therapy that refer to themselves as being "strategic" or "systemic" (though equally by no means confined to these).

When we say that we do not tell lies in therapy, this means that we do not misrepresent our views by claiming to believe things that we do not really believe; we do not claim to have done things that we have not done or to have consulted with people with whom we have not consulted or who do not even exist; we do not invent any "instant research," making up non-existent research studies that have supposedly demonstrated one thing or another; we do not claim to have people observing a session behind the one-way mirror who are not really there; we do not fabricate stories about "disagreements in the team" if we work with a team; we do not talk about "a client we had once" whom we never had; we do not, for the sake of therapeutic metaphor, invent stories about things that never happened to us; nor do we make up "positive connotations" or attribute spurious praiseworthy motives for behavior that we do not seriously hold as our considered view of the matter; nor do we profess to any "understanding" of a problem that we would not be prepared to share with colleagues or commit to print as representing our best clinical judgment of the situation. There is a technical term to cover all of these categories of intervention: The technical term is "lying."

The problems we can see with lying are these: It is unprofessional; it is unethical; it is potentially dangerous (as in the case we know of a nonmedical therapist who lied to reassure a client by saying he had an eminent neurologist behind the mirror); it is relatively ineffective as a form of communication; it can be exceedingly embarrassing for the therapist to be caught out in a lie; it is damaging to the integrity and credibility of the therapist, both as a therapist and as a trustworthy individual in her personal life; it is damaging to the credibility and integrity of the profession as a whole; and the toleration of such lying, in its very nature—like the thin end of the wedge—undermines the foundations of rational communication in society. Perhaps, just as "people get the government they deserve," lying might serve the public right for having put so much unquestioning faith in the so-called "helping professions," but in a society that already has put so much trust in the authority of "experts" and in the practitioners of a given profession, to betray that trust and take advantage of a powerful position is, in our view, inexcusable.

Arguments that have been put forward suggesting that "there is no such thing as truth anyway" (these arguments, if right, assert something that can then no longer be claimed to be true!) (P. Booth, personal communication, 1982) have no bearing on the question of whether or not it is possible to lie. Whether there is or isn't any "absolute truth" (whatever that is supposed to be, or not to be!), to profess to believe what one does not believe is lying. And as Samuel Johnson quipped, "If he does really think that there is no distinction between virtue and vice, why, sir, when he leaves our houses let us count our spoons."

Not Being Tricky

Again unlike some other therapists, many of whom we respect greatly, we try not to be tricky in doing therapy. We are not trying to do something to our clients. Our therapy would not be unsuccessful if our clients found out what we were doing. Our stance is emphatically *not* one of "tricking clients out of their problems." Trickiness is, in our view, disrespectful to the clients and totally unnecessary to carrying out effective psychotherapy.

Congruent Communication

One of us used to tell a particular Zen story in therapy from time to time, about an abbot and some monks; however, tailoring the story to what he took to be the limits of some of his clients' tolerances for the unconventional, he censored a few details by making it a Benedictine abbot and Benedictine monks. Although he thought the story was a powerful one, it seemed to fall pretty flat. As time went on, and the ethical and professional imperative of communicating congruently in therapy became increasingly important to him, and as he shook off more and more of our previous training not to be himself in therapy, he began to have the nerve to just "tell it like it is"— namely, as a Zen story. He was struck by the powerful impression the story now seemed to make on his clients, though he wasn't aware of telling it any differently apart from the identification of the religious order. And yet, somehow, this difference made a difference.

It is our experience—so far borne out only by the experience of some of our colleagues, and by anecdotal reports we've heard of research tending to the view that listeners can register (in galvanic skin responses, electroencephalograms, etc.) subliminal awareness of incongruent communication—that to communicate congruently is to communicate more effectively. Since we are interested in communicating ideas to our clients as effectively as possible, one of our operating stances is to communicate as congruently as possible. This goes beyond merely not lying and not being tricky. It means striving to represent an experience or relate a story as accurately as we can, down to the accuracy of whatever details we select for inclusion. We recognize that this is a counsel of perfection; that we are no more perfect in therapy than outside of therapy; and that therefore we are prone to get carried away with excitement or enthusiasm and either exaggerate some details or add others inadvertently from our imagination. Such is the nature of the "oral tradition." Congruent communication, however, is the ideal we continually aim for, and by keeping this goal in our sights we hope to attain nearer to it than we would otherwise.

Not Struggling

There was a time when we thought that when we found ourselves struggling in therapy it was because we were failing, and the time came when we realized that when we were failing in therapy it was often because we were struggling.

Therapy should never be a struggle. There is an *effortlessness* about effective psychotherapy, which does not imply that no effort is being made or energy expended. Rather, this effortlessness is more akin to the Zen concept of *wu-wei* or "nondoing." The orientation is an active one, not a passive one; yet it is one of not going against the grain of things. One moves with the current and not against it. In training psychotherapists, we find it useful, as a rule of thumb, to advise them that if they find themselves struggling, they should stop struggling, relax, and do something different. And they should go back to the basics:

"Have you got a complainant? What's the request? What are you trying to do? Since the client's goal is to do something different, and the only way to do that is to do that, and since the client doesn't need fixing or reforming and is just fine as she is, and since nothing needs to be done to her or about her or for her, what are you struggling for?" It is our belief that if the therapist is struggling, therapy has turned into some kind of a contest or a fight, and that is something other than therapy. When in doubt, the therapist should relax, observe the client, stay external, just be himself, and above all cultivate effortlessness; in this way, he can at least be in a position to do effective psychotherapy. As both John Weakland and Steve de Shazer (personal communications) have emphasized, the first rule of doing therapy briefly is this: To get rapid results, go slow. *Festina lente*: Hasten slowly.

Flexibility and an Individualized Approach

An important part of our operating stance is that of flexibility. Our approach is as flexible as possible and is customized and individualized to meet the uniqueness of each client. Erickson advised therapists to "invent a different psychotherapy for each patient." Moreover, the nature of that psychotherapy needs to be continually responsive to a client's moment-by-moment responses, continually shifting in quality. It must shift from being gentle, to confrontive, to supportive, to challenging, to joking, to serious, to teasing, to provoking, to doubting, to encouraging, and so on, all within a matter of minutes.

Voluntary Clients

We work with voluntary clients—people who come as complainants actively seeking our therapeutic help. Although in the past we have both borrowed and devised a number of creative ways for adapting these approaches to working with so-called "involuntary clients," our ethical and professional stance is one of only doing psychotherapy with people who actively seek it from us. Of course, not everything worth doing is psychotherapy; far from it! And there are many other ways of being useful to people—social work, probation work and aftercare, child protection services, and so on—that need not involve doing psychotherapy. The "social control" functions of many of the helping professions are, in our view, very important and are not to be despised. But to try to press psychotherapy on those who do not want it is something that we want to have as little to do with as possible.

No Cure

If people could have psychological diseases, we might be interested in curing those diseases. But since we do not subscribe to the "illness" metaphor, we can hardly claim to achieve psychotherapeutic "cures." There simply is nothing to cure. We do indeed do follow-ups (which we prefer to do by telephone to avoid getting back into "the land of psychotherapy,") and our success rate in the traditional sense seems to be remarkably high—far higher than the proverbial "one-third rule" of "one-third improved, one-third partially improved, and one-third failures." But we interpret this rather differently. Just as we do not believe in attaching any significance to chronicity, we do not attach any significance to the "durability" of results. People are perfectly capable of going back to old patterns of behavior any time they please. Sometimes we'll get phone calls informing us of such "relapses", and the only intervention necessary will be to tell such persons on the phone, "Don't do that. Remember what you did before, and how much better that worked? Right—do that instead." Or sometimes we may see them for a therapeutic follow-up session or even further therapy. The bottom line, however, always remains the same: The only way to do something different is to do something different, and people have a choice about that even though they sometimes act as if they did not.

Not Cheering

When clients achieve their goal, although we may show that we are pleased for them and pleased they don't need to see us any more, we do not do a lot of cheering and patting them or ourselves on the back. To do so is to imply that something extraordinary has occurred. In our view, the reason effective psychotherapy can achieve its results so rapidly—often in a single session—is because there is so little that needs to be done.

Similarly, in working with parents or consulting to schools, we emphasize that ordinary good behavior should never be praised or rewarded, but taken for granted—indeed, expected. It should be identified, so that a child can get to know the adults' standards and descriptive equivalence of "good behavior"—"That's what I want," or "fine"—but to praise little Johnny for finally doing what all the other kids already do is unavoidably to give Johnny the impression he's damaged.

Perhaps the nearest we come to cheering is simply to ask our clients, "Do you think you need to be here?", and we certainly cheer inwardly to hear them say they don't think they need to see us any more. Our pleasure in not being needed any more is pretty hard to disguise, and clients seem to find this cheering in itself.

MEDIA

Throughout this book, we have alluded to some of the media we make use of in our application of clinical epistemology in psychotherapy, and it remains to summarize a few general points here.

Forms of Parallel Communication

We make a lot of use of various forms of parallel communication in therapy—that is, communication that addresses two parallel subjects or themes at the same time. To put it another way, we use communication that on one level discusses overtly (or directly) some matter that parallels the subject that the communication is (more importantly) addressing itself to covertly (or indirectly) at another level. The forms of parallel communication we use include therapeutic metaphor, analogies, puns and word plays, and various forms of allusion. Haley (1973) gives the example of Erickson dealing with a couple in conflict over sexual matters who would seem to prefer not to discuss the conflict too directly. Erickson "might, for example, talk to them about having dinner together and draw them out on their preferences. He will discuss with them how the wife likes appetizers before dinner, while the husband prefers to dive right into the meat and potatoes. Or the wife might prefer a quiet and leisurely dinner, while the husband, who is quick and direct, just wants the meal over with" (p. 27). Sometimes we may make such analogies explicit, and sometimes, when we are being still more indirect, we may prefer to distract conscious attention away from such parallels.

We make extensive use of analogies and of plays on words that build bridges between two subjects so that it remains unclear which subject we are talking about. Also, by dropping out content in our own communications—using abstract nouns, unspecified verbs, and generally *violating* all of the injunctions of the "Index" (see Chapter Five)—we deliberately leave open the matter of what it is we are talking about. This puts clients in the position of having to keep their options open and hence to establish (and keep tentatively running) a number of parallel "tracks," thus creating a context in which the clients will construct for themselves a number of multiple levels of meaning, and thereby facilitate—or even initiate at their own end—the process of parallel communication.

The Therapeutic Uses of Stories and Anecdotes

A man wanted to know about mind, not in nature, but in his private large computer. He asked it (no doubt in his best Fortran), "do you compute that you will ever think like a human being?" The machine then set to work to analyze its own computational habits. Finally, the machine printed its answer on a piece of paper, as such machines do. The man ran to get the answer and found, neatly typed, the words: THAT REMINDS ME OF A STORY.

—Gregory Bateson

A story or an anecdote (which the dictionary defines as "a short narrative concerning an interesting or amusing incident or event") can be a powerful therapeutic tool. We frequently use stories and anecdotes in therapy, drawn from the most diverse sources: from our own or our friends' or our clients' or acquaintances' experiences; from newspapers and magazines, or television and radio; from literature or films; from Zen stories, Sufi stories, or Aesop's fables . . . the list could go on and on.

Our trainees often ask us what to do if they don't know

many stories. How do we remember them, and how do we seem to have so many on hand—"one for every occasion"? *The answer is that we deliberately collect them.* Every time we hear or read a story or anecdote, or have an experience we think might one day be worth relating to a client, we open a file in our brains labeled "stories and anecdotes for use in psychotherapy" and "record" it. Sometimes we write them down and keep them in literal files. And as we collect each story, we file it under a few different headings, corresponding to the circumstances under which we might tell such a story in therapy. For example, we might listen to a story, thinking, "That might be a good one to tell clients who are giving up too easily," or " . . . who need to learn to trust their unconscious," or " . . . who are striving in the wrong direction." Or we might have an experience, such as being caught in a particular traffic jam, and make a mental note of the circumstances in which the story of this experience might be therapeutically useful.

There are numerous therapeutic uses of stories and anecdotes, and we only list some of the more important ones relevant to our practice of clinical epistemology. Zeig (1980, pp. 3–27) provides an excellent discussion of Erickson's uses of anecdotes; we have found this discussion useful in constructing our own categories, and it includes a number of further therapeutic uses of anecdotes that we do not mention here. We have already discussed in some detail the use of stories in therapeutic metaphor, which, as we mention in our discussion, is but one of many uses of narratives as interventions in psychotherapy. Here are some of these uses:

1. *To make or illustrate a point.* Virtually any idea that can be conveyed straightforwardly in a declarative statement (or series of statements) can be conveyed through a story or series of stories. And of course it is common practice in everyday conversation to illustrate a point with a story or anecdote. Many of the reasons for choosing the more indirect, narrative form, are specified in the following paragraphs (2 through 15). Sometimes the therapist may precede or follow the story with the point or "punchline" or "moral of the story" stated in simple declarative form (as Erickson also sometimes did). Or the therapist might, alternatively, respond to the request for an explana-

tion by telling another story (to help the client understand the point by "putting it another way"). Whether or not the therapist offers to spell out the point of the story in plain language depends on how direct or indirect the therapist wishes to be: Does the therapist want the client at this point to have a clear conscious understanding to take away from the story, or is the therapist still in the process of indirectly "channeling" or "loading" the negotiations?

2. *To peg ideas* (or "tag the memory"; Zeig, 1980). This classic example (Watzlawick, 1978) provides a double-leveled illustration: Pages of description could not convey the ferocity of a storm as well as the single image of a straw driven through a solid oak door by the sheer force of the wind, an image that pegs the idea (and the idea of pegging an idea) unforgettably. As Zeig points out, it is often easier to remember the theme of a story than the same point made straightforwardly, the story making the idea "come alive" (1980, pp. 7–8).

3. *To seed ideas* (Haley, 1973, p. 34, p. 195, and passim). Stories or anecdotes can be used to prepare the ground for an intervention or idea that may not be harvested until much later, simply by broadcasting a few seeds (in the form of anecdotes) now here, now there, so that when the intervention is delivered it will not have appeared out of nowhere and risk being rejected, but will appear in a context in which it will already make sense. As Haley points out (1973), seeding diverse ideas earlier in the therapeutic interchange to build an elaborate groundwork that can be built on later allows the therapist to build in a number of different options (for intervening in different directions) that she can choose between or among when the opportunity arises. This choice will depend in part on the client's observable responses to the stories in which the ideas were seeded. (The seed metaphor is also nice because one can think of the stories as tempting fruit, containing the seeds of the ideas, to be eaten by birds who thereby ingest and digest those seeds in the process, while aware only of the luscious fruit.)

4. *To open up possibilities*. By offering illustrative tales the therapist can gently and indirectly introduce the client to possibilities that she may not have considered before. Without having to make explicit claims in the form of "You know, it really is possible for a person in your situation to achieve X,"

the therapist can simply and matter-of-factly tell a few anecdotes about people in the client's situation who really did
achieve *X*, thus at least opening up the possibility for the client's consideration.

5. *To normalize or otherwise recontextualize.* This use of
stories and anecdotes involves telling a series of tales that taken
together create a new context, within which the situation (or
complaint) described by the client takes on a new meaning altogether. The context woven by the stories is often one in which
the client's complaint appears quite normal. This is a context
intervention (see Chapter Eight), which does not depend on the
client's altering her view of anything in order for the intervention to succeed in altering the meaning of what the client has
described. To give a simple example: A young couple consult a
psychotherapist about their 2-year-old's (their first child's)
"temper tantrums" and describe a couple of recent instances.
The therapist responds by telling half a dozen comparable anecdotes about his own children when they too were in the "terrible 2's," chuckling over the reminiscences; he then inquires
what brings the parents to see him. Without any further ado,
the behavior of the couple's child has taken on a new meaning.
The therapist, who is supposedly knowledgeable from a professional point of view about the range of children's behavior, is
clearly amused by the incident in retrospect; moreover, the
therapist has survived. The stories themselves, together with
the stories taken in this therapy context, continue to create a
new context for the comparable behavior of the couple's child.

6. *To reframe or redefine a problem.* Here a single story is
used (and another one can then additionally be used, and so
on), to provide an alternative frame that the client can adopt to
see the problem differently. This is not a context intervention,
but a "frame intervention," and so depends for its effectiveness
on the client's actually "buying" (i.e., accepting, "taking on
board") the new frame proffered by the therapist. Typically,
again, the reframing takes the form of a wider frame within
which the client can see (1) the problem context and (2) the
context in which she already applies the required (potentially
problem-solving) know-how as two versions of the same thing.
By offering an "alternative class membership" for the problem
described by the client (Watzlawick *et al.*, 1974, p. 99), the

story or anecdote implicitly offers a new definition of the problem (and hence of the nature of its potential solution)—a definition that the client will either ultimately accept or not.

7. *To introduce doubt.* Very simply, a story or stories can be a powerful means of introducing doubt, often by means of offering a counterexample or "exception to the rule."

8. *To guide associations.* In order to get a client thinking in a particular direction, a narrative can be used to channel the client's thoughts (or "associations"). In other words, the therapist gets the client started thinking along certain lines. This is often a very simple matter. As Erickson was fond of pointing out, "If you want a person to talk about his brother, all you need to do is tell him or her a story about your own brother" (in Zeig, 1980, p. 11). This same principle can be applied to "start the little wheels turning" over particular kinds of solutions to the problem. For example, if the therapist wants parents to consider ways of adopting a more indirect and subtle approach to getting their children to behave, the therapist might simply tell a few anecdotes about parents who successfully "used a bit of psychology on" their children.

9. *For indirection.* In general, the narrative form can be preferred to the declarative form whenever the therapist wants a client to customize the proffered ideas and possible problem-solving approaches to fit his unique situation. For example, by offering a series of relevant stories instead of spelling out a specific task assignment, the therapist can engage the client in designing a "custom-tailored" solution that will fit his unique situation better than any "off-the-rack" solution would. "Indirection" essentially involves subtly directing clients to do their own thinking and to come up with their own ideas to solve their problems; the therapist provides a general framework or structure for the clients' thinking, but leaves out the specific details, which the clients are left to fill in.

10. *To suggest solutions.* Either general forms of solutions or even specific solutions can be suggested through an illustrative anecdote or story, or through a series of such narratives. Multiple anecdotes with a common theme or thread running through them (Zeig, 1980, pp. 9–10) can be used to suggest solutions very indirectly, so that it is the client who finally spontaneously "comes up with the idea." Erickson, who fre-

quently made use of this approach, told the story of how his son Burt tried to give his father a taste of his own medicine, trying to get Erickson to spontaneously get the idea to lend Burt the keys to the car; Burt (nearly, but not quite) achieved this by sharing a series of family reminiscences, all involving either automobile trips or keys (in Rossi, *et al.*, 1983, pp. 246–247).

11. *As therapeutic metaphor*. This particular means of suggesting solutions has already been discussed in some detail, and is an important use of narratives in therapy.

12. *To increase rapport*. On the simplest level, this use of stories means selecting stories about gardening if the client is a keen gardener, or about engineering systems if the client is an electrical engineer, and so on—in other words, selecting the stories one uses for therapeutic metaphor (or whatever) from areas with which the client is already familiar and at home. Also, as in everyday life, sharing anecdotes revealing what the speaker and listener have in common is a good way to establish and increase rapport. In therapy, this often takes the form of relating anecdotes that, among other things, take the therapist down from the "superior" position of the all-knowing "expert" and reveal the therapist to be a pretty ordinary, fallible, fellow human being (and one who doesn't mind letting the client know that!). Relating personal experiences and sharing the experiences of one's friends contributes to the therapist's "transparency" and to building rapport with the client.

13. *To lighten clients up*. In addition to jokes, humorous or light-hearted stories and anecdotes are a useful means of getting clients to "lighten up" about the issues being discussed. In our experience, if a client is still being melodramatic or deeply serious about the problem being discussed, often little can usefully be done to negotiate the problem. Equally, in our experience, there are few problems, however heavy or serious, about which a therapist cannot get a client to lighten up. There are a few clients, however "melancholic" at the moment, who cannot be lightened up within a short space of time, given sufficient therapeutic skill. The work of Farrelly and Brandsma (1974) provides some excellent illustrations of some ways of accomplishing this. Even anecdotes that aren't actually funny but are simply "light" can provide a lighter background against which to view the problem.

14. *To regain the floor*. If a therapist finds that a client is taking over the negotiations, the therapist can gently, politely, but powerfully regain the floor by telling a story. As the story is unknown to the client, the client cannot take over its telling, and since it is not clear what the point of the story is going to be, the client cannot begin to "contest" it. And one story can be followed by another. Human beings are marvelously responsive to stories. A favorite cartoon of ours shows one character saying, "I'd like to share this story with you." A second turns to a third and asks what that means, and the third replies, "It's polite for 'Shut up and listen.'" Stories thus provide a natural means of enabling the therapist to reassume control of the negotiations so that they can be steered in a more productive direction.

15. *To shift the subject or redirect the discussion*. Even if the therapist is not having any difficulty regaining the floor as such, but rather in redirecting the discussion onto another subject, stories provide a useful means of transition. A long story or long series of stories can provide an "intermission," leaving the previous subject well in the past, and/or can lead to the start of a new subject—one taking up from where the last of the stories left off. Meanwhile, the floor is safely in the therapist's hands.

Therapeutic Artifacts

An important medium of communication we make use of is that of "therapeutic artifacts" or objects—physical objects that make a point in themselves and have a story to tell (or, more accurately, that we can tell an interesting and therapeutically pointed story about). Therapeutic artifacts, like stories and jokes, we deliberately collect. We look out for them wherever we go. Such artifacts include greeting cards, posters, bumper stickers, postcards, wall plaques, children's toys, advertisements, puzzles, games, native crafts from different parts of the world, objects from nature (unusual stones, plants, etc.), photographs, etchings, sculptures, "executive toys," novelties, and so on. Almost anything that makes a point or that can be used to make a point can be adopted as a therapeutic artifact. This is a large topic, but here is a simple example: If a client is failing because he is struggling, a therapist can use the classic children's toy of "Chinese finger handcuffs"—a raffia tube into one end of which the therapist places a finger and invites the client to place a finger in the other end, and then asks him to "try and get away." The more the client pulls to get away, the tighter the tube gets and the more his finger is locked in; the only way for him to get out is to push his finger in further, so that the tube loosens and the finger can be gently slipped out. (This can also be used as a metaphor in various other situations and in different ways, and in marital therapy a couple can use the finger handcuffs on each other.) As another example, one can keep a "sensitive plant" (whose leaves fold up when touched) next to the driest, spindliest, most forbidding yellow cactus (an idea of Dr. Brian Roet's, a therapist friend of ours whose office is full of therapeutic artifacts) or one can have an "air plant" that draws all its sustenance directly from the air; these plants can be used to illustrate or make various points in various ways. Therapeutic artifacts are particularly useful for pegging ideas.

Entertaining New Ideas: Jokes, Humor, Irony, and Other Light Refreshments

In teaching, in therapy, you are very careful to use humor, because your patients bring in enough grief, and they don't need all that grief and sorrow. You better get them into a more pleasant frame of mind right away.—Milton H. Erickson (in Zeig, 1980, p. 52)

We make extensive use of jokes, humor, and other related approaches in our practice.

In a case in which the parents consulted us regarding their child's soiling, the parents presented their problem rather melodramatically, punctuated by the mother's periodically breaking down in tears. They described the soiling and smearing in graphic detail, repeatedly referring to how "horrible" it all was. We kept agreeing with them about how "horrible" it was. Then, when the mother described how the boy would sometimes come home from school "with it running down his legs," we said, with a pained and disgusted look, head in hands, and with a sense of intense dramatic build-up, "That sounds really horrible. . . . You know, one is reminded of that horrible, horrible, horrible joke—about the man who goes to his doctor and complains of diarrhea, and the doctor asks him, 'When did you first discover you had diarrhea?' and he replies, 'When I took my bicycle clips off.'" The parents collapsed with laughter, and continued chuckling over the joke. When, subsequent to the joke, we would deliberately use the word "horrible," the parents would start chuckling again and we'd ask, "What's so funny?" and they'd say something like "Sorry—I just thought of those bicycle clips again." From that point onward, the parents lightened up considerably. We were able to discuss the problem humorously and sensibly, and by the end of that session the parents felt sure they knew exactly what they needed to do to solve the problem, and solve it they did. At follow-up, the mother was particularly grateful to us for helping her and her husband to "see it all in perspective" and to "relax about it to the point where we could see what needed to be done," and we had another good laugh over the bicycle clips.

In addition to using jokes and humor, we sometimes make liberal use of irony, satire, playful teasing, and on occasion outright burlesque. A client in his late 40s who kept bemoaning his age, and who spoke of being "an old man," "over the hill," "too old a dog to learn new tricks," and so on, was, after a while, teased mercilessly. As he mentioned the phrase "Just after the war, we used to . . . " we interrupted to ask, "First World War or Second World War?"; we happened to refer to the Roman conquest (or something like that) and added, as an aside, "which of course you remember from your childhood"; and so on. Each time he laughed in self-recognition, and we continued until he "cried uncle" and said, laughing, "O.K., O.K., I take your point—maybe I'm overdoing this "old man" bit. But I am pushing 50, you know!" The "old man" routine was never repeated.

We find it most important when using teasing and burlesque—and the more outrageous it is, the more important this becomes—to use a clearly different voice tone and facial expression, which unmistakably marks out the communication as a humorous one. The master of humorous provocation in therapy, Frank Farrelly, was keenly aware of the importance of the "meta-communication" that "this is play" (Bateson, 1955). Farrelly and Brandsma write:

> Humorous personal interaction is one form of play that can either start out in a playful context or can suddenly be reorganized

into such a context at some point during the interaction. The playful context indicates that this particular communication process has meanings different from the one usually ascribed to its content. . . .

The metacommunicative aspects of the playful context are as necessary in . . . therapy as in play. These are communicated by non-verbal qualifiers such as a wink, a mock serious attitude, dialect, or the context itself. However, the framework that "this is not for real" is often suddenly erased when the therapist's sensitive humor proves to be quite "real" and personally relevant, and the client suddenly realizes that "the joke is on him." (1974, p. 99)

It is vitally important, too, to draw the line clearly between, on the one hand, humorous parody geared to lightening the client up and getting him off an extreme and untenable position, and, on the other hand, cynical ridicule that hardly conceals a hint of underlying contempt. Fowler, in *Modern English Usage*, also makes the relevant distinctions nicely (1980, pp. 252–253): "Cynicism," for which there is no place in psychotherapy, is aimed at an audience of "the respectable," operates in the realm of "morals," and aims at "self-justification" achieved through the "exposure of nakedness." "Humor" is directed toward a "sympathetic" audience, operates in the province of "human nature," and uses the method of "observation" to achieve its aim of "discovery." Farrelly (see Farrelly & Brandsma, 1974) was also very aware of the extent to which it is important that the therapist's love or "unconditional positive regard" be simultaneously plainly communicated to the client. As a rule of thumb, no teasing or burlesque is necessarily too outrageous in psychotherapy, so long as one would be prepared to similarly tease (i.e., with similar context, voice tone, facial expression, and, most importantly, similar attitude) one's own deeply loved grandmother or child.

At its best, psychotherapy should be highly entertaining for both therapist and client. Postman writes:

. . . I must avow my belief that the best defense against all varieties of crazy talk is our old friend a sense of humor, which is always available as an escort through hard and confusing times. I mean by a sense of humor an active appreciation of the fact that time's winged chariot is always at our backs and that therefore there is a profound and essential foolishness, transiency, and ineptitude to all our adventures, including the hardest of all, talking to each other. Without a sense of humor, almost any talk will, soon or late, descend into craziness, brought down by its own unrelieved gravity. I believe that a sense of humor is at the core of all our human impulses, and he who would make us mad must first exorcise our appreciation of human frailty, which is what a sense of humor is. (1976, p. 253)

Ordinary Conversation

Finally, in our discussion of media, we should emphasize once again that our main therapeutic communicational medium is ordinary conversation. A "fly on the wall" who did not know we were doing psychotherapy would not necessarily suspect that that was what we were doing; he would see and hear only an ordinary conversation. What defines the conversation as psychotherapy is simply our *goal* in conducting this conversation.

Footnote (If the Shoe Fits): Ericksonian Hypnosis

For those who are familiar with the naturalistic approaches to hypnosis and hypnotherapy developed by Erickson, and by those who have continued his work, there will be some point in mentioning that there lies another whole range of media fitting in elegantly with these approaches, and, incidentally, overlapping with a great many of the working methods we have been discussing. For those who are unfamiliar with these approaches, for us to say much more in this context (without going into an extended discussion) would, we suspect, only serve to confuse the subject. Suffice it to say, for the moment, that the subject of "Ericksonian hypnosis as clinical epistemology" is, in our view, a fertile one for further exploration, and a subject on which we may have something to say in the future.

METAPHORS FOR THERAPY AND THE THERAPIST'S ROLE

We have already, in various places in this book, made use of a number of metaphors for characterizing the role of the therapist in our approach. Here, however, are the three metaphors we find most useful.

Therapist as Consultant

Whatever the presenting complaint may be, we think of the psychotherapist not as a healer who actually carries out some therapeutic procedure, but rather as a consultant to the client. We make ourselves available to our clients, as consultants to them in their ongoing efforts to solve their "problems." They are the ones who are going to do the "therapy"; we merely consult to them, in order to assist them in their process of problem solving.

Therapist as Coach

Another and related metaphor is that of the sports coach. The clients are the athletes who are going to do the actual running, or golfing, or tennis serving, or what have you; we are merely there as their coaches, urging them to lift their knees higher, or suggesting a different turn of the wrist that might improve their swing, or reminding them to keep their eye on the ball. A coach does not explain why a player couldn't cut the muster or why the play was the wrong one to have chosen; that's the job of the "Monday morning quarterback" or sportswriter, analyzing and second-guessing. Our role is to coach our clients in various ways they can do something different in order to improve their performance and reach their goal.

Therapy as a Pit Stop

One of our supervisees (Case, 1983) has compared our therapeutic approach to a "pit stop" in automobile racing. When the car pulls into the pits, a highly skilled team, perfectly coordinated to do as many things at the same time as possible, changes the tires, cleans the windshield, takes care of any necessary repairs or alterations, and sends the car and the driver back onto the track in the shortest time possible. In our way of seeing things, psychotherapy is the pits, and each session is a pit stop; our goal is for a client to spend the least amount of time possible in the pits with us and as much time as possible out there on the track. The only rationale for a pit stop is to effect the minimum necessary adjustments to get the driver back on the track in peak performance, or, at least, at a sufficiently good level of performance to stay in the race. We want to get our clients "out there," living their lives as they want, as fast as we can.

CHAPTER EIGHT

BEYOND NEGOTIATION
An Introduction to
Contextual Approaches

Any good ecologist could inform you of the logic of your problem: a change in an environment is rarely only additive or linear. You seldom, if ever, have an old environment plus a new element. . . . What you have is a totally new environment requiring a whole new repertoire of survival strategies.—Neil Postman and Charles Weingartner

At this point some readers may be asking themselves, as some of our trainees ask, "Well, if you don't hypothesize and you don't think anything needs to be changed, what do you do to intervene if your initial negotiation doesn't dissolve the problem?" Well, we do intervene in situations after the initial negotiation, and we usually focus on the context of the presenting complaints, not on the alleged causes, meanings, functions, or present maintenance of the complaints. We have two distinct but overlapping ways of discussing these interventions. Each has its unique merit, as each suggests different ways to think about intervening in the context of the presenting complaint. The concepts we present here involve intervening in the patterns and contexts of the presenting complaint. First, we take up the notion of pattern in general.

OPTIONAL PATTERNING

Left to their own devices (and in our approach, clearly, they never are), clients tend to speak and act as if they and others were robots. People are not robots, and yet they often behave *as if* they were robots—that is, as if in a given situation at a given time, they had only one choice, which is to say, no choice at all.

People do behave in rigidly patterned ways, and in one sense and one sense only this patterning is not optional. This patterning is not optional insofar as behavior must be patterned more or less rigidly in *some* sort of a pattern. This is so because, as much of the work of both Gregory Bateson and Milton H. Erickson has emphasized, it just is not possible for any but a small portion of human (individual and social, let alone physiological) functioning to be under conscious, error-correcting direction. Most of our functioning goes on smoothly, autonomously, and unconsciously in rigid, automatically recurring patterns, nor could it be otherwise.

Bateson considers "the impossibility of constructing a television set which would report upon its screen *all* the workings of its component parts, especially those parts concerned in this reporting." He writes: "Consciousness, for obvious mechanical reasons, must always be limited to a rather small fraction of mental process. If useful at all, it must therefore be husbanded. The unconsciousness associated with habit is an economy both of thought and of consciousness; and the same is true of the inaccessibility of the processes of perception. The conscious organism does not require to know *how* it perceives—only to know *what* it perceives" (Bateson, 1978, pp. 108–110). Bateson goes on to draw attention to the fact of skill as "indicating the presence of large unconscious components in the performance."

Rigid patterning only becomes problematic in itself when difficulties arise. Intervention in a rigid pattern of individual behavior, or the larger interactional pattern (or "system"—the pattern considered metaphorically in terms of its "machine-like" sequenced automaticity) of which the individual's pattern (typically) forms a part, is called for when and only when (1) difficulties arise and (2) the pattern does not include the behavioral options necessary to resolve those difficulties and reach the desired outcome. In such instances, the individual finds her present pattern of behavior to be unsatisfactory and yet acts as if her behavioral options were limited. This illusion of limitations appears in perhaps its most compelling form where the individual's behavior has the appearance of being "locked in" with the behavior of others in an interactional "system," or where the "symptomatic" (i.e., undesired or undesirable) pattern in question is, according to prevailing cultural presuppositions, reified and regarded as involuntary and mechanistically determined.

In the most general terms, we can say that the aim of intervention in the pattern/system would be to extricate the individual from the rigid pattern or interactional system and facilitate her exercising alternative behavioral options. This then allows for a new, equally rigid, automatic, unconscious, autonomously functioning pattern or interactional system to be inaugurated. This new pattern, however, is nonproblematic; that is, it produces the desired results (the reaching of a particular outcome) and does not contain the "symptom" or any other undesired "symptom."

Interpersonal interaction, too, displays rigidly recurring patterns—invariant, sequenced automaticity—but this in no way constrains the individuals concerned from acting outside those patterns and just doing their own thing.

That there must be a good deal of rigid patterning—this much is *not* optional. But it is to a great extent purely optional as to which particular rigid pattern obtains. And even more importantly, the rigid patterning of human behavior and experience is a feature of organization, not of control. At every point in the pattern the individual is free to do something different, if she so chooses. In other words, the pattern may not *contain* certain options, but neither does it *constrain* the individual from exercising those options.

The "sequenced automaticity" of much of human behavior and experience is thus a descriptive rather than a prescriptive feature. Just because people often function as if they were machines, relying on unconscious automatic patterns (including recurrent interactional patterns), this does not mean that they cannot act outside those patterns at any point they choose.

In psychotherapy, we need to "get the facts" of the precise patterns in which our client's behavior and experience "around the problem" are organized. A map of the pattern—the invariant features of the recurring sequences—constitutes in and of itself a map specifying the numerous points at which the client has other choices potentially, imminently, available to her. If our process of asking about our clients' presenting complaints— "tacking into the wind"—is not sufficient in itself to enable the clients to see their way to exercising these options, we may need to provide them with strategies for doing so. We do this by means of pattern interventions and context interventions.

CONTEXTS AND CONTEXT-MARKERS

If communication is to happen, we require not merely messages, but an ordered situation in which messages can assume meaning.—Neil Postman

One of the most central among our own epistemological presuppositions, is that reality—for human beings, at least—is always necessarily contextual. As human beings, we do not simply live in a world of facts, still less in a billiard-ball world of forces and impacts, but in a world of facts and meanings in which "what a thing is" involves and includes what it *means* for us—its significance. On a biological level of explanation we might refer to its "signal value." What anything "is" for us as humans depends on the context in which we find "it"; that context, indeed, is part of what "it" is for us. (In Gregory Bateson's *double entendre*, "The pattern *is* the thing.") The same "thing" in different contexts will mean something different and therefore will *be* something different. An utterance, or action, or communication, or piece of interaction would have a completely different significance (and therefore would be something completely different) in a different context. Indeed, it is difficult even to talk about all this, precisely because the context is part of what something is; here "we are so befuddled by language that we cannot think straight," as Bateson points out (1978, p. 246).

A fist at the end of an outstretched arm with the thumb pointing heavenward may be a request for a car to stop to offer transportation to the thumb's owner. At least in some parts of Asia Minor, we hear, the same (physical) gesture may "be" (or will be taken to be) an obscene gesture employed as an aggressive insult. (Hence the mayhem that ensues when unsuspecting Western hitchhikers stick out their thumbs.) The "same" thumb may equally well "be" (at least in England) any of the following, depending on the context: a "good luck" wish; a parting salutation—"Goodbye, all the best!"; a confirmation that one has succeeded in the task at hand; an offer of congratulations; a reminder or affirmation of who is "number one"—usually, depending on the context, the thumb's owner or some group to

which he belongs (the recipient of the nonverbal communication is typically also a member of that group—e.g., "Up the
Lions!"); a display of affiliation (as in a political poster urging
one to "vote for Bloggs," illustrated by the ubiquitous thumb);
an "O.K." indicating the thumb's owner's acceptance of what
he has been requested to do; or a simple "thanks for your help."
In Yugoslavia, it is the sign used by pupils to ask to be excused
to use the lavatory (Philip Booth, personal communication,
1984). The earliest recorded upstanding thumb was a plea of
"let the Christian live" and an applauding of his bravery—a
signal from the crowd to the gladiator to "get off his case." (The
alternative was thumbs down and socially sanctioned murder.)[1]
And, needless to say, the thumb becomes a horse of a different
color as soon as its context is altered by dint of the bending of
the arm and juxtaposition of the thumb's owner's nose.

For human beings, context is a product of communication
between people, present and past, ongoing (as in kinesics) or
enduring (as in written traces such as stop signs). The communication may include not only ongoing verbal and nonverbal
communication and relatively durable features of the environment, but, equally, rules, laws, customs, traditions, institutions,
and even *Weltanschauungen*. We may, for heuristic purposes,
abstract from the stream of communication those aspects that
serve to signal, to classify, to differentiate contexts. Following
Bateson (1964/1971, p. 260), we will call these abstracted parts
of the communication "context-markers." As these context-
markers are artificial abstractions, something imposed on the
data by the observer, there is no question of ever being able to
count context-markers or to decide how many can dance on the
head of a pin. But we can consider the sources of information
heralding the news that this is one sort of context rather than
another. Bateson (1964/1971, p. 261) gives these examples from
among "the diverse set of events [falling] within the category of
context-markers":

1. The Pope's throne from which he makes announcements *ex cathedra*, which announcements are thereby
   endowed with a special order of validity.

---

1. Of course, this is how the story is usually told. In actuality, however,
it was the other way around: "Thumbs down" got the Christian off the hook,
and "thumbs up" was the go-ahead to finish him off.

2. The placebo, by which the doctor sets the stage for a change in the patient's subjective experience.
3. The shining object used by some hypnotists in "inducing trance."
4. The air raid siren and the "all clear."
5. The handshake of boxers before the fight.
6. The observances of etiquette.

Context is more like a hot-air balloon than a zeppelin, the former sort of airship requiring the constant input of heated air to maintain its distinctive shape. Contexts need to be maintained, either by a continuing stream of context-markers or by context-markers with some durability through time (such as police uniforms or stop signs or chessboards or houses of parliament). If not continually maintained, contexts tend to fade, wither, decay, evaporate, or generally evanesce in the special way contexts have of evanescing: They become ambiguous. Once ambiguous, the very context is at the mercy of the first unambiguous context-marker to happen along and exploit the situation by claiming the context for its own. Unmaintained contexts quickly come to be up for grabs.

Now, as Gregory Bateson has put it, "message-material" or information (a difference that makes a difference to the receiver) "comes out of a context into a context" (1978, p. 370). When in this book we refer without further qualification to "context," we are referring to the context the information comes *out of*—the "environmental" aspect, so to speak, of "context" in the wider sense. When we wish to refer to the "intraorganismic" counterpart of "context"-in-our-narrower-sense—that is, when we are speaking of the context the information comes *into*—we shall use (following Bateson) the term "frame." The "frame" is thus "the internal state of the organism into which the information must be received" (Bateson, 1978, p. 370)—a kind of "psychological" counterpart of context in our sense; it is the meaning the individual adds to the facts. (Bateson would perhaps rightly argue that even the "frame" isn't quite yet "psychological" either, but the "frame" is at least that part of the added meaning that is not supplied "from outside" by the semantic environment itself. Cf. also Bateson, 1955.)

What is essential to emphasize is that the "context" the information comes out of and the "frame" into which the individual receives it *are both equally negotiable*. And as clinical epistemologists, in the practice of psychotherapy, we are continually negotiating and manipulating both contexts and frames. In earlier chapters, we have described how an individual's "frame" (definition of the problem, attributed meanings, deductions and imperatives, supporting assumptions, etc.) can be negotiated through the "assessment" process, and in Chapter Seven we have considered the structure of "reframing" and of therapeutic metaphor. What we have not yet touched on, however, is the way in which the very context itself is negotiable and can be altered or abolished through the therapist's communications; this is the subject of "context intervention," to which we turn our attention in a later section of this chapter.

CONTEXTUAL APPROACHES: PATTERN INTERVENTION AND CONTEXT INTERVENTION

To reiterate: People have choices, though whether or not they exercise those choices is another matter. As we have said, our process of negotiating the presenting complaint will not always turn out to be sufficient in and of itself to enable the client to see his way to exercising the choices he has.

We may supplement this negotiation, however, by directly abolishing the pattern (or interactional system) or expanding it beyond recognition, thus throwing the individual back on his own devices (resources, ability, know-how) and initiating a search for new options. This mode of intervening further ("beyond" the negotiation of the presenting complaint) opens up an extraordinary variety of therapeutic options, and constitutes more than a mere set of working methods. For what we are considering is how to intervene therapeutically, not in the way the individual defines or frames the problem, but in the context of the problem situation itself. We are not talking here about particular therapeutic working methods or "techniques," but a whole range of *approaches*—which, we believe, have implications far beyond psychotherapy—for transforming and abolishing contexts. Rather than continue further with the negotiation process, the therapist may simply choose to cut the negotiations short and directly transform the problem context. In this transformed context, either further negotiation may prove to be un-necessary, or else the therapist will be negotiating on far firmer ground. We refer to this range of approaches for directly inter-vening in the context as "contextual approaches."

Contextual approaches can be described under the rubric either of "pattern intervention" or of "context intervention." As should become clear, we do not regard "pattern interven-tion" and "context intervention" as describing two distinct classes of intervention, but, rather, as two alternative ways of describing one broad class or mode of therapeutic intervention. Just as it may be useful in physics to describe light sometimes as particles and sometimes as waves, the focus and description are different depending on the frame for viewing the data. *Every pattern intervention is a context intervention, and every con-text intervention is a pattern intervention.*

If we are thinking of making a context intervention, we are considering the problem context in terms of those communica-tional features that serve to differentiate or classify or define the context as being one sort of context rather than another, in turn determining the meaning of the various elements within that context. We can then seek ways of manipulating context-mark-ers so as to abolish or transform the existing context and there-by transform the meaning—indeed, the very "nature"—of all the elements within it. If, on the other hand, we are thinking in terms of making a pattern intervention, we are looking at the problem context in terms of the pattern—that is, those generic (video-descriptive) elements that, from one occasion to the next of the occurrence of the difficulties, are invariant. We then seek ways of strategically varying some feature of the pattern so as to replace the old pattern with a new one from which the individual may more easily see his way to extricating himself. Or again, it may be that in the context of this new pattern "around the problem," the therapist will find herself on firmer ground for further negotiations.

CONTEXT INTERVENTION

A toddler whose screaming annoyed his mother would have the contextual rug pulled out from under him if his mother urged him to scream louder; his screaming would no longer be what it was, no longer a member of the class of "things that bother

Mother." We can alter the "fundamental nature" of any behavior, experience, or communication by introducing some communication altering the context.

To abolish any pattern or system all that is required is to transform the context. One option would be simply to abolish the present context and (as it were) leave the choice of new context up for grabs. To this option we will (if the reader will forgive us) assign the overlong and unnecessarily ugly term "decontextualization." The other option would be to transform the old context into a new one specifically preselected by us—with the new context, if we wish to be fanciful about it, rising like a phoenix from the ashes of the old. To this latter option we will give a term no shorter and no less ugly, "recontextualization" (Wilk, 1982/1985).

RECONTEXTUALIZATION

Recontextualization, transforming one context into another quite specific one, is accomplished through introducing new context-markers. This can be achieved either (1) by actually introducing new objects or behavior (through behavioral prescriptions) to serve as new context-markers; or (2) by giving a new sense to signs (including behavior) currently serving as markers of one context, in order to re-employ them as markers of an entirely new context.

Let us begin by considering the approach of introducing new context-markers altogether rather than recycling existing ones.

Recontextualizing by Introducing New Context-Markers

A child of 12 who was acutely afraid of the dark and of being on her own was given the giggly opportunity in a session to practice pulling silly faces, putting thumbs in the ears and waggling the fingers, and so on. She was then instructed to pull these faces whenever she was alone or in the dark and felt afraid, and to do so (simultaneously hopping up and down on one foot in extreme instances) until the fear subsided. She was to repeat this as necessary. This context-marker made it awfully difficult, if not impossible, for the fear context to be maintained. In the next session 3 weeks later, the child reported having to do the exercise only two or three times, thereafter having no opportunity "'cause I just don't get scared any more."

We frequently introduce the old-numbered and even-numbered days of the month as context-markers. For example, a 25-year-old woman had a lifelong history of being unable to get up in the morning and of rarely rising before midday—a severely disabling pattern that had resisted all previous attempts at "treatment." She was told that every morning when the alarm rang, she was to take note of the overwhelming feeling of wanting to go back to sleep. Then on odd-numbered days she was to give in to this feeling and go back to sleep, and on even-numbered days she was to get out of bed and start the day. Within a week she had altered the directions herself and was getting up on time every day, a pattern she has continued to maintain.

If it is seen as a new context-marker, it is easy to understand how any new behavior or other variation, however small, introduced into a previously invariant pattern, can have a dramatic effect. In a rigid, automatic, recurrent pattern of "symptomatic" (i.e., undesired) behavior, each step in the familiar sequence marks the context as one of compulsion and immutability, of behavior following its predictable and predetermined course. To introduce one small piece of new behavior—so small that the individual can readily incorporate it in the pattern—is to introduce a new context-marker. This marks the context as therapeutic, and as one of change, of choice, of mutability, and of subsuming an "automatic" pattern under voluntary control. (It also, incidentally, marks the context as one of hope rather than hopelessness.)

Recontextualizing by Re-Employing Existing Context-Markers

As we have mentioned earlier, new context-markers can be introduced by "recycling" existing ones, or, to be more precise, by re-employing signs that had previously been used as markers of one context as context-markers for another, quite different context.

A man who sought therapy for depression was in a rigid pattern of brooding for hours on end over the impossible situation with his married girlfriend. After extensive questioning, he explained that the way in which his problem got in the way of his daily life was this: He would get this powerful sinking feeling in his chest whenever thoughts of his relationship crossed his mind. If he was with his mother and grandfather at the time, he would start snapping at them and being rather nasty. If he was studying, he would abandon his work and go out on a binge of either drinking or spending. As a result, he was failing in his studies, getting into terrible rows with his mother and grandfather, and spending most of his time either broke or loaded or, in his words, "crawling on the floor."

We told him that for the next month, as soon as he got that sinking feeling in his chest, he was to write down the time in a little notebook and give himself exactly 5 minutes from that time to reach a decision: If he was studying, he was to decide whether to go on studying in spite of the feeling in his chest, or to go out drinking or spending. If he was with his relatives, he was to decide whether to be nasty or civil. Otherwise, he was to decide whether to "crawl on the floor" or to accomplish something useful. He was to write down the decision he reached at this "choice point." A month later he reported that he had only had to do this once, completing 4 solid hours of studying after this choice point. He said he had stopped snapping at his folks, got on with his studies, and stopped bingeing; he was "finding choice points all over the place" and not letting his feelings determine his behavior. Follow-up indicated that his depression had not recurred, although the situation with his girlfriend remained substantially unchanged and frought with difficulties.

DECONTEXTUALIZATION

During some road construction on the one-way traffic system in Oxford a few years ago, just before rush hour, a practical joker obscured a carefully selected detour sign. This resulted in the establishment of a loop that the diverted traffic could get on but not off. A bumper-to-bumper jam of cars soon formed a slow-moving complete circle; no further traffic could even get onto the loop, and thus traffic was snarled up throughout the city, virtually within minutes. Clearly, obscuring one judiciously selected context-marker can produce major ramifications reverberating throughout an entire system.

In *decontextualization*, the therapist obscures or obliterates existing context-markers and thus simply abolishes the old context through the introduction of ambiguity. This is more easily done than explained. In Bateson's famous definition, information is a difference that makes a difference. In other words, information is a perceptible difference that makes a difference to the receiver. Context-markers are information about context—differences that make a difference as to the context. Context-markers can thus be obscured/obliterated in one of two ways: by obscuring the perceptible difference *itself* (i.e., so that it is no longer perceptible *as a difference*), or by obscuring the difference it *makes* to the receiver.

Now when we speak of "the signaler" and "the receiver," it may well be, in a given instance, that the signaler and the receiver are the same person. Our considerations apply equally to this limiting case, for it is in the self-reflexive nature of human beings that we can both behave and be the observers/interpreters of our own behavior. We are at once producer, director, author, actor, audience, critic, and board of censors. It is sometimes simpler to deal with cases in which the signaler and the receiver are stationed in different bodies—though this is by no means a necessary requirement.

Obliterating the Difference (Signal) Itself

To obliterate the perceptible difference itself is to prevent reception of the signal in the first place by means of communication, in effect introducing other signs indistinguishable from the signs used in the signaling, so that the signal cannot any longer be differentiated as a signal—as in the story of the boy who cried wolf. The sign (in this case, the cry) that would have otherwise signaled a wolf context could not any longer be perceived as a context-marker of a wolf context because of all the preceding false alarms. In the story of "Ali Baba and the Forty Thieves," when Ali Baba's house is singled out for some sort of attack by a mark being placed on it, his wife puts an identical mark on all the other houses; when the plotters respond by putting a red mark on Ali Baba's house, his wife responds by putting such a red mark on all the other houses (Warner, 1983).

In radio communications, one speaks of "jamming"—preventing the reception of certain signals by sending out other signals of approximately the same frequency. Noise or "static" has thus been introduced. In counterespionage, one might speak of "disinformation"; Watzlawick (1976) devotes considerable discussion to examples drawn from cases of deception in wartime counterintelligence work.

In psychotherapy, there are two general strategies of introducing such "noisy" communication to prevent reception of the putative context-marker as a signal in the first place, two ways to camouflage the context-marker altogether: (1) arranging for the *actual introduction* of additional signs indistinguishable from those used in the signaling; or (2) simply *requesting* the introduction of such additional signs, doing so in front of both the "signaler" and the "receiver." In the latter case, even if the signaler disregards the request, noise will have been introduced for the receiver.

Merely Requesting the Introduction of Camouflage. In a case of Haley's (1963), a man referred for *ejaculatio praecox* had been crusading for years to give his wife an orgasm. The wife was told, in the husband's presence, that one day she might experience some sexual pleasure and "when she did she was to tell her husband that she did not enjoy it. If her husband insisted on her saying whether she had really not enjoyed it or was just following this directive, she should say she had really not enjoyed it" (1963, p. 143). Robbed of any source of information as to his wife's enjoyment, the husband no longer focused his attention on giving his wife an orgasm. His potency was soon restored, and with it, no doubt, his wife's pleasure in sex. In this case, the wife needed to do nothing in response to the intervention: The uttering of the directive itself was sufficient to obliterate existing context-markers, and so to abolish the old context and throw the husband back (quite literally) on his own devices.

If person *A* performs certain types of behavior serving as context-markers of context *X* for person *B*, we can merely request of *A* in the presence of *B* that *A* additionally perform that same type of behavior to signal news of context *Y* (where contexts *X* and *Y* are incompatible, and preferably require opposite courses of action from *B*). Whether *A* complies with this request or not, noise will have been introduced, just as broadcasting the news that large numbers of counterfeit $5 bills are about to be put into circulation will have the same effect, whether or not those bills are subsequently circulated. In a similar way, too, news of an impending fuel shortage will have the same effect of increasing fuel sales and decreasing available supplies, irrespective of whether the gross amount of supplies subsequently is diminished. Note that the behavior we have requested of *A* may now disappear altogether, perhaps in part because *B*, now robbed of information, behaves differently; this may break a communicational loop in which *B*'s behavior in response to *A*'s behavior in turn called forth more of that same behavior from *A*. (Again, note that *A* and *B* can be the same person; however, this kind of intervention can be more readily understood by looking at examples where *A* and *B* are different individuals.)

A boy of 14 had been stealing from home for many years, and recently had begun stealing from the family's shop and from elsewhere. We saw the boy on his own and told him all he needed was to learn how to resist temptation, and that we had a guaranteed, sure-fire way to teach him to resist temptation— but that he wouldn't like it a bit. We had already secured his desperate parents' agreement to carry out anything we asked of them, and we told him so. We told him we could either give his parents the sure-fire cure right now, or we could give him 2 months to see if he could teach himself to resist temptation; if he failed after the 2 months, his parents would teach him with the sure-fire method we would give them. We gave our somewhat reluctant, skeptical consent in response to his pleading to be given a 2-month period to try on his own, and we called his parents in.

We explained the deal, and in front of the boy we secured the parents' cooperation in helping him teach himself to resist temptation by providing as much temptation for him as possible. In front of the boy, we instructed them to leave money around for him to find, to leave doors or drawers or cash registers unlocked "accidentally on purpose," and so on. The parents were to conspire with other family members, friends, neighbors, school personnel, and local shopkeepers to provide this temptation for him, in ways so indirect and subtle that sometimes the boy would be unable to imagine any possible way the parents could have had anything to do with planting the temptation. At every opportunity they were to deny planting any temptation for him and to deny they were following this assignment at all. They were to keep careful records of how well he was succeeding in teaching himself to resist temptation, and to bring us the results in 2 months.

Note that the success of this intervention did not depend on the parents' actually doing anything at all, as the decontextualization was accomplished merely through the "noise" introduced in the delivery of the directive. Note also that this intervention can to some extent also be viewed as a recontextualization employing existing markers.

Arranging for Camouflage Actually to Be Introduced. As we have noted earlier, context-markers can be obscured as signals by arranging for additional signs indistinguishable from those used in the signaling actually to be introduced.

Here is an example of a decontextualization involving the actual introduction of camouflage (which could, however, have worked either way). In a case on which one of us consulted, there were violent arguments over trivial matters between the teenage identified patient and her stepmother, made worse by the father's "inability" to stay out of the middle of them. The therapist gave the family an assignment to help the father learn how to stay out of these fights. Stepmother and stepdaughter were to give him plenty of practice by deliberately picking fights with each other over the most trivial things and trying to draw him in. His job was to stay out. They were both to deny ever picking such a fight deliberately. If the two had managed to fight, the intervention would have worked through camouflaging the context-markers on which the father depended. However, it is possible that the context-markers for the start of a fight may have been obscured for both stepmother and stepdaughter, and they may never have managed to fight at all.

Obscuring the Difference That the Difference
(Signal) Makes

Since information is a difference that makes a difference, context-markers can be obscured not only by obscuring the difference (the signal itself) so that it can no longer be distinguished
as a signal, but, additionally, by obscuring the difference that
the signal makes. To obliterate the difference it makes is to
ensure that it makes no difference in terms of the response to
the signal—in other words, that the response elicited in its presence is no different from the response elicited in its absence.
With a well-functioning fire-alarm system, it may be announced
that a test will be carried out on such-and-such a day at such-
and-such a time; if a fire actually breaks out at that point, no
one may take the alarm seriously. (One of us can remember
thinking frequently as a child, when the town's air-raid siren
was tested every Saturday at 12:00 noon, "What a wonderful
time for the enemy to attack!") When some American cities
introduced the right turn on red, the red light could still be
distinguished as a detectable difference, but for the driver wanting to turn right, the red light no longer made a difference
distinct from the difference the green light made, at least once
the driver had briefly stopped. Thus such decontextualization
can be accomplished simply by attribution. The signal can still
be received, but it no longer makes a difference to the receiver:
Once again, the response required in its presence is no different
from the response required in its absence (Wilk, 1982, 1985).

Pragmatically, the net effect of this attributional communication is the same as that brought about by jamming the signal
altogether (in one of the two ways already described). An example of obscuring the difference itself would be the familiar story
of the boy who cried wolf: His false alarms obscured the genu-
ine S.O.S. Another example of obscuring the difference itself,
this time by merely requesting the introduction of camouflage,
would have been if the story had been rewritten as follows: "A
young shepherd boy in training, who needed further practice at
raising the wolf alarm, was instructed in front of the entire
assembled village to pretend to raise the alarm of 'wolf' at least
once in the coming week. The next day a real wolf came, and

the frightened shepherd boy raised the alarm, but of course no one came to his rescue." An example of *obscuring the difference that the difference makes* would be if the story had again been rewritten, this time as follows: "A young shepherd boy had never in his life raised any false alarms about wolves, but one day all the villagers heard on the radio that a disease was going around among shepherds that gave them vivid hallucinations of wolves; the next day a real wolf came and the frightened shepherd boy cried out, but no one came to his rescue."

The therapist can decontextualize a situation through obscuring the difference that the signal makes by attribution, thus making the pragmatic situation thoroughly ambiguous. For example, a mother felt that her son, Melvin, was always being "picked on" by her husband, the boy's stepfather. The stepfather would correct some small bit of misbehavior or bad manners; the boy would dig in his heels and persist all the more; the stepfather would get increasingly annoyed and become more insistent in his demands; and the cycle was punctuated frequently by the mother's demands that the stepfather "stop picking on Melvin." The results of this escalation could be pretty ugly.

In the second session with the mother and Melvin alone, the mother sought our help in getting her husband to stop picking on the boy. After getting a "video description" from the mother of each of the specific situations she was referring to, we told her this tallied well with the interaction we had witnessed in our office in the initial family session, and that we weren't sure if the stepfather was picking on Melvin. From what we saw and what she described, he *might* have been picking on him, and she might have been right that he disliked and resented Melvin. Yet it seemed equally possible that he loved Melvin very much and was trying to bring him up as if he was his own son, and was getting very frustrated in the process. If so, the best thing was to help her husband out; but if not, she'd better defend Melvin from being picked on. In the next session, the mother reported that she had stayed out of these battles and sometimes told Melvin to behave himself, and had found not only that her husband was going easier on the boy, but that most of the time he was right.

The distinction we have introduced between obscuring the difference and obscuring the difference that the difference makes is a purely heuristic distinction. There will be considerable overlap in practice, and often the same situation can be validly described from either point of view (though, of course, it does not cease to be true that black is distinct from white just because there are all shades of gray in between). Equally, there will be overlap of this kind between the (wider) category of obscuring existing context-markers (decontextualization) and the category of introducing new context-markers (recontextualization). It is our belief, however, that while the edges may be occasionally blurred, the therapist's familiarity with these fundamentally distinct modalities of abolishing and transforming contexts will increase the perceived options for intervening at any point in any given case. In the same way, even though every context intervention is a pattern intervention and vice versa, an awareness of the numerous modalities for intervening in patterns will provide the therapist with still further options.[2]

PATTERN INTERVENTION

. . . to expand the idea that maladies, whether psychogenic or organic, followed definite patterns of some sort, particularly in the psychogenic disorders; that a disruption of this pattern could be a most therapeutic measure; and that it often mattered little how small the disruption was, if introduced early enough.—Milton H. Erickson

But the pattern may be changed or broken by addition, by repetition, by anything that will force you to a new perception of it, and these changes can never be predicted with absolute certainty because they have not yet happened.—Gregory Bateson

Once you break through rigid, fixed patterns of behavior patients are forced to pick up the pieces to put them together; and they are forced to function in a totally different way.—Milton H. Erickson

THE TEMPLATE: PATTERN AS INVARIANCE

Sometime during the 14th century, the Old French word *patron*, meaning "patron," acquired the secondary sense of "a model." It entered late Middle English in the 15th century and eventually became "pattern"—a term first used chiefly in dress-

2. Context interventions are discussed in greater detail in Wilk (1985).

making, where it still has the same sense today. Equipped with a pattern or mold or template to serve as a guide, one can produce any number of duplicates of an original design. Where we can identify a "motif"—a distinctive and recurring form, shape, or figure in a design—we can speak of the design as being "patterned" in a particular way. One invariant "pattern" (in the sense of "model"), repetitiously applied, creates a recurring pattern.[3]

When we reflect on the etymology of "pattern," we have available to us a convenient way of conceptualizing the relation-

3. If one looks at traditional art forms such as certain oriental carpets or embroideries, one can observe a number of 'layers' of application of this concept in the manufacture: (1) the design was printed onto hessian using wooden blocks, thus allowing many copies of a design to be woven; (2) any given design itself included numerous recurring motifs (e.g., the ornamental border), so that the very design was created through numerous applications of only a few wooden blocks; (3) each wooden block was itself made up of recurring "submotifs." Like some modern floor tiles, where the designs on adjacent tiles blend together to form a continuous repeating design, the ends of the printing blocks were cut so that the end of the design printed by one application of the block would correspond perfectly with the beginning of the design printed by the next application.

Bateson (1978, passim) often spoke of pattern and redundancy in the same breath. The *predictability* of particular events within a larger aggregate of events ("redundancy"), made possible through the *repetition* of certain elements; the *recurrence* of a design within a larger design; the *regularity* of a given motif; and the *invariance* of a recurring pattern: these are concepts that are obviously closely intertwined. If we wish to consider a painter's characteristic style, we can compare a great number of his paintings and consider those features that recur from one painting to the next (i.e., that are "redundant," to use the engineer's terminology). Or, what is really the same thing, we can consider those features that, despite marked *differences between* the paintings, remain *invariant*. If we consider the *overall* pattern, in space, in time, or in space and time, and identify the motifs that are repeated throughout, we are considering pattern from the point of view of redundancy. If, on the other hand, we consider the individual occurrences that *make up* the broader pattern, and, comparing one with the other, identify those features that remain consistent (despite other differences) from one occasion or occurrence to the next, we are considering pattern from the point of view of invariance. The logic of invariance and the logic of redundancy are perfectly complementary. For something to be redundant, it must duplicate what occurs elsewhere, and hence certain features must be invariant from one occurrence to the next; and for certain features to be invariant from one occurrence to the next, those features must be duplicated and hence redundant.

ship between redundancy and invariance, consistency and recurrence. For whenever we observe pattern in the sense of "a repeating design" (say, on fabric), we can deduce what the pattern or "model" must have been like from which the design was created through repeated applications of the ("model") pattern. We can ask ourselves, "What is the smallest pattern that, if applied repeatedly, would produce this design?" Likewise, in observing human behavior and experience, whenever we notice (usually from the experience of recurrence or "here we go again") that "there seems to be a pattern here," and seek to identify the pattern, what we are seeking is the model, the mold, the template. And what is this template but the general abstracted from the particular, the general outline or form of what remains consistent or invariant, with all the episodic features or incidental details left out? The search for the pattern is a search for the outline, the general template. It is the search for the regular amidst the irregular, the invariant amidst variation, the unity in diversity. In cybernetic terms, we are looking for the "constraints" or "restraints" on variety—the limits within which the variables happen to vary; that which remains the same the more things change. If we can discover these limits on variance—and it is precisely those limits that are invariant—we can intervene to introduce variation going beyond these limits, thereby creating a new pattern.

Where can one intervene in a pattern to produce a new pattern in its place? The answer is "Wherever anything is invariant." Consider how the screwdriver has been reinvented many times. Screwdrivers may have come in many shapes, sizes, and colors, but what did they all have in common? A wooden handle that can be gripped by the hand, a round steel shaft, a flattening at the end to fit the slot of a screw. These features were invariant. *But none of them was necessary.* The shaft can be made square, so that it can be turned by an open-end wrench for greater leverage; the tip can be pointed with a cross-shaped cross-section to make a Phillips screwdriver; the handle can be replaced with an electric drill; and so on. Wherever there is consistency or invariance, there is an opportunity to introduce variance. And the more invariant ("rigid" or "stereotyped") the pattern—that is, the less variation there is within each set of limits—the easier it is for a small change to be significant. For example, if an obsessional hand-washing ritual has for many years been highly stereotyped down to the brand of soap, altering the brand of soap may be a difference that makes a big difference.[4]

CLASSES AND LIMITS: SEQUENCE
AND CIRCUMSTANCE

In psychotherapy, in negotiating a client's deductions and getting down to video descriptions of what happens and video descriptions of what the client actually does, we are aiming ultimately to get detailed factual information not only about particular episodes but about the general pattern—again, in terms of video descriptions. We want to determine what features of the particular episode are typical, and what the range of variation is. Therefore we ask a lot of questions on the order of "Is it always *X*?" "Would it ever be *Y*?" "What about *Z*?" "Would you say it's never *Z*?" *We seek sensory-based descriptions of the "always," the "usually," and the "never" with respect to every conceivable parameter of the "symptom."*

If we use the term "symptom" as shorthand for "undesired behavior or experience that the client is seeking to eliminate," there are numerous parameters of the symptom's occurrence that can be considered. We can obtain precise, detailed, sensory-based (video-descriptive) information about when, where, how, and how much it always, usually, or never occurs with respect to the following parameters or variables, among others:

4. It must be remembered that patterns are not "things." Yet they are the next best thing to "things": They are descriptive abstractions. When observing some facts, an observer can abstract patterns of facts. This does not involve theorizing or explaining the existence of these facts, what function they serve, or whatever. It is more like classifying organisms into species or objects into a set. But while the patterns abstracted are abstracted by an observer, it is our contention that the pattern distinctions drawn by the observer are not in the least arbitrary, and that the invariance is in the factual realm, independent of the observer's interpretations. This is in contradistinction to the views of some other systems theorists, who hold that any distinctions drawn by an observer reflect only the observer's way of drawing distinctions. For our part, we believe that the regularity of Nature is not due merely to the orderliness of observers, and we share Einstein's sentiment that "God does not play dice."

time of day, time of week, time of month, time of year, location in the world or in the body, frequency, rate, intensity, duration, the sequence of events in time (including all the events that redundantly occur along with the symptom—i.e., "the pattern around it"), who is present, and mode or quality (depending on the symptom: voice volume; whether sitting, standing, or lying down; type of food eaten on a binge; or whatever). These parameters of the symptom's occurrence concern the *sequence* (what follows what) and the *circumstances* (where, when, how, how often, how much, at what rate, with whom, etc.), all of which can be described in terms of "always, usually, or never."

It is sometimes helpful to think of a complete video description of "what the client does" and "what happens" as a series of answers to a hypothetical series of questions asked by someone with insatiable curiosity: "How often does it happen? In what rooms of the house? Sitting or standing? Who else is around? How much? How often? When exactly? What happens first? What about after that? And then what happens?" and so on. Once one has answered every conceivable question that can be answered with a video description, one can imagine the answers written out in the form of a list. Then for each item on the list, one can find out the *range* of other possible answers that can be given if one is describing other occurrences of the client's symptom. For each item, one will then be able to define the limits beyond which that particular variable never (in fact) varies. The therapist will thus be able to describe the "blow-by-blow" sequence of events and behavior, and the circumstances of their occurrence, in terms of the *class of possibilities* for each variable.

So if we are talking about the pattern—the sequence and circumstances described in terms of the features that vary within certain invariant limits—the diagram of the sequence would thus resemble not a series of linked dots but a series of linked circles, with many potential dots within each circle. To intervene in a pattern is to replace any variable with one falling outside the known limits, a dot falling outside one of the linked circles.

Let us return for a moment to our discussion of context-markers. In a sequence of events and behaviors *L-M-N-O-P, L* can be thought of as a context-marker marking the context as one in which M is the next step, and M may play the same role for N, and so on. Alternatively, it may be that it is the sequence L-M that is the context-marker "summoning up" N (rather than it being the occurrence of M alone), and so on. Therefore, to introduce a new behavior W (however small) between L and M (thus L-W-M-N-O-P) is to eliminate L as an unalterable context-marker for M, or L-M for N, and to set up W as the new context-marker signaling that it's time for M, or, as the case may be, that it's time for T. Because, as the next intervention, T can be prescribed to come after W and before M, and why not? W has only been "calling forth" M since the intervention in the previous session! Thus L-W-T-M-N-O-P. Eventually the pattern can be "derailed" altogether, so that it never gets to its ("symptomatic") destination. Likewise, one can insert L again just before the end: After several repetitions of L-M-N-O-L-P . . . L-M-N-O-L-P . . . L-M-N-O-L-P, eventually the client can just as easily go L-P . . . L-P . . . L-P (a modality of pattern intervention we call "short-circuiting").

What is important to emphasize, however, is that the letters (L, M, N, etc.) do not each refer to specific items of individual behavior or specific events. Each class M may comprise many possible alternative specific events or items of behavior (M_1, M_2, M_3, M_4), any of which may serve equally well as an "M context-marker." For example, at a certain point in a binge-eating pattern, a person may take a taste of some cake, or cookies, or bread, or ice cream, or chocolate (but never carrots, or celery, or cottage cheese, or hard-boiled eggs); she may then go on a binge including all of the former items but none of the latter items. That is, if she eats "forbidden," "fat," or "nondiet" foods, she typically or always binges, and she never binges on "good," "nonfattening" foods. The binge may be followed by self-induced vomiting in the toilet, or in the sink, or in the bath (but never in the garbage can, or in a bucket, or on the carpet). And in terms of the circumstances surrounding this part of the sequence, the initial taste may be taken standing up or walking around (but never sitting down or lying down). The binge-eating may take place in the kitchen or in the dining room (but never in the bedroom or in the backyard), and may occur in the middle of the night or in midafternoon (but never first thing in the morning or just before bed). It may always occur while the person is alone (and never with other people around), and usually while she is doing nothing else in particular or sometimes while watching TV (but never while talking on the telephone or feeding the cat and dog). The pattern will be a different range with different elements for each person, so a therapist cannot come up with some fixed "catalogue" of ranges or elements, or of interventions. For example, many binge-eaters binge only when alone, but some binge with others around occasionally or often. *The therapist needs to find out the limits of the class of things that would serve equally well to maintain the pattern as still being this pattern.* For there are many variations on the theme such that the theme remains the same theme; what the therapist wants to introduce are variations outside those class limits, that therefore define the theme as a new pattern. And in a new and unfamiliar pattern, anything might happen.

In asking questions about the pattern around a symptom, not only do we ask "When does it always occur and when does it never occur?" or "Is it always X, or is it ever Y?", but we also ask hypothetical questions of the form, "When would it always occur, and when would it never occur?" and "Would it always be X, or would it ever be Y?" Moreover, we "help the clients out" extensively by suggesting possible alternatives ourselves. Since clients are often unaware of what the pattern is, they frequently say, "well, there's no particular pattern to it," or "it could be just about anything," but careful questioning never fails to reveal, for most parameters, classes with fairly distinct limits. A mother who consulted us because of her 11-year-old daughter's "temper tantrums" (which we specified down to video descriptions) repeatedly insisted that "she could throw a tantrum over absolutely anything." By systematically ruling out the numerous circumstances we put forward as suggestions, we enabled the mother finally to know for certain that the tantrums always occurred in the kitchen or in the living room, and only when Diane was being cajoled into doing some chore that it was actually her sister's turn to do. But as there were many chores and as Diane's sister rarely took her turn, it genuinely *seemed* to the mother that the tantrum could be over "absolutely anything."

MODALITIES OF PATTERN INTERVENTION

Therapy is often a matter of tipping the first domino.—Milton H. Erickson

When you have a patient with some senseless phobia, sympathize with it, and somehow or other, get them to violate that phobia.—Milton H. Erickson (in Zeig, 1980, p. 253)

Our discussion thus far has led us to this conclusion: that any sensory-based descriptive statement of any invariant aspect of the sequence or circumstance of the "symptom" provides a recipe for *where* to intervene. "If it's invariant, vary it." In this section, we briefly discuss the matter of *how* to intervene in the sequence and circumstances of the symptom ("the pattern"), surveying some of the modalities of pattern intervention (*see* O'Hanlon, 1982b). The modalities we discuss here are these (again, we use "symptom" as shorthand for the undesired experience/behavior that occurs as part of a larger pattern, the "symptom pattern"):

1. Changing the frequency of the symptom/symptom pattern.
2. Changing the rate of the symptom/symptom pattern.
3. Changing the duration of the symptom/symptom pattern.
4. Changing the time (of day/week/month/year) of the symptom/symptom pattern.
5. Changing the location (in the body or in the world) of the symptom/symptom pattern.
6. Changing the intensity of the symptom/symptom pattern.
7. Changing some other quality or circumstance of the symptom.
8. Changing the sequence (order) of events around the symptom.
9. Creating a short-circuit in the sequence (i.e., a jump from the beginning of the sequence to the end).
10. Interrupting or otherwise preventing all or part of the sequence from occurring ("derailing").
11. Adding or subtracting (at least) one element to or from the sequence.

12. Breaking up any previously whole element into smaller elements.
13. Having the symptom additionally performed without the symptom pattern.
14. Having the symptom pattern additionally performed minus the symptom.
15. Linking the occurrence of the symptom pattern to another pattern—usually an undesired experience, an avoided activity, or a desired goal ("symptom-contingent task").

CASE EXAMPLES USING PATTERN INTERVENTION

That little hole in the dike [doesn't seem as if it will] flood the land, except that it will, because once you break through an altered pattern of behavior in some way, the cracks keep traveling.—Milton H. Erickson

What follow are some case examples to illustrate the use of pattern intervention. Each example is followed by a notation that refers the reader to the list of the 15 modalities (see above), for the (primary) type of intervention that was used in the case.

Case A. A boy of 12 who had a compulsive habit of blowing his nose was asked to obtain an average of how many times he blew his nose each day; this was found to be about 20, and never more than 25. He was instructed to blow his nose 35 times each day, and if he hadn't completed all 35 by bedtime, he had to fill his quota before going to bed. This number was alternately reduced and increased by the therapist until the symptom disappeared. (Frequency, #1.)

Case B. In a case of Erickson's, a 17-year-old retarded boy, recently placed in a school away from home, developed a symptom in which he rapidly alternated his right arm out in front of him at a rate of 135 times per minute (Erickson had the rate counted). Erickson got the boy to increase the rate to 145 times per minute. Over a course of some time, the rate was decreased, under Erickson's supervision, to 135 again, increased to 145, then decreased and increased by alternating an increase of 5 times per minute and a decrease of 10 times per minute until the movement was eliminated. (Rate, #2.)

Case C. A bulimic who reported that the very longest duration she'd managed for a bingeing episode was 1 hour was told that she must stretch the duration of bingeing (i.e., before vomiting) to 2 hours. She could increase this duration in any manner she wished. (Duration, #3.)

Case D. A bulimic told us that she only binged in the evenings. We told her that for the next week she could binge and vomit as often as she liked, provided she only did it between the time she arose and noon. (Time of day, #4.)

Case E. A couple who argued constantly, and who said they had trouble not falling into an argument even when both had the best of intentions not to fight, were told (by a student of ours) that if they got into an argument they were to head for the bathroom, where the husband was to remove his clothing and lie down in the bathtub while his wife was to sit (fully clothed) on the stool. They could then continue the argument. (Location in the world, #5.)

Case F. A 6-year-old thumbsucker who only sucked his left thumb was seen by Erickson. The boy was told that he was being unfair to his other digits, not giving them equal time. He was told to suck his right thumb, and, eventually, each of his other fingers. Erickson remarked that as soon as the boy divided his thumbsucking between his left and right thumbs, he had in effect reduced his habit by 50% (Rossi *et al.*, 1983, p. 117). (Location in the body, #5.)

Case G. A 13-year-old boy who talked to himself "constantly," much to the consternation of those around him, was instructed to continue to do so, but in a very quiet voice instead of his usual loud voice (Booth, 1984, personal communication). (Intensity, #6.)

Case H. A man came to Erickson and complained that he could only urinate through a wooden or iron pipe 8–10 inches long. Erickson had the man switch to a somewhat longer bamboo pipe, and, after he had used it for a while, told him to begin shortening it to 10 inches by degrees. He then had the man shorten it further gradually until the pipe was no longer needed (Haley, 1973). Quality or circumstances, #7.)

Case I. A couple sought therapy from Erickson for marital difficulties. They ran a small restaurant together and constantly quarreled about the best way to run it. The wife insisted that the husband should be in charge, as she'd rather stay home, but she feared that without her supervision, he'd ruin the business. So she continued to work alongside her husband and they continued to quarrel. Erickson gave them this assignment: Each morning, the husband was to go to the restaurant half an hour before his wife. When the wife now arrived, the husband had already successfully fulfilled many of her "irreplaceable" functions. She started coming in even later each morning and leaving before closing, until she finally rarely showed up at the restaurant. The bickering ceased (Haley, 1973). (Sequence, #8.)

Case J. A 13-year-old boy had had a "compulsive" pattern, since the age of 5, of running up to his mother and hitting her whenever she sneezed. The invariant sequence was that he would hear her (or see her) sneeze, jut his jaw forward and tighten up his face and neck until they trembled visibly, then run frantically up to his mother and hit her on her shoulder, and then relax completely and go off quite calmly until the next sneeze. In in-session practices and then in "real life," he was instructed to hear the sneeze, tense up his face and neck, run, hit his mother, then tense up again for a specified duration of time (with all jaw movements, etc.), and then relax completely. Since he now had a pattern (appended to the end of the sequence) of going straight from the face-tensing to the relaxing, he was next instructed to hear the sneeze, tense up, and relax completely. The duration of the tensing-up period was then gradually reduced. (Short-circuiting, #9.)

Case K. An 8-year-old soiler only soiled his pants while playing outside after school and often "forgot" to come in after school before going out to play. (When he did come in, his mother would get him to use the toilet before going out, and then he wouldn't soil.) The boy was instructed to "touch base" at home to collect his "TV ticket" (entitling him to watch TV that day), and the ticket could only be collected between his return from school and playtime (Adding a new element, #11.)

Case L. A binger was told that she could binge as usual, but that she must put a drop of tabasco sauce on every bit of food that she ate during the binge. (Derailing, #10.)

Case M. A couple who argued with no productive results,

calling each other names and generally saying things during fights that they later regretted, were told to have their next argument on paper. Once they realized they were fighting, they were to get a pad of paper and a single pen. No talking was allowed. They were to take turns saying their piece (peace) in written form. (Derailing, #10.)

Case N. A 23-year-old man with an obsessional "fixation" on the flow of saliva into and out of his mouth, who compulsively swallowed every couple of seconds to keep his mouth "free" of saliva, was asked whether he swallowed the saliva down the right side of his throat, or the left, or in the middle, or all three. He looked shocked and said, "You know, I have no idea." He was told to pay careful attention, each time he swallowed, to where the saliva was going, and to keep a log indicating each swallow as "r," "l," "m," or "all 3." (Breaking into smaller elements, #12.)

Case O. A bulimic was told to binge at least once in the next week when she didn't feel like bingeing. (Symptom without the symptom pattern, #13.)

Case P. A bulimic provided a highly detailed picture of the precise, stereotyped ritual for the bingeing and vomiting. She was instructed, in addition to her usual bingeing and vomiting, to carry out this entire ritual from the preparations for the setting out of the binge food to the cleaning up afterwards, and so on, but without actually bingeing or vomiting. (Symptom pattern without the symptom, #14.)

Case Q. A lawyer who wanted to quit smoking agreed that if he smoked a cigarette he would do 15 minutes of paperwork he had been putting off before he smoked any additional cigarettes. (Symptom-contingent task, #15.)

Case R. A couple sought marital therapy, and the main complaint was that the husband was a "workaholic" (they both agreed on this point). This led to terrible arguments almost every evening, as the husband constantly broke his promise to be home on time. The husband complained that his wife wanted ed him to spend his only day off visiting his or her parents. We agreed that instead of complaining, the wife would record the amount of time the husband was late during the week, and he would have to visit his or her parents for that amount of time on Sunday without complaining. (Symptom-contingent task, #15.)

AFTERWORD ON CONTEXTUAL APPROACHES IN PSYCHOTHERAPY

Clearly, many of the examples we have given of particular modalities of pattern intervention could just as well be cited as examples of other modalities. There is considerable overlap in practice. Moreover, when making a pattern intervention, we often simultaneously prescribe a number of alterations. The point of making all of these distinctions between modalities is simply to aid the practitioner in devising interventions by emphasizing the variety of choices available. Likewise, as we have pointed out earlier, every pattern intervention is a context intervention, and vice versa. The distinction between pattern intervention and context intervention, once again, is merely a heuristic distinction pertaining to how one thinks about where and how to intervene. In pattern intervention, one looks for the invariant aspects and seeks to introduce variance in one or more of the 15 modalities we have distinguished. In context intervention, one looks for context-markers defining the context as being one thing rather than another. One then seeks to manipulate context-markers in one or more of the varieties of ways we have distinguished in order to transform or abolish the context.

This chapter has provided a model for how to intervene therapeutically without searching for causes, functions, or explanations for the diffculties. As we have been contending throughout this book, behavior, symptoms, and complaints are embedded in contexts. Contexts are made up of patterns of behavior, language, interactions, objects, time and space components, and so on. Symptoms do not appear randomly; they appear only in certain contexts. We strive to alter, transform, or abolish the symptom context in order to eliminate the symptom.

Context and pattern interventions, we must re-emphasize, do not provide individuals with any choices that were not previously available to them. But (like virtually all of our therapeutic communication in the practice of clinical epistemology), by marking out new distinctions and obscuring old ones, these interventions enable individuals to see their way to exercising the choices they have always had.

CHAPTER NINE

CLOSING THE BOOK
Getting from Here to There

As therapists, clearly we have a duty. First, to achieve clarity in ourselves; and then to look for every sign of clarity in others and to implement them and reinforce them in whatever is sane in them.—Gregory Bateson (1969, "Pathologies of Epistemology")

We have endeavored to make this book as clear as possible and immediately useful for clinicians. We appreciate, however, that as clear as it is to us, it may not be obvious to our readers how to translate this book into their clinical settings. It is to speak to this translation effort that we are including some general hints for readers to use after closing the book.

CONTINUING AND SHIFTING APPROACHES

Once, after one of us had taught a course on clinical epistemology, a member of the audience remarked, "You've just destroyed my whole basis for doing psychotherapy! Now what am I to do?" We still practice psychotherapy and find it to be a very viable means of being useful to people. We do not view what we have written in this book as in any way an "attack" on psychotherapy or on any particular school of practice. Rather, we view it as a contribution to the psychotherapy field: We are endeavoring to make therapy more effective.

While we have taken a firm stand on what can be known and on what we have found to be a set of minimal assumptions that can generate effective psychotherapy, we intend this approach to be *inclusive*, rather than "siding" with certain schools and against others. We have found "mythologies" and highly objectionable ideas in every approach we have examined, and in each we have also found elements that are very much in line with clinical epistemology.

For example, let us consider, in some detail, an approach that might at first appear, in many ways, to be furthest removed from our own approach: psychoanalysis. Many therapists have been attracted to psychoanalysis because of some or all of the following features of the psychoanalytic approach:

- Its attempt to deal therapeutically with symptomatic behavior by placing that behavior in the context of the individual's unique life circumstances and idiosyncratic ways of construing experience, and to work therapeutically on that context rather than necessarily working directly on the symptom itself.
- Its emphasis on the distinction between the actual event or experience and the construction placed upon it by the individual, and its locating the difficulties or "problem" in the individual's construction rather than in the facts of the matter.
- Its central interest in looking for recurring themes or patterns, and for the pattern that connects the various patterns—in other words, both its search for patterns that repeat over time, and its search for abstractions describing invariant general patterns common to many specific patterns occurring simultaneously throughout many areas of the individual's life.
- Its attempt to get underneath the client's communications and behavior to the fundamental and habitual ways of construing experience, without which that behavior and communication would not make sense.
- The following back of objections to what the therapist proposes, until the last objections dissolve, as the favored way of liberation from self-imposed limitations.
- Its emphasis on how individuals keep seeing situations the same way and so keep acting the same way; and its attention to the recursive circle of presupposition, action, experience resulting from that action, interpretation of experience, and presupposition the next time around.

- Its view of the person's "past" as history or autobiography—an ongoing present construction or reconstruction; and hence its view, in contradistinction to more traditional psychiatry, of the past not as causally influential, but influential only as a present-day construction that forms the basis (often an irrational basis) for action.
- Its view of personal existence as consisting primarily of actions with multiple and transformable meanings (Schafer, 1978).
- Its therapeutic aim of transforming the meanings an individual places on experience;
- Its overriding interest in language, its subtleties, and multiple levels; its perspective on human beings as shaped by language and using it to create new worlds (Schafer, 1978).
- Its precision use of language to effect therapeutic change;
- Its insistence that it is the patient who does the therapy.

All of these features, in different ways, are common also to clinical epistemology; many, indeed, can be seen as central to it. Although we have clearly biased our selection to make this point, and although some may accuse us of being overcharitable to psychoanalysis, in our view these features of the psychoanalytic approach represent what is best in psychoanalysis, and what has attracted to it many of our finest minds. If it is these features of psychoanalysis that one finds valuable, one need not throw out the baby with the bath water. But, to our way of thinking, psychoanalysis has also contained an inordinate amount of (if we may be charitable again) bath water. When psychoanalysis was the only show in town that had these features, one could be tempted (to change our metaphor) to buy the whole package; however, that often meant buying a lot of features one did not necessarily want, or of whose value one was not entirely convinced. But if one were attracted to psychoanalysis for any or all of these reasons, one might find clinical epistemology attractive for similar reasons.

Again, many therapists have been attracted to behavior therapy and behavioral approaches because of some or all of the following features:

- Its relatively transparent approach, with the client seen as a cotherapist or "trainee" behavior therapist.
- Its emphasis on observables and on what can be verified empirically.
- The pre-eminent importance it attaches to behavior and to behavioral changes.
- Its view of behavior as autonomous—that is, in order for behavior to change, nothing other than behavior needs to change.
- The relative brevity of treatment.
- Its emphasis on starting out with clear outcome measures, and the way in which the therapist takes responsibility for achieving objectively demonstrable results, in terms of which the success or failure of treatment is exclusively measured.
- Its therapeutic use of task assignments, and its handing over to the patient the responsibility for handling the "spadework" of the therapy at home, between sessions.
- Its attempt to identify and modify *patterns* of behavior.
- Its insistence on explicit, specific, solvable "problems."
- Its problem-solving frame, taking complaints one at a time, and building on successes.
- Its approach of teaching clients strategies for dealing with problems, so that they can transfer skills across to other difficulties without further reliance on the therapist.
- Its demystification of therapy and the therapist's role.
- Its avoidance of interpreting or reading meaning into behavior.
- Its rigorous approach to case documentation and follow-up, and its willingness to test its claims empirically.

Once again, therapists who find behavioral approaches attractive for these reasons will most likely find clinical epistemology attractive for the same reasons.

Let us go on to consider, somewhat more briefly, a few of the many other approaches to psychotherapy, and the factors that have no doubt attracted a large number of therapists to these approaches.

Therapists who have been excited by the promise of humanistic psychology and related approaches to psychotherapy, because of the humanistic emphasis on the unrealized possibilities for people and on helping individuals to realize those possibilities in their lives here and now, and because of its optimism and creative approach to overcoming "illusory," self-imposed limitations, may be excited by the ways in which clinical epistemology fulfills that promise.

Therapists who liked Carl Rogers's "nondirective" counseling because of the respect shown for the client and its emphasis on acceptance will probably find our approach appealing for similar reasons—in particular, our avoidance of characterizing clients, our taking the clients' statements "at face value," and our courteous approach of accepting and utilizing whatever the clients offer. In short, such therapists might appreciate our attempt, in Erickson's words, to formulate psychotherapy "to meet the uniqueness of the individual's needs, rather than tailoring the person to fit the Procrustean bed of a hypothetical theory of human behavior" (quoted in Erickson Foundation brochure, 1979).

Therapists who have found family therapy to be an important development and a powerful approach because of its focus on the interactional context of symptomatic behavior and experience, its move away from the psychologizing of problems, its move from a lineal/causal view to a Batesonian cybernetic epistemology of form and pattern, its search for redundant sequences and attempts to intervene in patterns through the smallest necessary therapeutic communication, its extensive use of task assignments to intervene in patterns and contexts, and the increasing brevity of treatment, will probably find our approach congenial for these and a whole host of other interrelated reasons.

And, finally, therapists may appreciate Milton Erickson's work for its emphasis on observation and flexibility; its utilization of clients' behavior, beliefs, and symptoms in reaching therapeutic outcomes; its optimism and unswerving orientation toward the future; its individualizing of therapy to the uniqueness of each client; its de-emphasizing of hypothesizing, theorizing, and explaining; its preference for simple and commonplace solutions; its drawing on a client's existing repertoire of resources;

its naturalistic approach; its combination of directive therapy with indirection and indirectness; its view of therapy as providing only the climate or weather for clients, who have to do their own thinking and therapeutic work; its use of jokes, humor, and ordinary conversation; its unconcern with the cause, function, or meaning of symptoms; its emphasis on influencing the client to DO something; its delight in language and in the subtle use of multileveled communication; its orientation toward breaking rigid conscious sets and rigid patterns of behavior; its use of communication to abolish and transform contexts; its preference for unconscious learning and acquisition or application of skills and know-how instead of conscious insight; and its emphasis on how little therapy is really required to enable a person to bypass self-imposed limitations. Such therapists will appreciate the way in which clinical epistemology has embodied all these orientations. This is (need we say it?) no coincidence; Erickson, of course, has had a major influence on us, clinically, conceptually, and in terms of our actual working methods.

A couple of years ago, one of us met a colleague at a therapy conference, a colleague who was a fellow veteran of many of the same conferences and workshops and weekend courses over the years. He said something like this: "A few years ago we thought psychoanalysis was 'it'; then 'it' was group analysis, soon giving way to family therapy; then 'it' was strategic approaches and brief therapy; and now 'it's' Milton Erickson and Ericksonian approaches. But what next? And how do we know it won't be something else next year, or in 10 years?" After thinking it over, the answer we and our colleague came up with was this: Many of the same things that had attracted us to each approach had attracted us also to each of the others. In looking back, we discovered that we had not simply been fickle followers of ephemeral fashions and fads. There were some common threads or leads that we had been following in our quest for effectiveness in psychotherapy; between us, we and our colleague came up with themes such as the interest in language, in recurring pattern, in viewing limitations as self-imposed via one's habitual ways of construing experience, and in shifting contexts. That conversation with our colleague was quite a while ago now, but the same threads can still be discerned in our continuing search. Clinical epistemology, in its attempt to get underneath all of the psychotherapies to the foundations on which they all rest, represents simply a different and perhaps deeper level at which the two of us continue this quest for what is effective in psychotherapy.

The point we wish to stress is that therapists do not have to discard their previous ideas and working methods to apply clinical epistemology to their practice, nor does their adopting this general approach necessarily invalidate what they have been doing heretofore. In one of the first courses we ever taught on clinical epistemology, one of the trainees said, "You know, it's just dawned on me: I've *always* been a clinical epistemologist, only I didn't know it!"—a remark compared both by the therapist himself and by us to M. Jourdain's ecstatic discovery in Molière's *Le Bourgeois Gentilhomme* that he had been speaking prose all his life. Our actual current working methods (Chapter Seven), though readers may find some or all of them useful or at least worth trying out, are only our particular ways of working at the moment and are not essential to the practice of clinical epistemology. Therapists may find other ways that fit in more naturally with their current ways of working and personal therapeutic styles. Moreover, just as we do not expect our clients to "relinquish" every last epistemological presupposition with which we disagree or that we regard as potentially problem-engendering, therapists do not have to discard every presupposition that we ourselves have discarded (Chapter Six). A response we frequently get at the end of one of our courses—our favorite kind of feedback—is that "I realize I've been doing this all along, but I couldn't articulate what it was I was doing, and now that I think I can say what it was that is most effective in my work I can do it more deliberately, more skillfully, and more often."

All that a reader has to do to begin to apply clinical epistemology to his therapy practice is this: (1) begin making the distinction for himself between what is in the (sensory-based, video-descriptive) realm of fact and what is in the negotiable realm of attributed meaning (Chapter Two); (2) begin to be aware of what imperatives (particularly prerequisites), deductions, and supporting assumptions (Chapter Four) he brings to his work as a therapist and imposes on the facts of the clients' situations; (3) one by one, identify each one of his presuppositions (Chapter Six) that, if it turned out to be invalid or irrelevant, would leave his clients with more immediate options for reaching their desired outcomes; and (4) experiment—while otherwise continuing with his current approaches—with temporarily dropping now one presupposition, now another, acting in a way that is congruent with its being invalid or irrelevant, and observing the effect on his practice and on his results.

REALIZING POSSIBILITIES: THE PROOF OF THE PUDDING INTO PRACTICE

In the beginner's mind there are many possibilities; in the expert's mind there are few.—Shunryu Suzuki

Don't bite my finger, look where I am pointing.—Warren S. McCulloch

The proof of the pudding, as they say, is in the eating. We cannot prove to our readers that what we have offered here is valid or useful until they have had some experience with it in practice. Readers must try the pudding to find out whether it is really pudding at all, and, if it is, whether it is to their taste.

We have as yet conducted no empirical studies to statistically demonstrate the effectiveness of clinical epistemology. We are mainly clinicians and spend our professional time mainly seeing clients or supervising, teaching, and training other clinicians. We only have our inevitably subjective follow-up data at present. We would welcome appropriate, rigorous experimental examination of our work and results, but until such is forthcoming, all we can offer is our experience that it is possible to obtain successful results in therapy using this approach.

Our own subjective experience—as veterans, between us, of therapeutic approaches from across the whole range of individual, group, family, and marriage therapies—is that the approach presented in this book enables the clinician to achieve dramatic therapeutic successes more rapidly, more enduringly, more effortlessly, more pleasurably (for both client and therapist), and more reliably than any psychotherapeutic approach we have encountered. It is also our conviction, from our results so far, that most psychotherapeutic problems can in principle be resolved in a single therapeutic session, and that in practice, using this approach, it is rather the exceptional case that goes beyond three or four sessions; many are resolved in a single interview.

As Erickson has pointed out, though one case doesn't necessarily prove anything, it can sometimes indicate quite a bit:

> For example, a professor of internal medicine, after reading a psychiatric report upon a single patient, remarked that one case proves nothing. Reply was made that a single instance of an untried medication administered to only one patient with lethal results proved much more than could possibly be desired. The nature and character of a single finding can often be more informative and valuable than a voluminous aggregate of data whose meaning is dependent upon statistical manipulation. . . . Rather than proof of specific ideas, an illustration or portrayal of possibilities is often the proper goal of experimental work. (Erickson, 1980, Vol. 4, p. 246)

What single cases prove better than any amount of statistical evidence is *what is possible*. That first celebrated instance in which a surgically hopeless case of congenital ichthyosis (a serious scaly skin condition) was rapidly and completely resolved through hypnosis demonstrated beyond all doubt what was possible in the treatment of this once fundamentally "incurable" condition. The Wright brothers, once airborne, needed no statistical demonstration of the possibility of powered human flight, and of the possibility that—contrary to the prevailing scientific studies of the time—a machine heavier than air could indeed fly. And even if, in the absence of a sufficiently large statistical sample, the Apollo 11 mission was regarded as a fluke or "merely anecdotal," it proved that it was at least possible for a man to land on the moon. Statistical evidence, though valuable, is necessarily merely probabilistic; single cases, though insufficient to prove general "scientific laws," can nevertheless demonstrate possibilities with a degree of certainty unapproached by even the most convincing statistical studies.

What we have "proved," through our clinical work, is that it is possible to obtain results in psychotherapy in very brief amounts of time without reference to many of the assumptions of current therapeutic approaches. And what we suggest is that, at times, all one needs to do in order to challenge one's tightly held assumptions about therapy is to have one experience contrary to that assumption. That is, if a therapist's client were to get lasting results without having insight, or without discovering the cause of the present "dysfunctional" pattern, or without altering the family structure, or without a change in the contingencies of reinforcement, the therapist would at least know that it was possible to achieve lasting results in this way. Frank Farrelly, the originator of "provocative therapy" and a former Rogerian therapist, illustrates this when recounting how a "serendipitous" experience with one client, then another, and then another led him to question both his standard techniques and his assumptions about therapy (Farrelly & Brandsma, 1974, pp. 3–31).

In this book, what we have been aiming for is to open up possibilities for therapists and clients where before there has been both verbal and behavioral closure. We have been pointing to an approach to psychotherapy that offers new possibilities, but our words can *only point to* the possibilities. The burden is now upon the reader to close the book and to try out the approaches suggested here in a clinical setting.

POTENTIAL BARRIERS

No young lady ever lost her virtue by reading a book.—Al Smith

We have noticed a few "traps" or "barriers" that clinicians typically encounter when learning this approach, and so we would like to send up some warning flares to help our readers to avoid them or surmount them.

One of the traps is to dismiss this material with the attitude: "Oh, this is just like X" or "This is just the old X wine in new (clinical epistemology) bottles." We have heard this from trainees and colleagues from time to time, and we reiterate that clinical epistemology isn't "just X," whatever one might select X to be. We have tried in this chapter to highlight some of the affinities of this approach with other approaches, and we hope that readers will discover further affinities to still other approaches, but clinical epistemology cannot be assimilated to any of these or to any combination of these. Clinical epistemology, once again, is at a level (as it were) lying beneath all of these approaches.

Another trap is that of not trying any of this because one does not believe it is possible. Such a person probably will not get to discover whether it is possible or not if she never tries it. As they say in Las Vegas, "You can't win if you are not at the table." As we were completing the writing of this book, one of us wanted to complete a certain chapter by a certain deadline, and the other claimed that that was impossible. In the end, we agreed that the most sensible way of finding out whether it was possible or not was to start action toward discovering whether what we claimed was possible was indeed possible. The motto for coauthors, clients, and therapists alike might be, "TAKE AC-TION TOWARD THE GOAL first, and then tell me what is or isn't possible."

If readers do "try it out," of course, we do not guarantee success. As most gamblers know, merely being at the table, although it gives them the opportunity to win, does not mean that they will win. Paul Watzlawick (1978, p. 160), in a similar connection, reminds us of the joke about the man who declares that piano playing does not exist, because he tried it and nothing came of it. Readers should beware the trap of concluding that what we say is impossible on the basis of one or even several tries. The application of these approaches, like any other, involves numerous skills that can only be acquired and perfected through practice.

Another barrier is that of dismissing what we have been saying as merely stating the obvious. For that is what we have attempted to do—to state the unstated (and, as Moshe Felden-krais [1984] adds, "elusive") obvious. We earnestly hope that the main points we have been making will appear obvious once we have made them. As Whitehead once observed, the analysis of the obvious has produced some of mankind's most dramatic intellectual accomplishments.

Finally, one last barrier that is sometimes encountered that we would like to draw attention to is that of explaining away successful results as "flukes" or simply not noticing or not believing successful outcomes. We ourselves *began* by regarding one-session therapeutic successes as flukes, and as the "flukes" became too frequent and predictable they could no longer be so easily dismissed; we *ended up* writing the book that our readers, and we, are now about to close.

DISPATCH FROM THE FRONTIER

We regard this book as a beginning, a report of a new world. We have roughly indicated the location of the territory and have sketched out the coastline so that others may follow, but only time and further explorations will fill in the gaps and correct the distortions.

We expect (and hope) that in some years this book will be obsolete—not proved fundamentally wrong, however, for when explorers find themselves in a new world, whether they have misidentified it or placed it incorrectly on the map, they know for certain, at least, that they have landed. And certainly there were those who sought (and perhaps found) this land before us, for we have seen signs of them and have gained valuable directions from their records. We hope that this will be seen as a landmark and as groundbreaking work to be followed by other explorers, pioneers, and settlers who will help to realize its potential and to increase our knowledge of the area. In the meantime, we shall not cease from exploration.

EPISTEMOLOGY AND CLINICAL EPISTEMOLOGY

In this appendix, we add a little to our discussion in Chapter One, for the sake of those who are interested, particularly with regard to three ends we have left deliberately loose in that chapter: the concept of presupposition; the question of how our use of "epistemology" relates to how Bateson and others have used the term; and the relationship of clinical epistemology to epistemology proper. First, however, a definition of "epistemology proper" is in order.

EPISTEMOLOGY: THE REAL MCCOY

In recent years, the term "epistemology" has been bandied about in the psychotherapy field with alarming variations in meaning, most of the muddle being historically traceable to Gregory Bateson, who introduced the term. The therapy field has unfortunately inherited Bateson's conceptual and terminological muddles along with his valuable insights. Bateson himself inherited some of the muddle from the team of scientists in Warren S. McCulloch's neurophysiological laboratory at MIT, who, not without some justification, coined the term "experimental epistemology" for their experimental study of "how organisms know, think, and decide," beginning with their work on what the frog's eye tells the frog's brain. But all this was in some ways a rather different matter from the concerns of epistemology proper. So let us begin by considering "the real McCoy," and return to Bateson's contribution (and terminological variations) later.

Epistemology, or "the theory of knowledge," is the branch of philosophy concerned with the nature and scope of knowledge, its limits and validity, its presuppositions and basis, and the general reliability of claims to knowledge. As a branch of philosophy, epistemology is concerned not with how or why human beings come to hold the beliefs that they do or to make the claims to knowledge that they make, but rather with questions of whether we are justified in claiming knowledge of some particular class of truths—in other words, whether some kinds of knowledge are even possible at all.

An epistemological claim is defined as any claim to know something, such as, for example, the claim that "it is probable that smoking leads to increased risk of heart disease," or the claim that "we know that John has a depressive personality." For those who would like a more rigorous philosophical definition, an epistemological claim is any statement that logically entails another statement to the effect that "it is reasonable or warranted for a person N to place more confidence in P's being true than in Q's being true," where P and Q are propositions that can be either true or false; thus, any claim logically entailing a statement that it is more reasonable or warranted to believe one thing than another is a claim to know something.

Epistemology is concerned with the general principles for appraising the acceptability—the reasonableness or warrantability—of epistemological claims. Epistemological analysis is thus involved with assessing how we can go about deciding whether or not such claims are justified. Ultimately, the epistemologist seeks to lay down general principles or standards for deciding whether epistemological claims (claims to knowledge) are justified or warranted. In practice, epistemologists have tended to demarcate certain kinds of knowledge as being *bona fide* knowledge: what we can really, reliably claim to know; the real McCoy. Other kinds of knowledge are thus regarded as derived, with varying degrees of reliability or unreliability, from the more basic kind of knowledge, or, worse, are thought not "really" to be knowledge at all.

PRESUPPOSITION AND EPISTEMOLOGICAL CLAIMS

We are concerned throughout this book, and in many ways, with the unstated assumptions that provide the necessary ground for clients' and therapists' explicit statements. In this section, therefore, we attempt to arrive at a simple, coherent way of characterizing these unstated assumptions, and to indicate how such assumptions enter into one's epistemological account of how to appraise the justifiability of claims to know something. It is often useful to distinguish between (1) what a person explicitly states or asserts when she utters certain words in certain circumstances, and (2) to what further statements she nevertheless commits herself in uttering those words in those circumstances, even if she does not explicitly assert them.

ENTAILMENT, CONTEXTUAL IMPLICATION, AND PRESUPPOSITION

In his 1955 William James lectures at Harvard, "How to Do Things With Words" (published in book form in 1962), J. L. Austin (1962, pp. 47–52) distinguished three ways in which we commit ourselves in uttering a statement.

If we say "all men blush," this logically entails "some men blush," and if we say "The cat is on top of the mat," this logically entails "the mat is under the cat," because we cannot logically assert one statement of each pair while denying the other. Under the rules of formal logic, it is flatly contradictory to say "All men blush, but there are not any men that blush," or "the cat is on top of the mat, but the mat is not under the cat." So making one statement can logically commit us to making another, insofar as the truth of the statement we do make depends, logically, on the truth of some statement one doesn't actually make. This is known as logical *entailment*.

Now if we say "John's children are bald," this presupposes that John has children, but "John's children are not bald" equally presupposes that John has children; and so this is quite different from entailment, in that "the cat is on the mat" and "the cat is not on the mat" do not equally presuppose that the mat is under the cat. In *presupposition*, making one statement commits us to making another, insofar as the truth or falsity of the statement we make depends on the truth of some statement we do not actually make. The presupposed statement thus enables the explicit statement to even have the *possibility* of being true. The notion of presupposition is probably due above all to the work of P. F. Strawson, who, in his *Introduction to Logical Theory* (1952, p. 175), defined the relation of presupposition as follows: A statement S presupposes a further statement S' ("S-prime") if S' is a necessary precondition of the truth-or-falsity of S. So in his example, it is a necessary condition of "All John's children are asleep" being either true or false, that "John has children." "John has children" is thus presupposed by, or is a presupposition of, "All John's children are asleep." *Presupposition, then, is a concept referring to the class of statements that are true or false, and what conditions must be satisfied if we are to regard a given statement as being either true or false.*

Both logical entailment and presupposition are different again from the kind of commitment involved in what Austin called "implication," which has come to be more generally known in philosophy as "*contextual implication*": If we say "the cat is on the mat," this contextually implies that we believe that the cat is on the mat, unless we are taken to be lying or deliberately deceiving someone. The notion of contextual implication was clearly distinguished from presupposition by the philosopher Isabel Hungerland in her paper "Contextual Implication" (1960, p. 239). She expressed the relation between the two concepts by saying that whenever S presupposes S', a speaker, in making the statement S, contextually implies that he believes that S'. *Contextual implication is thus a concept referring to the class of beliefs held by the speaker, and what we are entitled to infer about those beliefs from the statement he makes in a certain context.*

Let us try to clarify the difference between presupposition and contextual implication further. If we say, "The psychotherapist next door does hypnosis," this contextually implies that we believe there is a psychotherapist next door, and unless we are taken to be lying or deliberately deceiving someone, one is entitled to infer from our statement that we at least believe there is a psychotherapist next door. Now whether there actually is a psychotherapist next door is quite another matter. However, for it to be either true or false that "The psychotherapist next door does hypnosis"—that is, for it to be the case either that the psychotherapist next door does or doesn't do hypnosis—it must be true that there is a psychotherapist next door. Thus this latter statement (that there is a psychotherapist next door) is presupposed by the former.

OUR USE OF THE TERM "PRESUPPOSITION" IN THIS BOOK

We are concerned throughout this book both (1) with what the making of a given statement in a given context entitles us to infer about the speaker's (client's or therapist's) beliefs—contextual implication; and (2) with what further statements (or "claims") have to be true for a given statement to be either true or false (and therefore to have even the possibility of being true)—presupposition. For the sake of simplicity, we use the terms "presupposition" and "to presuppose" to cover both contextual implication and presupposition in the stricter sense. In our usage of the term, then, *presuppositions are the underlying, supporting, or background assumptions that we are entitled to infer as having to be true if a given statement is either to be true or false, or that we are entitled to infer as being held implicitly as a belief by a person asserting the statement.*

A statement S shall be said to presuppose another statement S', if S' needs to be true for either S or the contradiction of S to be true, or if we are entitled to infer the speaker's belief in the truth of S' from his uttering of S in a given context.

The main exception to this usage is in Chapter Four, Part Two, when we refered to the "supporting assumptions." These are all in fact presuppositions in our broader sense, but for the sake of clarity we divide these into three subcategories: (1) presuppositions (in the stricter sense—what must be true for the statement to be either true or false), and (2) the evaluations and (3) the expectations contextually implied by the person's making these statements.

EPISTEMOLOGICAL PRESUPPOSITIONS

As we state at the outset of Chapter One, whenever a person makes any epistemological claim (any claim to know something), this claim, whether it is true or false, asserted or denied, usually presupposes a considerable number of other statements. Both the truth and falsity of the claim depend upon the truth of these presupposed statements. And again, whether a person asserts or denies an epistemological claim, she is implicitly affirming the truth of these presuppositions.

Any statement that is presupposed by a given epistemological claim, we call an *epistemological presupposition* of that claim. These epistemological presuppositions will include presuppositions about what can be known, about the existence of certain classes of entities of which a person can claim to have knowledge, and about certain general posited relationships that are deemed to hold in human mental life or in the universe as a whole. Whatever has to be true for the epistemological claim to be either true or false, or whatever we are normally entitled to infer that the maker of the claim believes (however implicitly) to be the case (i.e., assumes), is regarded as an epistemological presupposition involved in the claim.

If whole classes of such epistemological presuppositions come to be regarded, according to a given viewpoint, as invalid (e.g., assumptions involving positing the work of demons as the cause of psychological problems, or involving the notion of lineal chains of cause and effect in human mental life), that viewpoint will provide at least a partial set of standards or principles for appraising the warrantability of epistemolgoical claims. In other words, any claims involving any of the discredited epistemological presuppositions will themselves be regarded as unwarrantable or unjustifiable. So one's set of standards for appraising whether or not a given epistemological claim has a logical possibility of being true will depend on the views one holds in general. As we stress in Chapter One, which sets of epistemological presuppositions one holds in general as fundamental assumptions, and which sets one regards as invalid or otherwise unacceptable, will play a large part in forming the principles by which one appraises the reasonableness of any claim to know something.

EPISTEMOLOGY AND BATESON'S PLURALISM

It would be convenient to have a term with which to refer to these sets of epistemological standards or principles together with the fundamental assumptions forming one's epistemological presuppositions— the whole epistemological kit and caboodle that one uses in appraising claims to know. Bateson referred to such a set of principles and assumptions as "an epistemology," and introduced the plural into the discussion by speaking of alternative "epistemologies." Thus one could speak of "rationalist epistemologies" versus "empiricist epistemologies," "epistemologies of form and pattern" versus "epistemologies of force and impact," and so on.

An important part of Bateson's contribution was his attempt to conceptualize alternative epistemologies as alternative ways of preferentially dividing up or "punctuating" reality. Bateson argued for one such way of punctuating reality—a "cybernetic" or "nonlineal" epistemology utilizing the metaphors of form and pattern, information and organization, instead of the metaphors of substance and force, matter and energy native to a "traditional lineal" epistemology (Keeney, 1982, p. 155; 1983, p. 14). Bateson's own epistemology involved the notion that human knowledge is fundamentally knowledge of differences, of pattern and relationship, of recurring patterns of patterns, and patterns of patterns of patterns. Much of Bateson's work can be seen as concerned directly or indirectly with the (in his view) often disastrous conceptual and pragmatic consequences of introducing other metaphors and presuppositions into one's epistemology—especially such metaphors as substance and energy, cause and effect, power and control.

Bateson used the term "epistemology" in a plurality of ways (cf. Dell, 1981a, pp. 2–8): (1) as the theory of knowledge; (2) as the experimental study of how organisms or systems "know, think, and decide"; (3) as the set of epistemological standards, principles, and presuppositions that one uses to appraise claims to know; (4) by extension, as the entire set of premises from which one operates, a broad paradigm for understanding and acting (hence "Newtonian epistemology" or "Occidental epistemology"); (5) as Bateson's own monist "biological cosmology" (Dell, 1981a, pp. 4–5), based on a cybernetic "epistemology" (in the third and/or fourth sense); and (6) as an individual's personal "epistemology" (in the third and/or fourth sense)—"a body of habitual assumptions" that Bateson in turn equated with character structure. Regarding the relationship (in a person's functioning in the world) between questions of ontology (the branch of philosophy dealing with what there is) and epistemological matters, Bateson wrote:

> In the natural history of the living human being, ontology and epistemology cannot be separated. His (commonly unconscious) beliefs about what sort of world it is will determine how he sees it and acts within it, and his ways of perceiving and acting will determine his beliefs about its nature. The living man is thus bound within a net of epistemological and ontological premises which—regardless of ultimate truth or falsity—become partially self validating for him.
>
> It is awkward to refer constantly to both epistemology and ontology and incorrect to suggest that they are separable in human natural history. There seems to be no convenient word to cover the combination of these two concepts. The nearest approximations are "cognitive structure" or "character structure," but these terms fail to suggest that what is important is a body of habitual assumptions or premises implicit in the relationship between man and environment, and that these premises may be true or false. I shall therefore use the single term "epistemology" in this essay to cover both aspects of the net of premises which govern adaptation (or maladaptation) to the human and physical environment. (1978, p. 285)

One could argue, of course, that here (of all places!), Bateson was being overly apologetic about his use of the term "epistemology," for the study of the presuppositions that form the necessary basis of epistemological claims is very much within the province of epistemology in the traditional sense, and always has been. Moreover, the general sort of criticism to which Bateson usually subjected the assumptions he regarded (not incorrectly) as "ontological" (concerned with what there is) was primarily epistemological criticism—aimed at the alleged basis for "knowing" of the existence of the entities in question.

There are many strands connecting Bateson's numerous uses of the term "epistemology," but these do not concern us here. The point we wish to note is simply Bateson's awareness of the recursive interconnectedness of our presuppositions about what there is in the world and how we can come to know the truth of these presuppositions, influencing how we perceive the world and act within it, in turn influencing our presuppositions about what there is in the world. Bradford Keeney, who has given (1983) the most complete and coherent formulation to date of a "Batesonian" cybernetic epistemology, which he has offered as a theoretical foundation for family therapy, has been concerned above all with this feature of recursiveness in the various forms in which it occurs. On the matter we have been discussing, he writes, "any act of epistemology affects how you act as well as perceive—the two are linked as a recursive process" (p. 98).

If we confine our use of "epistemology," preceded by the indefinite article (or in plural form—"epistemologies"), to the sense in which "an epistemology" is to be understood to mean a set of epistemological standards or principles for appraising the warrantability of epistemological claims, together with the fundamental assumptions forming a person's stock of epistemological presuppositions, we can consider the implications of shifts from one epistemology to another. Or, on a more limited, less ambitious scale, we can consider what differences in a person's judgments and actions would follow from a shift from one given epistemological presupposition to another. And in particular, we can consider specific examples in the clinical realm, such as what difference it would make to a clinician's therapeutic approach to depression, let's say, if he were to replace the presupposition that emotions are feelings or internal states with the presupposition that emotions are . . . ; here the blank might be filled in with, for example, "patterns of interaction involving at least two people." Clearly, such a shift would have implications for the kinds of epistemological claims this clinician would make, for his appraisal of epistemological claims, for how he would act in relation to depression (including, for example, his therapeutic approach), and so on. In the course of intervening therapeutically now in a different way, the response to the intervention (what the clinician would now "see" following his action) would recursively influence his assumptions about depression, and so on.

Whether we are thinking primarily about the therapist and the therapist's presuppositions, or about the client and the client's presuppositions, does not particularly seem to matter here. In either case, we can look at the recursive process in which epistemological presuppositions influence the kind of things the therapist or client might claim to know about the situation, how seriously the therapist treats his own epistemological claims or "hunches" about the situation (e.g., how he goes about dealing with his own or his client's "depression"), how he views the results of those actions, and how his views of those results (including "lack of results") come to bear on his presuppositions.

EPISTEMOLOGY AND CLINICAL
EPISTEMOLOGY: REPRISE

Throughout this book, in many different ways, we have explorerd the relationship between therapeutic problems and the client's and therapist's epistemological presuppositions. But at the risk of oversimplification, let us state this interrelationship in the simplest possible terms by way of concluding the present discussion (begun in Chapter One) of what on earth clinical epistemology, on the one hand, has to do with epistemology in the philosopher's sense, on the other hand. At one level, clinical epistemology (the therapeutic discipline) stands to epistemology (the academic philosophical discipline) as clinical psychology stands to academic psychology. Clinical epistemology is clinically applied epistemology. And, indeed, every clinical psychotherapeutic problem has at its heart an epistemological problem; every quandary that brings a client to psychotherapy exists only because of epistemological muddle—what Bateson calls "epistemological error." For every client (with or without a therapist) wrestling with some psychotherapeutic problem, there is some epistemological claim without which the problem simply could not exist.

Consider an "agoraphobic" client who wants to go out of the house and doesn't go out of the house. If asked, say, by an epistemological researcher, "Well, what stops you from just going out the door?", the client might reply that she gets scared. If asked, "How does being scared stop you from going out? Why not just be scared and go out?", she might reply, "Well, I'm afraid I might pass out—I feel like I'm about to pass out." If asked, "Well, why not just be scared, go out, and either pass out or not? You can pass out and then come around later," she might reply, "Well, I feel like I might pass out and never come around—I'm afraid I might die." If asked, "How can you tell the difference between feeling like you're about to die and feeling like you're simply about to pass out?", she might reply, "I've never thought about that before—I don't know, it just feels like that." If asked, "Well, since you'll probably always continue to be scared about going out—and with good reason, after all these years at home—at least until you are used to going out of the house regularly, don't you think you'll eventually have to take the risk and go out?", she might reply, "Yes, eventually, I guess I'll have to take the risk." If our researcher then asks the client, "Since you don't want to take the risk at the wrong time and end up dying, how will you know when it's safe to take the risk?", she might reply, "I guess I'll never know it's safe." At this point our bewildered epistemological researcher might be forgiven for asking, "Well, since you say you don't want to stay confined to the house forever, how will you ever decide to go out?''

Notice all of the epistemological muddles here at the heart of our agoraphobic straw man's quandary: (1) that being scared and then not going out indicates that her fear stops her from going out (she is presupposing, too, that feelings can cause actions); (2) that even if she could know from a feeling that she would faint if she went outside, such "knowledge" entails that she knows she cannot go out of the house; (3) that she can know from a feeling of lightheadedness or a thought about dying that she is on the verge of dying as distinct from just passing out; and (4) that she can reasonably wait until it is safe to take a risk, even in the absence of any conceivable indicators (any possible way of knowing) that it is safe to take that risk. Remove almost any one of these epistemological muddles, and our client would not be in a quandary; upon taking the appropriate simple action, she would soon no longer have any "symptoms."

Or consider the client who "knows" from the fact that he feels himself getting angrier and angrier the more he thinks angrily about some situation ("'I'll be judge, I'll be jury,' said cunning old Fury," in Lewis Carroll's apt characterization) that something called "anger" is getting bottled up inside him. This, of course, leads to the notion that he had better let it out somehow or it will come out somewhere else, or in the wrong way, or will reach explosion point, or will cause him to (physically or mentally) rupture internally.

Or consider the wife who no longer knows whether she still loves her husband, because she remembers feeling much more amorous toward him when they were first courting 15 years ago. Or the husband who wonders whether his wife still loves him, but when asked cannot at first specify any hypothetical indicators that would be "outward and visible signs of [this] inward and spiritual grace" (the definition of "sacrament" whose central relevance to epistemology Bateson seems to have recognized).

Or consider the client who has sat for years by the window waiting to die, because he once heard a voice in his head telling him he was doomed. Or consider the depressed client who does not get out of bed all day because she is depressed, and knows she is depressed because she stays in bed all day.

Or consider the parents who know their child is disturbed and needs psychotherapy because he throws violent temper tantrums when they try to discipline him in certain ways; or who know their child is hyperactive and needs medication because he runs wild despite their protestations, and who don't even consider educating him through discipline to behave himself, because what's the use if he suffers from hyperactivity?

Or consider the alcoholic who knows that "once an alcoholic, always an alcoholic," because every time he has one drink, he goes on from there to get drunk. Or the heroin addict who knows she needs a lot more psychotherapy and a lot more insight into her problems, because no matter how much therapy she has, she still goes and sticks that needle in her arm.

The list is as endless as the list of variations of the complaints that clients bring, or might bring but don't bring, to psychotherapy. This book, in its entirety, could constitute a guide to identifying and disentangling the epistemological knots at the heart of every therapeutic problem. It should, moreover, not be at all surprising that such a large number of the questions we ourselves ask in psychotherapy begin with "How do you know . . . " or "How will you know . . . " or "How would you know . . . ". Sometimes all that we need to do is to get clients to specify how they will know their problems have been solved—in other words, to specify the "outward and visible signs of an inward and spiritual grace"—and then get the clients to do something different and look out for those signs. This is where our work links up with the work of de Shazer (1985). One of our favorite de Shazer questions is this: "If a miracle happened in the middle of the night, while you were sleeping, and your problem was solved [or your marriage was the way you would like it to be, or whatever], how would you know in the morning, and as you went through the day, that this miracle had occurred?" (personal communication to Wilk). For oftentimes the difficulty is not that spurious epistemological connections have been made between certain signs and some (positive or negative) grace, but that the client is seeking after some grace without ever having specified to herself the relevant outward and visible signs.

Here too is where clinical epistemology links up with General Semantics (see Chapter Four and Appendix II) and with the work of Wittgenstein and Austin and their students in philosophy: These epistemological knots can only be tied in language, and often seem to come about because people "get taken in by a form of language" and confine themselves to the map of the territory sketched by their chosen metaphors. A person's "epistemology," in Bateson's sense, is basically the way that person punctuates or construes or represents, the way the person chooses to *talk about* reality. Clients, often aided and abetted by therapists, have talked themselves *into* problems—often with exceedingly serious consequences—and it is the job of clinical epistemologists, like the job of every practitioner of effective "talking therapy," to talk their clients *out*.

THE STRUCTURE OF
SELF-IMPOSED LIMITATIONS
Problem Talk

What, in general, are some of the means by which forms of language can either facilitate or frustrate the problem-solving process, by opening up or closing off possible avenues of approach? In Chapter Four, Part One, we survey a few of the more important general ways. In this appendix, we continue that discussion by surveying some further important ways in which language structures the problem-solving process for better or for worse. In the course of this discussion, here as in Chapter Four, we draw extensively on the work of the General Semanticist Neil Postman (Postman, 1976; Postman & Weingartner, 1969) in order to illuminate our own views. But while we must credit Professor Postman with some of the illumination, he can in no way be held responsible for any inadvertent obscurity in our own presentation, or indeed for the use to which his ideas have been put, though we have endeavored to apply them judiciously and present them clearly.

SPECIFICITY, CONTENT, AND PURPOSE IN DISCOURSE: GETTING WHAT YOU ASK FOR

There is a time for specificity and a time for abstractions, and a great deal of nonsense is generated by people who do not know what time it is.—Neil Postman

PURPOSE AND SPECIFICITY

Whether or not a form of language is "appropriate" depends on the purpose it is intended to serve. Poetic language is appropriate for writing verse; persuasive language serves well in advertising; but for purposes of problem solving, language needs to be descriptive and to distinguish clearly between what is in the realm of potentially verifiable fact and what is not. It is this latter feature of effective problem-solving language that makes its use of description nearer to scientific description than to poetic description, in that it is observationally based. Likewise, although people often confuse descriptive and prescriptive language, conflating "ought" with "is," effective problem solving requires a clear distinction to be maintained. If a person has been waiting 40 minutes for a number 37 bus, and asks the driver of a number 202 bus whether there is a number 37 close behind, it is not much use to be told (as one typically is) that "there should be one along every 7 minutes." However, this is just the sort of is–ought confusion that often brings about major hold-ups in the problem-solving process. And, to make things worse, it is not always apparent that the client who has been asked for a description is in fact giving a prescription—how things "are supposed to be" rather than how they are.

Not only must effective problem-solving talk be factual, descriptive, and observationally based, but it must be as specific as possible, keeping ambiguity to a minimum. One ought not to underestimate how far clients are prepared to go on speaking in vague generalities without realizing that they are failing to communicate any content whatsoever. Language is so full of ambiguity that it is very easy to run the risk of failing to communicate anything at all. The difficulty is this: The speaker may know what she is talking about—what she intends her words to mean—but she may fail to give the listener sufficient clues to enable him to reconstruct that same meaning. And the danger is that the listener might (and probably will!) make up his own content for the speaker's communication without realizing that he is doing so or that he has failed to grasp the meaning the speaker had intended to convey. For example, the speaker can say to the listener, "I have had so many experiences like this that I've learned to just relax and resign myself to the situation," and the listener can "understand" her (a nicely ambiguous word) to be referring to the experience of failing to communicate content to another person, whereas the speaker was in fact talking about standing out in the rain waiting for a bus for 40 minutes (where speaker and listener happen to be discussing communication). It is not only that words and phrases are frequently ambiguous (some, like the word "run"—as Milton Erickson was fond of pointing out—have literally scores of recognized dictionary meanings), but, more importantly, that a speaker's language may be too abstract and general to convey the particular events, objects, people, and so on that she may have in mind. As a result, it is very easy for speaker and listener (in therapy, client and therapist) to spend much or most of their time talking at cross-purposes.

But there is an even more important problem about language that fails to specify: It makes it difficult (if not impossible) for even the speaker to know what she is talking about. For there are no general solutions; solutions, in practice, are always specific (although, in the planning stage, a person can rough out a general plan and fill in the details later, and call this perhaps a "general" solution). A speaker cannot arrive at specific solutions through discussion of broad generalities and abstractions (as in the joke about the statistician who drowned while wading across a river with an average depth of 2 feet), and so for purposes of problem solving she may (literally) not know what she is talking about until she herself can move from abstractions and generalities to detailed specifics.

IMPORTANT QUESTIONS

It should be evident that in order for content to be adequately specified, the listener—the therapist—must ask some questions, and not just any questions. The questions asked must be sufficiently specific and worded with sufficient precision. "The type of words used in a question will determine the type of words used in the answer. In particular, question-words that are vague, subjective, and not rooted in any verifiable reality will produce their own kind in the answer" (Postman, 1976, p. 147).

This is an important point in itself, but it leads us to the further point that "all the answers we ever get are responses to questions" (Postman, 1976, p. 144), and that these questions are often implicit and unstated (Postman, 1976, pp. 143–152 passim). The significance, relevance, aptness, and felicity or infelicity of the client's statements; their truth and their consequences; whether they further or impede progress toward the therapeutic goal; whether they are part of the problem or part of the solution—all these depend (in part) on what implicit questions the statements can be regarded as being answers to. To take a trivial example, if one person says "It's raining out," the other may accept that as a constructive contribution if it is intended as an answer to the implicit question "Do we need an umbrella?", but as an unhelpful or even annoying remark if it is an answer to the implicit question "Shall we go, or change our minds and stay home?" In therapy, suppose that the therapist suggests a task and the client says, "Good God! I could never do that! How awful—not on your life!" and then immediately composes himself and says, "Sorry for the outburst.

I have an instant aversion to the suggestion of trying anything new."
Now the italicized statement may, we hope, be regarded as a perfectly
good affirmative answer to the unasked question, "Would you be
willing to try it anyway, in spite of your initial shock or reluctance?",
but, equally likely, it may more accurately be regarded as an affirmative answer to some such unasked question as "Are you somehow
constitutionally incapable of carrying out this task?"

The point is that a therapist may not know the meaning of any
given assertion until she knows more about the context—including
what question it may be regarded as being an answer to. Many of the
"answers" with which clients come into therapy are so vague and
unhelpful in part because they are intended as answers to unspecified
questions that are in fact unanswerable and that it would be problem-
engendering to attempt to answer at all. Often this is because these
questions are formulated at such high levels of abstraction. Postman,
writing from a point of view well outside the psychotherapy field,
states:

> Concrete, "operationalized" questions [about why one lost one's job or
> why one's marriage ended in divorce, rather than the abstract "Why am
> I a failure?"] are more approachable than loose-ended questions that
> imply one's nature is marred by some nondefinable affliction called
> "failure." It is characteristic of the talk of troubled people that they will
> resist bringing their [implicit] questions down to a level of answerability.
> If fanaticism is falling in love with an irrefutable answer, then a neurosis
> is falling in love with an unanswerable question. (1976, p. 145)

As Postman goes on to point out, many of the abstract, unanswerable
implicit questions "troubled people" attempt to answer ("Why are
people always trying to cheat me?" "Why does whatever I do, no
matter how hard I try, never get me anywhere anyway?") are never
really intended as questions to start with, in spite of their interrogative
form, but are merely disclaimers of any responsibility for their lives;
"one may well be deceived into trying to answer [them], which will
lead to continuous frustration and demoralization" (1976, p. 145).

Questions, whether implicit or explicit, can, by their very form,
either facilitate or impede the problem-solving process through their
implicit presuppositions. In Chapter Five we consider ways of using
presupposition in questions therapeutically, employing questions "as
instruments to open engaged minds to unsuspected possibilities"
(Postman & Weingartner, 1969, p. 44). Here, however, we wish to
draw attention to the ways in which questions can impose unnecessary limitations through their structure. Therapists and clients alike
tend for example, to use singular rather than plural forms, asking,

"What is the reason for . . . ?", "What is the cause of . . . ?", "What is the result of . . . ?", thus encouraging shallow, either–or responses or else a fruitless search for impossible cut-and-dried answers—to the extent, at least, that they allow the form of such questions to go unchallenged (Postman, 1976, p. 148). In a similar way, most Western languages are inherently biased toward "either–or-ness" ("Is it this or that?"), so that our question-asking language tends to encourage us "to think of things in terms of their singular opposites rather than as part of a continuum of multiple alternatives" (Postman, 1976, p. 148).

But there are a whole host of more crucial and less subtle ways in which questions can smuggle in all kinds of questionable assumptions through the use of syntactic presupposition, and in such a way that these assumptions are not readily open to consideration and criticism. If the listener stops and asks herself, "What would have to be the case, what would have to be true, for this question even to make sense?", she can readily tease out the unstated but presupposed assumptions and then proceed to check their validity. That is precisely what the therapist needs to do with the client's (explicit, including once-implicit) questions, and what the therapist should be attuned to in her own questions. The therapeutic interview will thus necessarily consist of a nested series of digressions, as presuppositions are teased out and challenged. It is, if anything, truer in therapy than in everyday life that

> once you start discussing these assumptions, you may never get back to the original question, and may even find it has disappeared, to everyone's relief. . . . The point is that if you proceed to answer questions without reviewing the assumptions implicit in them, you may end up in never-never land without quite knowing how you got there. My favorite invitation to never-never land, incidentally, was extended to me by a young woman who asked, "Why do you think the extraterrestrials are coming in such large numbers to Earth?" (Postman, 1976, pp. 150–151)

THE LEXICON: NAMES AND EPITHETS

Naming selects, discriminates, identifies, locates, orders, arranges, systematizes. Such activities as these are attributed to "thought" by older forms of expression, but they are much more properly attributed to language when language is seen as the living behavior of men.—John Dewey and F. F. Bentley (*Knowing and the Known*)

The structure of our language is relentless in forcing upon us "thing" conceptions. In English, we can transform any process or relationship into a thing by the simple expedient of naming it into a noun.—Neil Postman and Charles Weingartner

There is a basic scheme of classification *built into* our common speech and language. This built-in classification system directs us so that we observe the things we can readily classify with the names we know, while we tend strongly to overlook or disregard everything else.—Wendell Johnson

VOCABULARIES AND IMPLICIT TAXONOMIES

It is by now well known that Eskimos have more words for "snow" than even skiers have, or even snow-bound drivers trying to get home in rush hour. A book on the clinical practice of psychotherapy, however, is hardly the place to wax poetic over the multifarious ways in which the in-built biases of our English (or other) language restrict from the outset the ways in which we can conceive of things. Granted, it has been recognized by many writers, from Sapir and Whorf to others after them (and before, no doubt), that the structure of our language limits us more than somewhat through the way in which it slices up the kaleidoscopic flux of experience and the phenomenal flow of the universe. But, like it or not, short of teaching clients Chinese or Hopi or Jungianese (a lengthy process that may create as many problems as it solves), we as therapists are stuck with the natural language we and our clients happen to share in common, and we might as well make the best of it. Besides, at the risk of being unfashionable (and of our mentor, Gregory Bateson, turning over in his grave), we must confess that English, for all its admitted shortcomings, is as good a language as any we know of for solving difficult human problems with a great deal of precision, subtlety, and ecological soundness.

The real question is how we are to use this little language of ours. It is not that there are insufficient (or the wrong) tools in the toolbox, but that clients tend to use hammers to put in screws or screwdrivers to drive in nails. There are plenty of words available in the Great Lexicon in the Sky, but clients' selection may tend to be both rather limited and hence rather limiting. The names that clients (or for that matter, therapists) choose to select aspects of their experience; to discriminate and identify features of the situation; to locate, order, arrange, and systematize—all these will determine to a great extent how situations are conceived and dealt with. The facts remain untouched, but the naming and classifying process determines what one makes of it all. As Postman and Weingartner conclude, "whatever is out there isn't anything until we make it something, and then it 'is' whatever we make it. Most of our 'making something' activity consists essentially of naming things. Korzybski reminded us that whatever we say something is, it is not. But in a certain sense, whatever we say something is, it is. Because we have said it, and because of having said it, we will perceive it as such" (1969, p. 101). One of the chief ways in which we add (negotiable) meanings to the facts of a situation is through the really quite arbitrary naming of various aspects ("anxiety," "guilt," "self-punishment," "disobedience") or of the whole kit and caboodle ("insomnia," "depression," "bulimia," "behavior problem").

The names, epithets, and metaphors that constitute our own personal lexicon for "describing" (really, attributing meaning to) the facts of a situation can limit how we construe and respond to those facts, and the remedy may consist either in amending the lexicon (by addition and/or deletion) or by applying the "entries" in a different way or in different combinations. It need not be a matter of finding "one best way" to formulate a description of a given situation; rather, "the principle is that the more flexible you are in conceiving alternative names for things, the better you will be able to control your responses to situations" (Postman, 1976, p. 60).

It is not for nothing that Alfred North Whitehead gave to taxonomy the epithet "the death of science". The taxonomies or classification systems we bring to our observations and use to structure them, these hierarchies of general class names, serve both to make certain distinctions and to blur other distinctions. By categorizing our experience in one way, we preclude the infinite possibilities for categorizing it in other ways. General class names or categories serve to introduce distinctions between classes but to blur differences within classes. Both this distinguishing and this blurring can be quite useful, of course; together, they permit us to ignore differences that are irrelevant to our purposes and to concentrate on those and only those differences that really make a difference to our particular projects. But as soon as our purposes change, we may find some distinctions no longer relevant, and others now far from irrelevant. But we don't always bother to redraw the class lines, and so our investigations may be misdirected in consequence.

What makes class names revealing also makes them potentially misleading. They are revealing, insofar as instead of having to consider each instance *de novo*, we can, through the judicious use of the knowledge of general regularities enshrined in our linguistic competence in the use of class names, select our responses on the basis of the individual item's being one of a particular class of items, a class we already know how to deal with. For example, there are certain red-, black-, and yellow-striped species of snakes that are highly poisonous, and some clever mimics among other snake species that are quite harmless; although they all have red, black, and yellow stripes, the poisonous and nonpoisonous groups can be distinguished by the order of colors, which one remembers through the folk rhyme, "Red next to black is a friend of Jack, but red next to yellow can kill a fellow." Or again, we may wish to make use of our knowledge that brown bread will tend to have a higher dietary fiber content than white bread. Even here, however, our reliance on the class names "white bread" and "brown bread" may deceive us, as the latter fails to enable us to distinguish between bread made from whole-grain flour and bread dyed brown with molasses. We can, though, go on to ask further questions. Our competence in the use of what in fact constitutes a hierarchy of class names allows us to locate an individual item at some point in a hypothetical "branching tree" diagram, as it were, through our asking a series of either–or questions designed to discriminate relevant characteristics that serve to identify membership in a class or subclass (e.g., "Is it animal, vegetable, or mineral? Vertebrate or invertebrate? Furry, scaly, or feathered?" and so on). From knowledge of an individual item's class membership, we can extrapolate to know all kinds of other things about it that we would not otherwise know without extensive further investigation. But knowing whether a fish is freshwater or seawater won't help us decide whether it's all right to eat it, and knowing that it is usually served fried in batter won't tell us where we can catch it. Whether or not a difference makes a difference is entirely relative to our purposes.

Blurring certain distinctions can create problems, and equally, so can making certain other distinctions. If a clinician does not distinguish between a child's bedwetting that occurs as an involuntary voiding of the bladder during sleep, and bedwetting accomplished while the child is fully awake (but, for instance, afraid to get out of bed in the dark), the clinician's ability to be of therapeutic assistance may be limited. And a client who does not distinguish between say, boredom and hunger, may, through this blurring, be contributing to his own overweight problem. On the other hand, the parents who had successfully applied sensible discipline to teach their 9-year-old how not to be messy at the dinner table (see Chapter Seven, pp. 137–138) felt overwhelmed and helpless about not being able to do anything about his smearing feces in the bathroom, because they were drawing an arbitrary and unhelpful distinction between tidiness in the kitchen and in the bathroom; blurring this distinction was sufficient to resolve the problem in the first session. *Much of the process of negotiation in psychotherapy consists of the therapist's making new distinctions and blurring old ones, thus reclassifying or recategorizing experience and hence reformulating the situation such that it is no longer a problematic one for the client.*

All naming involves an implicit taxonomy. To select one name rather than another would have no point if selection of the name did not draw attention to different features, and how can a name—"a mere word"—do that except by identifying the item in question as being one of such-and-such a kind rather than simply being one of a kind? The implicit rules governing the use of the name, and hence in a sense determining the name's place in a "taxonomic hierarchy" of names, allow the referent of the name to be classified in certain definable ways. We might say, "*Vocabulary recapitulates taxonomy.*" And the classification implicit in a name permits us to extrapolate "beyond the information given" to draw conclusions that will form the basis for our responses. However, it is precisely in virtue of all the excess baggage a name thus carries with it that our progress may be hindered, as we may be encumbered by a whole load of implicit distinctions, classifications, and subclassifications that are irrelevant, unnecessary, and misleading. And the very distinctions that could enable us to take effective action are nowhere among our luggage. Sometimes it is as if we might as well set off into the desert with two great oxygen cylinders strapped to our belts or set off scuba diving with two 2-gallon canteens on our backs.

"If a conceptual distinction is to be made," wrote N. R. Hanson in *Patterns of Discovery*, " . . . the machinery for making it ought to show itself in language. If a distinction cannot be made in language it cannot be made conceptually." It is in virtue of the languaging process of dividing up our experience (splitting) and attaching particular names to particular results of this division (linking) that we are able to make distinctions at all. In the process of naming parts of our experience we both make and blur distinctions, and it is on the basis of the distinctions we do and don't end up with—the differences that we do or do not allow to make a difference—that we will provide ourselves with the information on which to act. "This is why in discussing what words we shall use in describing an event," writes Postman, "we are not engaging in 'mere semantics.' We are engaged in trying to control the perceptions and responses of others (as well as ourselves) to the character of the event itself. . . . The way in which 'it' is named reveals not the way it is but how the namer wishes to see it or how he is capable of seeing it. And . . . how it has been named becomes the reality for the namer and all who accept the name. But it need not be *our* reality" (1976, p. 57).

REIFYING AND EPITHETS

As many writers have pointed out (most notably perhaps Whorf, Bateson, and Harley Shands), one of the most serious of the problems that result from the naming process is that particular processes, interactions, and relationships get reified and spoken of as if they were things. As Bateson has written, "[We] abstract from relationship and from the experience of interaction to create 'objects' and to endow them with 'characteristics'." Patterns, however repetitive or long-standing, are potentially relatively fluid and can, given the right input, give way to other patterns; what's more, when described simply as patterns, they sound that way too! But substitute, for a blow-by-blow video description of a sequence of behavior involving two people, some such characterization of one or other of the parties to the inter-action as "aggressive," "passive," "domineering," or "bitchy," or of the relationship as "enmeshed," "sadomasochistic," or "shaky," and already 'it' even sounds like a much more permanent and entrenched state of affairs.

In a series of leaps, we move from the experience of pattern to the punctuation of pattern; to the abstraction of particular patterns of interest to us; to the reification of these abstracted patterns such that we speak of them as entities; to speaking of these named entities as belonging to particular individuals (i.e., as attributes of persons); and finally to the characterization of these individuals in terms of these purportedly characteristic, representative, more or less endur-ing, and intrinsic attributes. In the end, the posited attributes tend to take over. In our use of an epithet (which the *Random House Diction-ary* defines as "any word or phrase replacing or added to the name of a person or thing to describe a characteristic attribute"), we create a "bully" or a "coward," a "passive–aggressive" husband or a "castrat-ing" wife, an "anorexic" girl or an "overinvolved" mother. In short, we create all manner of "things," which we can then classify accord-ing to the human taxonomy of our choice. And, using this taxonomy, we can go on to draw all kinds of remote and specious inferences about the "things" so classified—inferences as spurious and yet insidi-ously plausible as the pronouncements of astrologers and crystal-gaz-ers.

When epithets are used in characterization—the attribution of relatively fixed and enduring abstract characteristics to individuals—they are often clearly metaphorical or synecdochal in nature. That is, they are often clearly (i.e., recognizably, though not always recog-nized as such!) of the form of figures of speech. If the use of the epithet is synecdochal, a (reified) partial aspect is used to go proxy for the whole; this is particularly so when the epithet is used in noun form rather than as an attributive adjective ("bully," "hysteric," "womanizer," "pedant," "stirrer"). If the use of the epithet is meta-phorical, one kind of thing is described in terms of another, thus imposing on the subject matter a specific model or system of imagery derived from another area of discourse ("inflexible," "spineless," "uncultivated," "weak," "frigid," "rebellious," "sadistic," "tyrannical"). And an epithet may be used both synecdochally and metaphorically at the same time ("a tough customer," "a big head," "a scavenger," "a martyr," "a con man," "a pushover").

Characterizations can be terribly limiting. In the first place, they tend either to describe a person globally in terms of some partial aspect, or to impose a metaphorical model that restricts one to the range of possibilities available in the relevant analogue. For example, if one person is seen by another as "tyrannical," the other tends to be limited to thinking in terms of how to appease or depose the presumed tyrant; if a client's "problem" is that he is "weak," a therapist's efforts may be directed to giving him "ego strength"; and so on. But quite apart from these considerations, and just as disastrously, characterizations convert malleable patterns into apparently fixed and unalterable givens with which an individual and those around them are more or less stuck. This is a particularly pernicious instance of what Postman and Weingartner have called the "photographic effect of language": "Out of this maelstrom of happenings we abstract certain bits to attend to. We snapshot these bits by naming them. Then we begin responding to the names as if they are the bits we have named, thus obscuring the effects of change. The names we use tend to 'fix' that which is named, particularly if the names also carry emotional connotations" (1969, pp. 108–109).

A common source of problems is that people tend to characterize not only others (including their intimates), but also themselves. They abstract from certain repeating patterns that they have noticed in their past behavior in interaction with others (punctuated in a particular way), and attribute various traits to themselves, which they then sum up into what they call "my character" or "my personality," itself further reified and often, with charming logic, regarded as the source or cause of these various patterns. They then regard themselves as limited to these particular patterns, short of somehow "changing my personality." The explanations, justifications, and rationalizations that they then supply for their limited behavior thus have the form of what Bateson (1978, pp. 25–26) called "dormitive hypotheses," after Molière's doctoral candidate who gave as the reason why opium puts people to sleep, "Because there is in it a *virtus dormitiva* (dormitive principle)." The explanation is "dormitive" in that it does no work. All characterological explanations are "dormitive" explanations or pseudoexplanations, including both the "amateur," pop psychology self-characterizations of clients, and the more sophisticated but equally sophistical characterizations of clients made by therapists. Self-characterization is a problem for which a therapist's characterization is no solution. This linguistic self-characterization is a common variety of verbal closure into which psychotherapists need to intervene. Unfortunately, more frequently, they contribute to its further and more intricate elaboration.

Another class of epithets consists of what Postman calls "key words"—simple nontechnical words whose meanings shift according to the semantic environment in which they occur. Examples of these (which we prefer to call "slippery epithets") would be "true," "false," "right," "wrong," "good," "bad," "better," "responsible," "dangerous," "law," "progress," "improvement," "failure," "success," "problem," and "solution." One chair may be heavier than another, or more expensive, or darker in color, but whether or not it is "better" depends on whether a person intends to use it, say, as a deck chair or a desk chair. And what it is for something to be "dangerous" depends more than somewhat on whether it is a guard dog, or a rabid wild dog, or an old car, or a tribal territory, or a weir, or a political party, or a proposed statute, or a line of argument, or an intersection, or a mistake. And two guard dogs may both be rightly regarded as "dangerous"—but one from the point of view of a prospective intruder because it is vicious and trained to kill, and another from the point of view of a vulnerable householder because it is deaf or lazy or affectionate towards black-masked strangers who enter through windows. The meaning of slippery epithets is largely relative to one's purposes in the context in which they are used. Their meaning is therefore continually shifting, and they can become problematic where they are used uncritically without reference to purpose and context, and as if they denoted qualities rather than having more to do with contingent relationships and relative values.

CONFUSING WORDS AND THINGS

VARIETIES OF REIFICATION

In Chapter Four, we quote Rapoport's remarks about the abuse of language that results when the linguistic representation is identified with the thing represented. This is a major subject that is perhaps as close as one can come to the heart of this book, although it would take an entire book on the subject in its own right to do justice to it. The subject of reification—confusing words with the things they refer to—is a vast one indeed. Reification as a phenomenon is ubiquitous in the languaging process and occurs in a bewildering variety of forms, and there is much to be said for the view that "[O]ne of man's deepest intuitions is to respond to the symbols he invents as if they 'are' whatever it is that he invented them to symbolize" (Postman, 1976, p. 136).

We have already touched on a number of instances of reification that are important to psychotherapy. For instance, we begin Chapter Four with a discussion of the way in which it is, as Epictetus put it in his oft-quoted aphorism, "not things themselves that trouble us, but the opinions that we have about those things." Psychotherapeutic problems and solutions have less to do with the facts of clients' situations than with the clients' ways of talking about those facts. This is but a special instance of the general phenomenon that people respond not to the facts of the situation but to their linguistic representation of those facts—not to "things" but to their talk about them, so to speak.

Our discussion of abstract nouns has introduced the notion that such words do not have content by virtue of picking out specific items in the world in the way that concrete nouns do; rather, their content depends on the meanings intended by the speaker and read in by the listener (which typically will be different), and hence will vary— sometimes considerably—from one occasion of a word's use to another. The particular, idiosyncratic meaning given to an abstract noun by the speaker will correspond to the speaker's idiosyncratic way of punctuating and abstracting from her experience—her way of epistemologically dividing up the world. What she means by a particular abstract noun on a particular occasion will depend on a number of things: on the conditions under which she would use the word in general; on the "content equivalences" that she would be prepared to assign to the word in general or in this particular instance (i.e., of the form "$X = Y$": "Love is helping me with the shopping, giving me a cuddle at night, and occasionally bringing me flowers"; "Respect is looking at me when I speak, addressing me as 'sir', never questioning my decisions, and not leaving his bike in the driveway"; etc.); as well as on the particular facts of the speaker's experience referred to on this particular occasion of the word's use; and the arbitrary significances added to those facts through the naming process. Reification occurs when either the speaker or the listener regards such abstract nouns as referring to distinct items in the world, and taking the "content equivalences" ("$X = Y$") literally (e.g., as specifying what "love" or "respect" "really is").

The naming process itself, as we have seen, is an essentially reifying process, insofar as a portion of patterned experience is punctuated into particular patterns, abstracted, and turned into a kind of "thing" by being named into a noun—a "thing" that (in the case of "things" to do with human relations) is often assigned as an attribute to only one of the two or more parties to the interaction. The process of character-ization, as we have discussed earlier, takes this reifying process still further, the end product being the linguistic creation of more or less enduring intrinsic personal qualities with which the person himself is then often crudely equated. Bateson has addressed himself to this and related matters in a number of places, for example:

> It is said that Mr. Jones is dependent, hostile, fey, finicky, anxious, exhi-bitionistic, narcissistic, passive, competitive, energetic, bold, cowardly, fatalistic, humorous, playful, canny, optimistic, perfectionistic, careless, careful, casual, etc. . . . [These adjectives] which purport to describe individual character are really not strictly applicable to the individual but rather describe transactions between the individual and his material and human environment. No man is "resourceful" or "dependent" or "fatalistic" in a vacuum. His characteristic, whatever it be, is not his but is rather a characteristic of what goes on between him and something (or somebody) else. (1964/1971, pp. 268–269)

Bradford P. Keeney summarizes this succinctly: "[A]ll descriptions of personality characteristics consist of extracted halves of larger rela-tionship patterns" (1983, p. 38).

We have already encountered many instances in which the verb "to be" is somehow to be "implicated" in the reifying process. "The principal grammatical instrument through which reification is accom-plished," writes Postman, "is the verb *to be* and its various forms. And since this verb comprises about one-third of all the verbs used in normal English discourse, we are all in constant danger of being af-flicted" (1976, p. 135). Whenever we catch ourselves or our clients saying that something or someone "is" thus-and-so or "is" a such-and-such, we should be on the lookout for some rather dubious and possibly misleading or even problem-making reification going on, and look to this as an opportunity for potentially rewarding negotiation of arbitrarily assigned meaning. The use of slippery epithets, as when we say that something is or isn't good, better, progress, a problem, a sin, or dangerous, can (as we have discussed) prove to be particularly hazardous bends in the stream of discourse, as the meaning of such slippery epithets—ever relative, evaluative, and contingent upon our particular purposes—is continually shifting from one context to an-other, even though the expressions in question sound like rather mat-ter-of-fact ascriptions of absolute qualities. "Everything is what it is and not another thing," preached the good Bishop Butler, and this is a sermon worth paying heed to. And we would do well to remind ourselves here of Korzybski's (1933) reminder that whatever we say something is, it is not.

If we can speak of there being a single most problem-engendering variety of reification, it is probably the literal interpretation of metaphor. It is all very well to speak metaphorically (and very difficult not to!), but only so long as we distinguish between speaking metaphorically and speaking literally. Problems are often constructed in discourse by a person's using metaphors in description, and then going on to base his actions (or his perceived range of options for action) on the model implicit in a literal interpretation of the metaphorical expressions. In Chapter Four, we consider an example of this, in the use of water, steam, and pressure-cooker metaphors for "anger," followed by attempts at "letting off steam" (i.e., speaking and behaving angrily) so as to magically get rid of the anger, thus ignoring the possibility that expressing anger only serves to increase it. (Imagine a person who swears constantly in an attempt to get all the bad language out of his system.) Another and not dissimilar example is that of someone who ruminates over unhappy thoughts as a way of dealing with being depressed over such unhappy thoughts, out of fear that if she turns her mind to happier thoughts and the brighter side of things, she would only be repressing the unhappy thoughts, with the implication that such thoughts would (according to the Freudian metaphor) go underground and live a subversive life of their own, wreaking havoc beneath the surface, perhaps gnawing away at the foundations of her mental stability. Using such metaphors, the person cannot easily perceive the obviousness of dealing with thinking unhappy thoughts by thinking happier thoughts in their stead. Again, using the metaphor "the mind as a brittle object" may lead a person to treating a depressed friend or relative "with kid gloves" in a way that helps only to perpetuate the interactional and behavioral patterns labeled "depression," rather than initiating actions that will tend to disrupt those patterns and replace them with more positive ones.

The literal interpretation of metaphor is also a fertile source of "dormitive principles" and "dormitive explanations" or pseudoexplanations: "He just cracked up," "I couldn't hold it in any longer—I blew my top when the pressure inside became too great," "She needs to stay in bed all day because of the fragility of her mental state," "That was his real personality coming out," "His family lacked firm enough boundaries to contain his aggression," "She is suffocated by a smothering mother, and any interest in life we may kindle in her will only be snuffed out," and so on. Psychotherapy is full of such nonsense, either more or less disguised. Taking such metaphors literally and acting on them is in many ways on a par with asking rhetorical questions ("Why am I such a failure?" "Why does this only happen to me?") and trying to find answers to them—which we could arguably classify as yet another variety of reification.

TOKEN AND TABOO

Many of the forms of reification that humans, as languaging beings, often uncritically engage in seem to be based on (indeed, seem to presuppose) a primitive, magical, superstitious view of language. In this naive understanding of language, the linguistic tokens or signs— the words we use—are regarded almost with a kind of Bronze Age fetishism, an attitude not far removed from the attitude of primitives who are afraid to have their pictures taken for fear that their souls will be captured, or to give their names for fear that they will be handing over some magical control over their destiny. Although it does not always take on so crude a form as the following, the view of language we are alluding to includes the ideas that words "contain meaning"; that they have "a real meaning" that can be known or discovered or only speculated about; that for every word there is some correspond- ing reality; and that (cases of homonymy apart) the same word always "points to" the same reality, the same entity. In this atavistic, magical view of language, moreover, words can be powerful and frightening, and capable of inspiring awe. Some sacred words ("democracy," "life," "love," "equality," "freedom," etc.) denote good and holy things that are only to be admired, respected, esteemed, and upheld and with which one wishes only to align oneself; other, profane words ("racism," "fascism," "communism," "killing," "inequality," "cen- sorship," etc.) denote wicked and evil things, abominations that are only to be despised, derided, scorned, and eradicated, and with which it would be anathema to be even verbally associated.

The notion that meaning is *in* words, that each word has a real meaning, runs deep in our culture—possibly, if we may speculate here, because such a large part of the function of language is to influ- ence other people; to have some kind of consensually agreed domin- ion over how words are to be defined, over what they "really" mean, is to increase the extent of one's influence. And so politicians and journalists, prosecuting and defending attorneys, governments and their opposition parties, pressure groups and bureaucracies, students and faculty, unions and management, all lay claim to the true meaning of things. This "laying claim," however, can only take place, the game can only go on, if the illusion of meaning-in-words and "real" mean- ing is maintained. Therefore it is rarely in the interests of an individual or group with an axe to grind to throw the whole matter into ques- tion. To take a couple of examples used by Postman (1976): The terror- ists who claim to be "urban guerrillas" or "revolutionaries" or "free- dom fighters" or a "people's army" are countered not by the government's reasoned forays into General Semantics, but by claims that the terrorists are not "really" "freedom fighters," but are "really" "common criminals" or "murderers" or "psychopaths." Likewise, garbage men are not "really" "garbage men" any more than they are "really" "sanitation engineers." Or, again, the antiabortionists who say that abortion "really" is "murder" are talking nonsense, but so are their proabortion opponents who say that abortion is "really not" "murder." The essence of propaganda is the use of language to evoke an immediate, emphatic, emotional, either–or response, and to compel belief rather than consideration (Postman, 1976, p. 170, and pp. 166–177 passim). Propaganda usually operates on the basis of slippery epithets and content-free abstract nouns carrying strong emotional connotations: "It is distinct from language which stimulates curiosity, reveals its assumptions, causes us to ask questions, invites us to seek further information and to search for error" (Postman, 1976, p. 170). Words do not have "real" meanings, because they do not "have" meanings at all. Individual tokens ("words" considered in the sense of particular instances of the use of a word) don't quite have meanings either, but people have meanings for them; and, once again, the meaning intended by a speaker and that "understood" by a listener may not coincide.

There is nothing magical about definitions. As I. A. Richards has put it, "We want to do something, and a definition is a means of doing it. If we want certain results, then we must use certain meanings (or definitions). But no definition has any authority apart from a purpose, or to bar us from other purposes" (1929). It is always worth finding out what definition the other person has in mind. "It depends on what you mean by . . . " is not "being pedantic" if the purpose of the discussion is something along the lines of critical inquiry; not asking for the definition may mean that words are only being tossed to and fro.

It is so difficult to get beyond the illusion that racism and democracy and freedom exist in the world much as do such "medium-sized dry goods" as chairs and briefcases and pencils. In the course of heated debate, it often takes a conscious effort not to respond in an emotional, reflex way (with what some semanticists call a "signal reaction") to such words as "racism" and "freedom" and to remember that they are both merely made-up concepts of most variable meaning. Until we know what a speaker means by "racism," we do not really know whether to regard it as a good, bad, or merely indifferent thing. Racism is not some real entity in the world that happens to have been given the name "racism" in English, nor is it possible to discover or to learn what racism "really is." Racism is a mere concept, a linguistic creation. That is not to say that it is not potentially a useful concept, although, as it happens, it is *not* particularly useful insofar as "racism" is one of those words that has been so inflated in meaning—so broadened in its use—that it has become difficult to know what it is supposed to mean (if, indeed, it any longer means anything at all). If the meaning of a word is stretched far enough, the word loses any recognizable shape. "The important idea about verbal inflation," writes Postman, "is that as it increases, distinctions become less accessible. A word not only suggests meanings; it excludes other meanings. The more meanings a word is allowed to suggest, the less usable it becomes for precision talking" (1976, p. 226). If we make a word do too much work, we are exploiting it, even if like Lewis Carroll's Humpty Dumpty, we make sure to pay it extra; the overworked word soon becomes of no use to anyone.

If by "racist" a speaker means what used to be meant by that word—namely, someone who expresses hatred or intolerance toward another race or races, or holds attitudes proceeding from the assumption that some "races" (n.b.: itself a mere concept) are inherently superior to others—then most people would agree that to be a racist is certainly a despicable thing. But if "racist" is used differently, it is no longer clear that, on the new definition, there is anything wrong with being a racist. For example, the word "racist" was recently used explicitly by an extremist pressure group in North London to denote *any* "white" member of "this society dominated by a white-supremacist power structure" (itself a charmingly quaint piece of presupposition), regardless of that person's views or behavior. According to this new definition, to be a "racist" is simply to be any "white" person living in Britain, where "white" is itself given the special meaning of "non-Asian Caucasoid type." A "racist," on this new definition, is now a perfectly fine and dandy thing to be. Anyone can, and pressure groups and politicians typically do, play Humpty Dumpty with words, giving them a brand-new meaning and relying on the signal reaction to the sound of the word itself, due to a hangover from its old meaning. In Malaysia, to take another example, you might even be branded a "SHIT," which is the immigration authority's official acronym for "Suspected Hippie In Transit." This term is itself defined in such a way that any males with hair extending over their shirt collars might come under this classification, in which case a "SHIT" isn't necessarily such a terrible thing to be (at least if you don't mind being asked to leave such a country and having "SHIT" stamped in your passport). No doubt, the Malaysian authorities had a lot of fun in their selection of this term, with its built-in derogatory connotations.

The relevance of all this to psychotherapy may by now be painfully obvious: *Clients get terribly hung up over words that they themselves or others around them or society at large have reified and*

inflated beyond recognition. And unless therapists can shake themselves out of the illusion that these words denote "real" things, it
becomes difficult to ask the $64,000 question: "So what?" But this is
the question that above all needs to be asked.

Related to this is the unfortunate tendency of some therapists to
"blind clients with science" in their use of mystifying, terrifying
multisyllabic technical terms to denote simple, easily soluble ordinary
difficulties, thus instantly taking the problem out of the realm of the
clients' competence to solve. We recently had referred to us a 7-year-
old who would run around the block or ride his bike when it was time
to come in for dinner, and who wouldn't pay attention to his parents'
requests that he do something if he did not want to do it. The referrer
had told the parents and us that the boy was "suffering from a behavioral disorder revealed by investigations to be spasmodic hyperkinesis
complicated by an attention deficit disorder"—which meant that the
boy wouldn't behave himself, and that the referrer's opinion from a
short interview with the parents was that the boy was running around
and not paying attention. But once the shaman had uttered this spell,
the "problem" became, to the parents, something that required the
work of the referring shaman or other shamans, and probably the
prescription of magic potions; it was clearly not a matter to be handled by mere parents. This verbal mystification, as Postman and others
have called it, is possible precisely because people still have a rather
primitive, magical view of words. And words, thanks to this self-
fulfilling belief in their power, can actually exercise a good deal of
power over the faithful.

However, the most general and far-reaching way in which this
naive view of language can create problems in discourse, and the most
important consequence of all of this for psychotherapy, is that people
tend to respond to assertions by agreeing or disagreeing (Postman,
1976, pp. 153–157 passim). Occasionally people will not be sure if
they do agree or disagree, as if to say they've not made up their minds
about the matter (like not being sure whether one wants the hot fudge
sundae or the strawberry cheesecake). But rarely are they aware that
they do not yet have sufficient information, not merely about the facts
but about what on earth a speaker might mean by an assertion. The
"What do you mean?" question gets bypassed, and they go straight on
to the question, "Do I agree or disagree?" They assume that a speaker
means by his words on this particular occasion what they would
themselves mean by these words if they used them on this occasion,
and so they skip over the whole matter of clarification. And it should
also be noted that an assertion, like a question, can often be rhetorical
and not an invitation to serious discussion, serving merely as what S.

I. Hayakawa (1939/1978) has called "snarling" and "purring," in which case it might be more appropriate to "snarl" or "purr" in response than to ask for clarification. But sometimes it is important to know what another person means by his words. Of course, we could not talk to each other at all if we did not to some extent rely on an assumption of shared meanings and some stability in usage, but "we must remember that this is only an assumption, that at any given moment a coin of the realm may not be worth quite what we imagined. And, naturally, our purposes will be short-changed" (Postman, 1976, p. 157).

Yet there is more to this matter of "bypassing" (issues of clarification) than this. First, *by agreeing or disagreeing with an assertion, we necessarily take on board the presuppositions "contained" in that assertion.* As science fiction writer Frank Herbert put it in his *Children of Dune*, "When you believe something is right or wrong, true or false, you believe the assumptions in the words which express the arguments." Whether we agree or disagree that "women have been victimized by our male-dominated society," as long as we do one or the other, we accept the presupposition that our society is male-dominated. Now that presupposition may itself be highly questionable indeed, depending on what on earth is meant by it. For instance, if it means not merely that men tend to have a greater number of important positions in management than women (a statistical question), but that men have historically conspired to keep women from these positions (or some such thing), the presupposition that our society is male-dominated becomes, on the face of it, rather dubious. But we bypass these critical issues in the act of agreeing or disagreeing.

Second, *there is more to knowing what is meant by an assertion than knowing what a speaker means by all the words in the assertion. Unless and until we know what further consequences are supposed to follow from this assertion, we do not yet know what is intended by it, and therefore it is too early to agree or disagree.* The assertion may be O.K. as it stands, but it may be insufficient to bear all the deductive weight that the speaker is going to go on to place upon it. When we then find ourselves led logically to some unacceptable or questionable conclusion, we may find, it we retrace our steps, that we have accepted a premise that sounded unexceptionable at the time but that now, though only in retrospect, does not pass muster. Often this is because there may be a weaker and a stronger version of a particular doctrine, and while there may have been sufficient grounds for provisionally accepting the weaker version, the subsequent course of argument has relied on the stronger version. In psychotherapy, this (usually perfectly innocently intentioned but no less insidious) logical legerdemain is not infrequently to be found at the heart of clients' well-argued objections to their being able to do the things they need to do to eliminate their problems. But the quickness of the "and" deceives the "I," and therapists as well as clients can be taken in by the false logic if they do not continually shake themselves out of the illusion that words "have" meaning. "I'm not sure yet—it depends what you're going to go on to say," and simply (the much-feared) "I don't know," can often be salutary thoughts to think and to communicate to clients.

Finally, a word should be said about another variety of reification that is closely related to these issues involving the magical view of language (and that involves expressions often used only for "snarling" or "purring," but that may then be interpreted as serious statements and discussed as such): the use of sweeping generalizations. Any reference we make to general classes, particularly of people, is bound to be biting off more than we can chew (cf. Postman, 1976, p. 206). If we take seriously such more or less arbitrary class names as "blacks," "Irish Catholics," "the unions," "the Third World," "the Internal Revenue," "big business," "anorexics," "alcoholics," "delinquents," "patients," "therapists," or "clinical epistemologists," and regard these concretely as entities in the world, we are overgeneralizing in a way that blinds us to the differences among the members of the class and that generates a good deal of nonsense. *And just because we can make generalized statements about such abstracted classes for one purpose doesn't mean that the class can be spoken of in general terms for another purpose.* Just because all Irish Catholics are of Irish ancestry (if indeed they are), or have certain accents, or whatever, this doesn't mean that we can generalize about them in other respects. To be awake to such nonsense in psychotherapy interviews, we need to be awake to the tendency to confuse words with what they are intended—always for specific purposes—to represent.

CAUSAL TALK

Finally, let us consider one last way in which forms of language can structure the problem-solving process in such a way as to lead toward or away from solutions. The forms of language we use to pose a problem unavoidably involve presuppositions concerning the punctuation of patterns or sequences in our experience. There are (at least) three "levels" of punctuation we can discuss:

1. Our presuppositions about how a particular sequence or pattern is to be punctuated (e.g., "She nags because he withdraws" vs. "He withdraws because she nags" or "The client is resisting" vs. "The therapist is getting too pushy").
2. Our presuppositions about how such sequences are in general to be punctuated (e.g., "One's feeling depressed makes one behave in a depressed way," vs. "One's behaving in a depressed way makes one feel depressed," or "He's yelling at her over something so trivial because he's feeling angry," vs. "He's feeling angry as a result of yelling at her over something so trivial").
3. Our most general schemata for "preferentially" punctuating experience (e.g., punctuating "lineally" [either "*A* because *B*" or "*B* because *A*"] vs. punctuating circularly or "cybernetically" ["*A* then *B* then *A* then *B* . . . "]).

These most general schemata (level 3) for preferentially punctuating experience have been referred to, respectively, as involving a "lineal epistemology" and a "cybernetic epistemology" (Keeney, 1983, p. 14). To put it all in perhaps less grand terms, the question is one of our semantic preferences—what kind of words we prefer to use to describe events. We might prefer to use words to draw inferences about causal connections, which we assert or presuppose in our verbal descriptions of events. Or we might prefer to use words rather less ambitiously to describe events in the most neutral possible terms, referring only to a repeating pattern that we can abstract. The former, more ambitious ("lineal") choice of description can be limiting, for in asserting or presupposing a one-way causal connection between events, we are stuck with a picture in which *A* causes *B*; if we want to do something about *B*, we must first deal with the antecedent "cause," *A*. A sequence of events described in this way thus seems to be rather fixed and (in varying degrees) immutable, like the movement of cogs in clockwork. If, on the other hand, we choose to limit ourselves to the less ambitious description, we are less likely to limit ourselves. For, described in more neutral terms as merely a repeating sequence we can abstract, the sequence no longer appears quite so fixed and machine-like, insofar as the sequence is regarded as rather arbitrary, the constant conjunction more or less incidental. (There is a certain irony here, in that cybernetics has tended to make use above all of machine analogies!) In the problem-solving process, then, we can avoid using words describing individual events as links in a causal chain, thus leading ourselves to seek out antecedent causes and struggle to "eliminate" them before anything else productive can be done. Instead, we can use words to describe the overall pattern of events. Appreciating how very delicately it all holds together, we can seek ways of gently intervening—now here, now there—to dissolve the pattern and replace it with a more desirable one.

Of course, if we lived in a lineal universe of antecedent causes, where cause-and-effect relationships were "just the way things are," we might, like it or not, have to go back and tackle those causes. However, the universe does not seem to be quite like that, and even if it were, it is much more clear to us that human conduct at least *only seems* to be like that. It might be that a circular, cybernetic epistemology of form and pattern is more "adaptive" than a lineal, causal epistemology, in a universe that in general seems to be (judging by the responses to our interventions in the world) deceptively "circular" (Bateson, 1978, 1979). But be that as it may, when it comes to the specific realm of human conduct and the very practical business of psychotherapy, three things seem certain.

First, even if the notion of cause had any useful, nonmisleading application in human psychology (and we seriously doubt that it does, ever has, or ever will), such "causes" as there might be in the realm of human behavior are never, ever as fixed and determinate as they appear to be. Second, nothing can even appear to "cause" a person to act in a particular way without the help of that person's believing that it can or must have such causal power. A person might use causal language to talk about her own behavior (e.g., to talk about her actions as being caused by certain feelings or thoughts or past events or the behavior of others); if she gets taken in by that causal form of language and acts accordingly (often by failing to act), she will indeed act as if her behavior were causally determined and beyond her control. Thus causal talk becomes a kind of self-fulfilling prophecy, and such talk can give a person cause for inaction. And third, it is not necessary in psychotherapy to deal with supposed antecedent causes in order to eliminate any undesired experience or behavior; rather, it seems sufficient simply to intervene in small ways in the pattern or patterns of which it forms a part.

We have discussed these three ideas more fully in Chapters Six and Eight, and we only mention them now in connection with the one point we wish to make here: that in the problem-solving process, to choose descriptions of pattern is to open up possibilities of solving the problem, whereas to choose causal descriptions is to introduce verbal closure and thus impede its solution. The choice of words reveals or conceals the available choices for action.

THE ONE-MINUTE SUPERVISOR
Challenging Imperatives

Most human problems require us to make choices and to find solutions. We mean by a "choice," the selection of one possibility from among several. This is a much more complicated and rigorous process than making a decision. We have to include more, recognize more, consider more, and provide for more—of everything. A solution is an answer we come up with as a result of seeing about as openly as a human being can.—Neil Postman and Charles Weingartner

Some counselors are expert at distracting people from their goals and getting them to focus on largely irrelevant, though interesting, topics. Many fascinating conversations may result, and if you enjoy them that's your business. On the other hand, if your main desire is to achieve a certain goal, find someone who's willing to help you keep it in sight and to help you reach it in a direct way.—Bernie Zilbergeld

CLINICAL EPISTEMOLOGY
AS SUPERVISION

This appendix is about clinical supervision, but we do not have much to say about the matter here. The main reason is that, in an important sense, *this entire book has been about supervision*. One way of thinking about clinical epistemology is as a model of supervising both other therapists and oneself. The negotiation process of distinguishing sensory-based descriptions from attributions of meaning, and challenging those attributions, is for us the essence of the supervisory process when it works well—that is, when it actually helps free the therapist to do something different that will make a difference to the client's progress toward that goal.

BEYOND THE SELF-CONFIRMING SYSTEM

In 1919, when the philosopher Karl Popper was working with "deprived" children, he was having difficulty with a case and brought it to Alfred Adler for supervision. He wrote:

> I reported to him a case which to me did not seem particularly Adlerian, but which he found no difficulty in analyzing in terms of his theory of inferiority feelings, although he had not even seen the child. Slightly shocked, I asked him how he could be so sure. "Because of my thousand-fold experience," he replied; whereupon I could not help saying: "and with this case, I suppose, your experience has become thousand-and-one-fold." (Popper, 1963, p. 35; (brought to our attention by Booth, 1984)

Traditionally, much supervision has implicitly or explicitly taken the form of the supervisor helping the therapist to see how the case under discussion, or the therapist's "incorrect" way of working, can be explained by the particular theory of psychotherapy to which the supervisor subscribes. The case is thus fit into a self-confirming system of belief, and at the same time constitutes further confirmation of the system of belief according to which it has just been "successfully" explained. Equipped with the "correct" theoretical understanding of the case, the therapist is then expected to adjust his approach to the case accordingly. Theory provides a way of understanding the case "material," and provides some kind of more or less rough guide to what the therapist is "really" dealing with and therefore how the therapist ought generally to proceed in the case. When the therapist is stuck, the problem is often seen as a matter of the therapist's missing vital clues, perhaps due to inexperience or to a personal blind spot or "countertransference." Alternatively, the culprit is variously alleged to be the misapplication of the theory to the case "material," inadequate understanding of the theory, mistranslation of the theory into technique, or inadequate technique. Thus has the supervisor's work traditionally been cut out for her.

Clearly, from the point of view of clinical epistemology, the tasks and goals of supervision are seen rather differently.

THE TASKS OF SUPERVISION

We can group the major tasks and goals of supervision in psychotherapy into three broad categories:

1. *Providing training/guidance in specific clinical skills.* Supervision is often used to teach novice therapists the actual clinical skills involved in therapeutic intervention, or to pass along more advanced clinical skills to intermediate and advanced practitioners.

2. *Assisting the therapist to master approaches based on presuppositions that are different from the ones with which the therapist currently operates.* The supervisor can familiarize the therapist with the presuppositions of the approach, and can help the therapist grasp the rather different set of imperatives (what he should do) derived from these presuppositions. This will include encouraging the therapist to behave differently in sessions, in keeping with this different set of presuppositions—doing things he would not previously have done, and not doing other things that he would previously have done.

3. *Getting beyond barriers to results in therapy.* Therapists often seek supervision to assist them in working with specific cases in which they are "stuck," or to move beyond "stuck" areas with specific clients or with clients in general.

Although the negotiation process described throughout this book provides the basic model for carrying out these three main tasks of supervision, and though in a way we may have little to add to this, this appendix offers a couple of hints to assist the reader in translating our presentation of clinical epistemology to the supervision setting.

SUPERVISING OTHERS

TEACHING SKILLS

One of the challenges in supervision is in the passing along of specific clinical skills. Before the widespread use of cotherapy, one-way mirrors, and video- and audiotaping, therapists often learned their trade through anecdote, theoretical discussion, or personal experience as clients. All of these teaching methods have their value, but are of limited use in specifying the actions that make up clinical interventions. The questions in most beginning therapists' minds, "What do I say?" and "What do I do?" (questions by no means confined to beginners!), are not readily or most usefully answered by these means. One of the strengths of clinical epistemology, as presented in this book, is its emphasis on description and observation as the core of any assessment. This emphasis lends itself well to the area of passing along specific skills in supervision.

The observational methods—audiotape, videotape, one-way mirror, "live" ("in-the-room") observation without a one-way mirror, and cotherapy—can be used by the supervisor either to instruct the therapist by showing examples of specific interventions, or to give the therapist specific corrective comments on the therapist's own use of the skills. The descriptive method (i.e., specifying with a "video description") can be used to impart specific "action steps" that make up a clinical intervention. In addition, sensory-based descriptions can be used in place of observations if necessary, to gather specific information on the interventions given and the responses that follow. The supervisor's discussing cases in appropriate video-descriptive terms, and getting the therapist to report his cases in terms of video descriptions, can enable both the therapist and the supervisor to know what the other is talking about.

THE MASTERY OF SHIFTING PRESUPPOSITIONS

Identifying and specifying the underlying presuppositions and associated imperatives of a particular approach to therapy is a way to avoid many of the struggles of supervision. Often supervisor and therapist are playing "dueling paradigms," each operating from a different set of assumptions and guidelines for results and not recognizing the area of disagreement. It is sometimes as if the therapist learning a new approach to therapy has to "get it" by osmosis, rather than explicit guidance and understanding.

The emphasis in clinical epistemology on being able to specify presuppositions and imperatives makes it easier for the supervisor to specify the underlying premises and guidelines of any particular approach and to ferret out those of the therapist that are in conflict with the approach being offered. In this way, the therapist can be aided in mastering the necessary shift from one set of presuppositions to another, and in mastering the very process of shifting presuppositions more easily.

Where the therapist's range of behavior or specific actions seems to be dictated by the imperatives (and hence the presuppositions) of some approach to therapy other than the one in which the supervisor is offering training, the supervisor can make explicit the links between the relevant presuppositions, imperatives, and behavior both of the new approach and of the one the therapist has been explicitly or implicitly following. One way of going about this is simply for the supervisor to request the desired behavior and negotiate the therapist's objections, either before or after the therapist has carried out the directive.

FREEING INTERVENTION

The third main task of supervision is getting therapists "unstuck" who are "stuck." As we say with regard to clients, therapists who aren't getting the results they want should do something different or differently, or stop doing something they are currently doing. In essence, everything we have been describing under the rubric of therapeutic intervention is applicable to the supervision setting, with the therapist–client "system" as the "client" in this case (cf. Liddle & Saba, 1983, on the isomorphic relationship between therapy and therapy training). The beginning—"What brings you here?"—is the same as in therapy, and the problem is negotiated in the same way, with the supervisor eliciting video descriptions of what happens in therapy and what the therapist actually does, negotiating the therapist's imperatives and deductions, and teasing out and challenging the therapist's presuppositions, evaluations, and expectations. The supervisor can then go on to give directives that intervene in the pattern or context. Or, frequently, the supervisor can simply offer numerous alternatives for intervention that are open to the therapist but that the therapist may previously not have been open to. For example, she can suggest a dozen or so different ways of intervening in the pattern and a half dozen ways to intervene in the context, or can simply give the therapist the benefit of her greater experience in the particular therapeutic approach, relating examples of what has been done in other cases in order to open up possibilities for the therapist.

CHALLENGING IMPERATIVES: QUESTIONING BEHAVIOR

The process of challenging the therapist's imperatives is one string to the supervisor's bow in reaching the three targets of supervision. The supervisor, having obtained video descriptions of what happens and what the therapist does in therapy, can question the therapist's behavior and suggest, "Why not just do this . . . ?" The supervisor can then negotiate the therapist's imperatives: (1) what the therapist believes he has to do first or has to happen first, either before he can do the suggested behavior or before the client can reach her goal (prerequisites); (2) what the therapist believes he must do or what must happen as a result of what has already happened in therapy or in the client's life (causal imperatives); and (3) what the therapist must do "on principle" (normative imperatives), including imperatives about what is *de rigeur* in therapy. As in therapy, negotiation of these imperatives (Chapter Four, Part Two) can lead to the teasing out and challenging of the therapist's evaluations, expectations, and epistemological presuppositions.

CHALLENGING IMPERATIVES: DIRECTING BEHAVIOR

The second string to the supervisor's bow is to give the therapist specific directives—in effect, simply to say, "Just do this, and then see what happens." This "imperative" or directive to do the required behavior can be without a rationale, or without one going beyond "If you want to learn how to do this kind of therapy, you need to do this, so do this and see how it goes." The successful carrying out of this directive (which might at first seem to be a difficult or challenging task), and the results that follow, will often in themselves provide a challenge to the therapist's presuppositions. The required behavior or intervention can be specified by the supervisor in video descriptions, as can the supervisor's "criteria for successful results" for carrying out the directive.

SELF-SUPERVISION

For us, one of the most exciting aspects of the use of clinical epistemology is the possibility it opens up for self-supervision. In accomplishing each of the three main tasks of supervision, clinical epistemology offers specific resources that individuals can use successfully to help themselves evolve as therapists through the self-supervisory process.

Therapists can supervise themselves through audiotapes and videotapes, listening for unchallenged presuppositions, imperatives, characterizations, and so on (both their clients' and their own). They can also use the tapes or recollections of the sessions (described to themselves in sensory-based terms) to note patterns of their own behavior, and can then vary these to find whether they have any effect on therapeutic outcome. If we are not getting results in a case, we may experiment by finding any regularity in our behavior and varying it to discover whether this alteration results in any beneficial effect.

THE ONE-MINUTE SUPERVISOR

Clinical epistemology offers the therapist a number of specific frameworks for supervising her own work in individual cases:

• The therapist can use the observation/description frame to sift facts from meanings (Chapter Two).

• She can return to "the bottom line" in psychotherapy (Chapter Three) and apply a measure of benevolent skepticism to the matter of whether there is anything at all stopping her client from reaching his goal right now.

• She can identify the client's or her own ways of *talking about* the facts of the problem situation, and can identify how these ways of describing the situation prematurely close off possibilities of solving it (Chapter Four, Part One; Appendix II).

• She can identify areas of missing content; ways in which the client or she herself has been implicitly seeking answers to an unanswerable question; limitations introduced through the names or classifications given to aspects of experience by her or by the client; instances of reification and pseudoexplanations; metaphors adopted by the client or herself that limit possibilities for solution to options available within the adopted metaphors; unchallenged ways in which the client has gotten hung up over particular words (the unasked "So what?"); instances of bypassing what the client actually means by certain expressions; irrelevant issues that are being worked on; the client's self-confirming beliefs; and unchallenged claims by the client to "know what ain't so" (Chapter Four, Part One; Appendix II).

• She can remind herself that "what the problem is" has been the outcome of a negotiation process, not a "given" (Chapters Four and Five).

• She can use "the problem map" to chart a course both through the client's self-imposed limitations and through her own (Chapter Four, Part Two).

• She can check to ensure that she has secured all the conditions for workable psychotherapy—a therapist, a complainant, a complaint, a request, and criteria for successful results (Chapter Five).

• She can use the "Index" to check for items that have gone unchallenged (Chapter Five).

• She can review the variety of possible classes of options for abolishing or transforming the context (Chapter Eight).

• She can run the symptom-pattern through the 15 modalities of pattern intervention to discover untried means of intervening. (Chapter Eight).

• She can check her presuppositional "furniture" against our inventory (Chapter Six), identify any unidentified presuppositions, and consider acting as if that presupposition were irrelevant or invalid.

• Finally, she can supervise her supervision of herself by running down this list of resources for self-supervision, as well as the suggestions for uses of audiotapes and videotapes in the self-supervisory process.

Cosupervision groups can be set up so that, when individual therapists run out of ideas or would like some further stimulation to keep their own work from becoming stale, they can supervise each other by "staffing" cases along these lines. And there is always the option remaining of seeking an appropriate supervisor, or seeking someone to consult on a case either in cotherapy or while one (i.e., the client's regular therapist) observes.

We find self-supervision to be, for the most part, the only supervision we seek in our work, though occasionally we will discuss cases with others or consult on each other's cases. Other therapists may be more comfortable, however, with supervision received from others. Such supervision has certainly had its place in our own training, but a great deal depends on the nature and quality of the supervision being offered, and we found all too often that we were expected to accept and believe the supervisor's presuppositions and imperatives "lock, stock, and barrel" in order to receive the benefit of the supervision. We often found oursleves wanting to give our supervisors a quick course in clinical epistemology (at least the descriptive frame) before we discussed cases with them, except that in those days we'd never "heard of" clinical epistemology and were only groping toward being able to articulate the answer that to "be flexible enough" to take on board more presuppositions (i.e., the supervisor's) often made one less flexible and not more so, just as "being flexible enough" to adopt a few more self-imposed limitations is not to be more flexible but to become more inflexible.

THE SUPERVISION OF SUPERVISION

The supervision and training of clinical supervisors is a subject of great interest to us, and again the proposed model is similar. However, in our view, *all* supervision ought to be supervision of supervision: *The aim of supervision of clinical work ought to be supervision of the therapist's own self-supervision.* As Confucius said, "Give a man a fish and you feed him for a day; teach him to fish and you feed him for a hundred years."

AFTERWORD

A Conversation between the Authors Recorded at Studley Priory,
Horton-cum-Studley, Oxfordshire, August 1986

JW: For me, this book is the culmination of a quest, though I hate to use the word "culmination" because it's still continuing. That quest began back in 1971 with the germ of an idea when I was first embarking on a serious study of the philosophical work of J. L. Austin and the so-called Oxford School of philosophy, and the work of Ludwig Wittgenstein and the so-called Cambridge School.

Now, what the two schools of thought had in common, despite their differences, was an interest not in solving philosophical problems, but in *dissolving* them by examining the language in which the problems were posed and questioning the underlying presuppositions on which they rested. This was often done by critiquing the way in which the very "existence" of the problem depended upon taking language more seriously than it was intended to be taken, and making it bear more weight than it could possibly bear.

Thus the Cambridge philosophers looked at such odd questions as "Can one play chess without the queen?" and "If my cat started to preach the gospel, what would we say—is it a cat or isn't it?" Well, look—language just isn't so precisely structured and defined as to enable us to give a definite answer to any questions of that kind. They are unanswerable.

Back in the forties, Austin's tutor at Oxford, Gilbert Ryle, in *The Concept of Mind* and elsewhere, was looking at the ways in which we have all these *metaphors* with which we discuss mental issues, and we reify these things and take them very seriously and create all sorts of pseudo-problems in philosophy. So the aim of these guys was not to solve those problems but, again, to dissolve them. Wittgenstein made an analogy to psychotherapy, saying that a philosophical problem was a kind of neurosis—"a disease of the understanding"—in which we are bedevilled by a form of words, and the aim of philosophical analysis was to cure the person of their "neurosis."

So here comes the germ of an idea that I had at the time: I wanted to turn the analogy around the other way and say that a psychotherapeutic problem had at the core of it a philosophical mistake, if you like. People in psychotherapy were supposedly troubled by all sorts of stuff to do with their mind, et cetera, and here I was reading Ryle saying all this talk was deep in metaphor land, and there's no such thing as a mind anyway (as a kind of ghost in the machine or whatever). It occurred to me that a lot of the problems people brought to psychotherapists, *they simply couldn't have* if, so to speak, they'd "had a damn good lesson in linguistic philosophy," or so I might have put it, tougue-in-cheek, back then. The germ of an idea was that it ought to be possible, by applying a procedure *parallel to* the philosophical procedures of J. L. Austin [particularly as in such papers as "A Plea for Excuses" or "Three Ways of Spilling Ink"], to take apart the language used to describe these things, and it ought to be possible in this way to do psychotherapy *very quickly*. I thought it ought to be like going to the doctor with an earache: You might go once or perhaps you'd need to go back again or just for a follow-up, but you wouldn't expect to embark on a program of therapy requiring years of appointments.

It's not that I thought psychotherapy should be like philosophical analysis; on the contrary. The critical approach to language found, for example, in Austin's work and directed at *dissolving* philosophical quandaries could serve as a model, I thought, for *dissolving* "psychological" quandaries in a clinical setting. If one is dissolving unsolvable problems rather than struggling to solve them, why should more than a session or two be needed?

But back in 1971/1972 this was still only a pious hope. As you know, it took me the better part of ten years to get to a point where I definitely *knew* how to *do* psychotherapy that quickly and in that kind of a way, and longer still before I could articulate the connections between my clinical practice and that old philosophical stuff that originally gave rise to that germ of an idea. Because the route was a circuitous one, nothing to do with philosophy at all, I was as surprised as anyone to end up back at my starting point.

BOH: I guess I came at it from an entirely different angle. Certainly I had some interest in philosophy; it wasn't totally lost on me. But I mainly came into it by dribs and drabs I suppose, little pieces that started to come together later in this kind of formulation.

I suppose the biggest pieces I can think of at this point are my interest in and knowledge of family therapy. I was a "family therapy convert" early on—the early seventies, mid-seventies—and I was certainly converted by good teachers: Family Therapy was the *only* way to do therapy; it was the most effective way to do therapy. All problems occurred in a context, and that context was a family context. And if you didn't revise or alter that context then you might as well forget it, because the problems would just keep recurring. Even if you were able to make a bit of a difference, when they'd go back in their old context, the context would "reimpose itself" on the clients, and then they would continue to have the symptoms or the difficulties, or someone else in the system would get a symptom.

So after a period of time of thinking further in this interactional/systemic/family therapy sort of way, I really was able to understand it, integrate it, and live it and have it be a part of me. And as I did, something very strange happened. That is, I realized that if indeed we were to take family therapy theory very seriously, or systemic or interactional theory very seriously then we really were saying this: We would come into a session and we would never again be able to see anything objective out there; that there was this myth of objectivity like what was talked about in the philosophy of science: One couldn't come into a therapy session and *not* influence the data that one observed, because things were interactionally influenced. The way they were influenced interactionally was through a process of language and nonverbal interactions and other contextual elements. So if this was the case, I realized—and from various experiences it became clearer—that we didn't really discover problems out there in therapy sessions. Rather, we came in, in cooperation with clients, and together co-created problems, we negotiated problems, and some problems we negotiated were easier to solve than others. "The problem" was something we negotiated from the raw data of what people brought in, the language and context that they brought forward through speaking, the way we interacted with them, and things like that. Once I *realized* this—and through various experiences *confirmed* this—I was convinced there must be a way to articulate this for other people. There were other people around who were articulating similar things: Paul Dell and Brad Keeney and some people who were interested in Maturana and cybernetics and epistemology. The main objection I've had to all that stuff is that I've had a bias, ever since I first went into the therapy field, toward the practical aspect: How do I use this every day? And I found that missing in these more philosophical tracts.

JW: The old, "What do I say? What do I do?"

BOH: That's right.

JW: Lynn Segal [of the Mental Research Institute (MRI)] put it a few years ago that, like most clinicians until recently, he was brought up on Otto Fenichel's *Psychoanalytic Theory of Neurosis,* a big fat volume; and if you were stuck in a case and didn't know what to do, you had to go back and read the whole damn book—all 885 pages. What nobody talked about, what nobody taught, was the "What do you say? What do you do?"

In a workshop I was teaching I once summed it up by saying, "The *theory* of psychotherapy is a branch of philosophy; the *practice* of psychotherapy is a branch of Home Economics." I would talk about the clinical side on a much more practical and brass tacks ("Home Ec") level than most people were talking about therapy. I think the most notable exception in the field over the years has been the MRI, where—in the way they trained therapists, and talked about therapy, and *did* therapy in the Brief Therapy Center—they tended to see therapy as a very *mundane* business. And yet at the same time they were working on all these philosophical issues about the nature of reality. . . . and how much we are talking about a solid reality out there or talking about our own constructions. At another level, of *doing* therapy, it was much more mundane than people might like to imagine psychotherapy to be. People would watch John Weakland doing a case and it would all seem to be at the level of Home Ec. And as we talk about in the book, that's precisely the level at which you and I like to do therapy.

Both of us have shared that background of having been family therapy converts, and also, I think, we both had the experience of working in largish clinics where there were a lot of other people who came from different orientations to therapy. And when it came to staffing cases or even daring to talk about our own work, we found that the same observations, the same "video descriptions" as we call them, would give rise to such totally different views of what it was one was working with. When you have that experience, of working with people who come at the problem from such totally different presuppositions, then you almost *have to* believe that a large part of what we're talking about is up for grabs, a matter for negotiation.

BOH: I can agree with that observation. When I was working in a large clinic, it was common knowledge—as it's probably common knowledge for many people who are reading this—that if clients came into the mental health center clinic and got assigned to one person's office, then they would be likely to follow a certain course, that would be likely to include ending up on medication or in a hospital, having multiple crises or possibly becoming suicidal, and things like that, along the course of therapy. And if they stumbled into someone else's office they would be likely to have a different course. They might end up talking to empty chairs or, you know, *whatever* it may be, but this course of therapy would typically be shorter and typically wouldn't include medication or hospitalization. And they would seem to do better. Basically, there was kind of a random assignment of people but there certainly was not a random outcome. Added to this was the fact that, over the years, I—and I'm sure, you—went, through a number of conceptual, technical, and philosophical changes with regard to therapy, and as a result "saw" different problems and got different results. And I think that brought home the point that later on we tried to articulate in this book and that we've been articulating for some time: namely, thinking very seriously about the presuppositions that one brings to therapy, challenging those presuppositions, and finding ones that support results—quicker results, better results—are very valuable things to do in therapy.

JW: Yes

BOH: I think that the other influence on both of us has been the work of Milton Erickson.

JW: Very much so.

BOH: And Erickson was a strange person in that, to a certain extent, he has been called one of the fathers of family therapy (along with Bateson who has also been a big influence on both of us). Although Erickson was doing something that seemed to be genuinely interactional/systemic/contextual, nevertheless he often didn't see whole families in his office, and that seemed strange at first to the two of us who were raised in family therapy, with the dictum that one had to see the whole family.

JW: . . . *at least try* to get them all in!

BOH: Even if one didn't get them all in and one was to see a "sub-system" of the family, the family was really the focus of treatment because that was where most problems "really" arose, and where most problems were maintained. Erickson seemed to be working in a much different way. He did indeed seem to be working interactionally, contextually, systemically. And I think that both of us, by that point having had a lot of experience with Ericksonian work, had a different vision of what so-called "systemic therapy" was. To a certain extent this book is a "re-visioning" or reworking of systemic therapy. We think it's been much too narrowly conceived. Many people including the Milan Group and Paul Dell and Brad Keeney have helped to make the point—but, again, not in a very pragmatic way—that the therapist is so much a part of the therapy context, and that there's no such thing as an objective problem without the therapist being there to co-construct one for or with the client.

JW: This is what we talk about in the book by saying that the therapy problem does not exist outside the therapist's office. When we talk about "the problem," that's where it is, that's where it is co-constructed, co-created.

And I want to come back to your point about systemic therapy, because I think it's an important one. Again, one thing that we had both come to before we started working together, was seeing things in a very systemic way whilst working primarily with individuals. I was very much influenced, as you were, by Bateson's cybernetics and that whole tradition, and whilst I was thinking cybernetically, systemically, my preference was for working one-to-one. Partly that was because I couldn't get people in, and partly because I found I was more personally effective—when working in an Ericksonian way—if I was working one-to-one as opposed to one-to-two. There wasn't so much to have to try and throw in "the old computer" at the same time. Applying cybernetic thinking, systemic thinking in that setting led to the kinds of therapy that we talk about and that for me are *at least as systemic* (you know, sort of like "more systemic than thou," right?), at least as systemic as anything that goes on, say, in family therapy, systemic family therapy.

But the funny thing is, I was talking to a colleague a couple of weeks ago who is waiting to see a manuscript of our book, and the following happened: I said that when you and I stepped back from what we'd done when we'd produced the first final draft and looked at it, a couple of things that we thought about it were, number one, it didn't look a whole lot like psychotherapy (which maybe wasn't surprising). When you look at what we actually did and how we talked about it, it didn't look like psychotherapy as we were brought up to think about psychotherapy. And second, one thing that we had here was a generic approach to problem-solving consultation that wasn't necessarily confined to therapy: It was a systemic way of going about solving problems. And the third thing (especially when you take the stuff on patterns and contexts toward the end of the book into account), was that we had a generic approach to bringing about change in systems of any description, as long as there was someone—an observer—describing them (which, by definition, there always is !). This is an approach to systems change, transformation, that could be applied almost anywhere. So this was a sort of overall systemic methodology. And the guy I was talking to was someone who I thought would really like this book because he was really committed to a systemic view. A couple days later I got the manuscript in the mail for a final proof reading, and when I re-read it I thought, this guy is really going to doubt my judgment. Because I thought, reading through it, I found it's all very much talking about individuals, and talking about language, talking about the interpretations that people make, talking about. . . . Well, it occurred to me that whilst *you* could see and *I* could see how this is a systemic methodology, the guy I was going to be giving the manuscript to—would *he* see it? And the only thing that reassured me of this was a book he'd written a couple of years ago. The first time he and I met he said to me, "When you read the book it seems to be mainly talking about individuals, but you have to understand that this comes from a systemic viewpoint strictly." So I think something that doesn't necessarily come across loud and clear in the book and that's worth saying, is how we relate to the whole systemic tradition.

BOH: That's important because I think that both of us are *extremely* committed to a systemic point of view and the interactional point of view. We *do* have one ! And people find it hard to see sometimes—they kind of lose it in the mix because we don't talk about *the family* so much, or even couples. . . .

JW: . . . or *"the system"*.

BOH: Yeah, "the system"—we don't like to use those kinds of words. When you read the book you'll probably understand why we don't use that term, but I guess the telling thing for me is this: Initially I started out as a therapist, I was very much a family therapist, and as I mentioned before, a family therapy *convert*—"That's the *only* way to work"—and I felt alienated from my psychodynamic, individually oriented colleagues. It would be like talking two different languages, and I couldn't get along with them, and I'd get angry at them and they'd get angry at me. After a time of working that way, I started to feel alienated from the family therapists as well—I had no colleagues to speak to! I had the individual, psychodynamic therapists with whom I didn't agree; most of the things they talked about were like ghosts in the machine, very much ethereal, abstract, nonexistent entities. . . .

JW: . . . that somebody made up.

BOH: Right. And unfortunately I came to the same view about family therapists because they had "things" like *enmeshment* and *coalitions*—things that no one could see or hear. You know, they could just as well be talking about families that had three Leos and two Pisces, and just about as checkable as that. I mean, they were based on *some* observations, but they're pretty specious. So, alienated from the individual, psychodynamic therapists and alienated from the so-called systemic *family* therapists, where did we go from there? And I think that what we *had* to do, by necessity, was to look for colleagues, and since then we have found other people who had a similar kind of disaffection from or dissatisfaction with both of those approaches. But having stood on the shoulders of both of those points of view, having stood on the shoulders of the family therapists, having stood on the shoulders of the psychodynamic therapists, we can see something that *isn't completely compatible with* either point of view but incorporates some ideas from *each*. We hope that what we have is a new kind of integration: a systemic integration that doesn't necessarily focus on any *family* aspects, but that *is* focused on how people *act*; and only individuals can be actors and speakers.

JW: Sure.

BOH: My orientation, I think, is an orientation toward the individual, although I certainly see couples and families in my practice. There's a story I think we tell in the book. I gave a lecture on epistemology and after the lecture this person said, "I'm a new psychotherapist; I've just completed my training and I'm just about to start practice. And you've just destroyed the whole basis for doing psychotherapy for me." And I said, "Certainly not for *me*: This is what I do for a living, it's my career. I teach it and I do it." I don't see anything that we've done to destroy it. Hopefully, ultimately, there'll be a *lot* of psychotherapy that will just disappear, because I think much of it is useless and too expensive and not very effective, and so I wish *most* of it would go away. I just want the *successful* therapy to go on, the stuff that does make contributions to people's lives. I've seen that there is a use for psychotherapy in this world and in our culture (at least so long as we have these philosohpical mistakes, if you will, inherent in our culture) because people get trapped in conundrums based on these mistakes.

JW: And that's the Alan Watts quote from *Psychotherapy East and West* with which this book opens: "the unrealized nonsense problems which lie in its social context."

BOH: The assumptions.

JW: Psychotherapy is very much a going concern, and where it starts getting interesting *for us* is where a lot of the bits that have for so long fascinated other people are sort of put to one side and we say, O.K., now what do we say, and what do we do, and how do we get this person out of our office as quickly as possible.

BOH: That's it.

REFERENCES

Angelo, C. (1981). The Use of Metaphoric Objects in Family Therapy. *American Journal of Family Therapy, 9*(1); 69–78.

Austin, J. L. (1957). A Plea for Excuses. In *Philosophical Papers* (J. O. Urmson & G. J. Warnock, Eds., pp. 175–204). London: Oxford University Press, 1970.

Austin, J. L. (1962). *How to do Things with Words.* London: Oxford University Press.

Austin, J. L. (1966). Three Ways of Spilling Ink. In *Philosophical Papers* (J. O. Urmson & G. J. Warnock, Eds., pp. 272–287). London: Oxford University Press, 1970.

Austin, J. L. (1970). *Philosophical Papers* (J. O. Urmson & G. J. Warnock, Eds.). London: Oxford University Press.

Bandler, R., & Grinder, J. (1975). *The Structure of Magic* (Vol. 1). Palo Alto, CA: Science and Behavior Books.

Bateson, G. (1955). A Theory of Play and Fantasy. In *Steps to an Ecology of Mind* (pp. 150–166). London: Paladin Books, 1978.

Bateson, G. (1964/1971). The Logical Categories of Learning and Communication. In *Steps to an Ecology of Mind* (pp. 250–279). London: Paladin Books, 1978.

Bateson, G. (1969). Pathologies of Epistemology. In *Steps to an Ecology of Mind* (pp. 454–463). London: Paladin Books, 1978.

Bateson, G. (1978). *Steps to an Ecology of Mind.* London: Paladin Books. (Originally published, 1972).

Bateson, G. (1979). *Mind and Nature: A Necessary Unity.* London: Wildwood House.

Beahrs, J. (1982). Understanding Erickson's Approach. In J. Zeig (Ed.) *Ericksonian Approaches to Hypnosis and Psychotherapy* (pp. 58–84). New York: Brunner/Mazel.

Berkeley, G. (1710). *The Principles of Human Knowledge* (G. J. Warnock, Ed.). London: Fontana, 1972.

Colapinto, J. (1979). The Relative Value of Empirical Evidence. *Family Process, 18,* 427–441.

Dell, P. (1980a). The Hopi Family Therapist and the Aristotelian Parents. *Journal of Marital and Family Therapy,* 1980, 123–130.

Dell, P. (1980b). Researching the Family Theories of Schizophrenia: An Exercise in Epistemological Confusion. *Family Process, 19,* 321–335.

Dell, P. (1981a, September). *From Systemic to Clinical Epistemology*. Plenary lecture presented to the Seventh International Symposium of the Institut für Ehe und Familie, Zurich, Switzerland.

Dell, P. (1981b). Some Irreverent Thoughts on Paradox. *Family Process, 20*, 37–42.

Dell, P. (1982). Beyond Homeostasis: Toward a Concept of Coherence. *Family Process, 21*, 21–41.

de Shazer, S. (1982a). *Patterns of Brief Family Therapy*. New York: Guilford Press.

de Shazer, S. (1982b). Some Conceptual Distinctions Are More Useful than Others. *Family Process, 21*, 71–84.

de Shazer, S. (1985). *Keys to Solution in Brief Therapy*. New York: Norton.

Einstein, A. (1961). *Relativity: The Special and General Theory*. (Robert W. Lawson, Trans.). New York: Crown.

Eliot, T. S. (1943). *The Four Quartets*. New York: Harcourt, Brace & World.

Erickson Foundation. (1979). Brochure for the First International Erickson Congress.

Erickson, M. H. (1973). Psychotherapy Achieved by a Reversal of the Neurotic Processes in a Case of Ejaculatio Praecox. In *Collected Papers* (E. L. Rossi, Ed., Vol 4, pp. 348–355). New York: Irvington, 1980.

Erickson, M. H. (1980). *Collected Papers* (E. L. Rossi, Ed., 4 vols.). New York: Irvington.

Erickson, M. H., & Rossi, E. L. (1979). *Hypnotherapy: An Exploratory Casebook*. New York: Irvington.

Erickson, M. H., & Rossi, E. L. (1979). *Experiencing Hypnosis*. New York: Irvington.

Erickson, M. H., Rossi, E. L., & Rossi, S. I. (1976). *Hypnotic Realities*. New York: Irvington.

Farrelly, F., & Brandsma, J. (1974). *Provocative Therapy*. Cupertino, CA: Meta.

Fisch, R., Weakland, J., & Segal, L. (1982). *Tactics of Change*. San Francisco: Jossey-Bass.

Fowler, H. W. (1980). *Modern English Usage* (2nd ed., E. Gowers, Ed.). London: Oxford University Press.

Gordon, D., & Myers-Anderson, M. (1981). *Phoenix: Therapeutic Patterns of Milton H. Erickson*. Cupertino, CA: Meta.

Gurman, A. (1984). The Name Game. *Family Therapy News, 15*(1), pp. 8.

Haley, J. (1963). *Strategies of Psychotherapy*. New York: Grune & Stratton.

Haley, J. (1967). Commentary on the Writings of Milton H. Erickson, M.D. In J. Haley (Ed.), *Advanced Techniques of Hypnosis and Psychotherapy: Selected Papers of Milton H. Erickson, M.D.*, New York: Grune & Stratton.

Haley, J. (1973). *Uncommon Therapy: The Psychiatric Techniques of Milton H. Erickson, M.D.* New York: Norton.

Haley, J. (1976). *Problem Solving Therapy*. New York: Harper & Row.

Haley, J., & Weakland, J. (1983). *Remembering Erickson* (video tape available from the Family Institute of Washington, DC).

Haley, J. (1985). *Conversations with Milton H. Erickson, M.D.* (Vol. 1). New York: Triangle (Norton).

Hungerland, I. (1960). Contextual Implication. *Inquiry, 4,* 211–258.

Huxley, A. (1940). *Words and Their Meanings.* Los Angeles: Jake Zeitlin.

Jackson, D. (1961). Interactional Psychotherapy. In D. Jackson (Ed.), *Therapy, Communication, and Change* Palo Alto, CA: Science and Behavior Books, 1968.

Keeney, B. P. (1982). "What Is an Epistemology of Family Therapy?" *Family Therapy, 21,* 153–168.

Keeney, B. P. (1983). *Aesthetics of Change.* New York: Guilford Press.

Korzybski, A. (1933). *Science and Sanity.* Lakeville, CT: International Non-Aristotelian Library.

Lakoff, G., & Johnson, M. (1980). *Metaphors We Live By.* Chicago: University of Chicago Press.

LeShan, L., & Margenau, H. (1982). *Einstein's Space and Van Gogh's Sky: Physical Reality and Beyond.* New York: Macmillan.

Liddle, H., & Saba, G. (1983). On Context Replication: The Isomorphic Relationship of Training and Therapy. *Journal of Strategic and Systemic Therapies, 2*(2), 3–11.

Liddle, H., & Schwartz, R. (1983). Live Supervision/Consultation: Conceptual and Pragmatic Guidelines for Family Therapy Trainers. *Family Process, 22*(4), 477–490.

O'Hanlon, B. (1982a). Splitting and Linking: Two Generic Patterns in Ericksonian Therapy. *Journal of Strategic and Systemic Therapies, 1*(4), 21–25.

O'Hanlon, B. (1982b). Strategic Pattern Intervention: An Integration of Individual and Family Therapies Based on the Work of Milton H. Erickson, M.D. *Journal of Strategic and Systemic Therapies, 1*(4), 26–33.

Popper, K. (1963). *Conjectures and Refutations.* New York: Basic Books.

Postman, N. (1976). *Crazy Talk, Stupid Talk.* New York: Delacorte.

Postman, N. &Weingartner, C. (1969). *Teaching as a Subversive Activity.* New York: Penguin.

Rabkin, R. (1977). *Strategic Psychotherapy.* New York: Basic Books.

Rapoport, A. (1953). *Operational Philosophy.* New York: Harper.

Richards, I. A. (1929). *Practical Criticism.* London: Routledge & Kegan Paul, 1982.

Rosen, S. (Ed.). (1982). *My Voice Will Go With You: The Teaching Tales of Milton H. Erickson, M.D.* New York: Norton.

Rossi, E. L., Ryan, M. & Sharp, F. (Eds.). (1983). *Healing in Hypnosis.* New York: Irvington.

Schafer, R. (1978). *Language and Insight.* New Haven, CT: Yale University Press.

Scheflen, A. (1972). *Body Language and Social Order.* Englewood Cliffs, NJ: Prentice-Hall.

Scheflen, A. (1973). *How Behavior Means.* New York: Gordon & Breach.

Shands, H. (1971). *The War With Words.* The Hague/Paris: Houghton.

Strawson, P. F. (1952). *Introduction to Logical Theory.* London: Methuen.

Suzuki, S. (1970). *Zen Mind, Beginner's Mind.* New York: Weatherhill.

Tavris, C. (1982). *Anger: The Misunderstood Emotion.* New York: Simon & Schuster.

Thomas, L. (1974). *The Lives of a Cell.* New York: Viking Press.

Watts, A. (1954). *The Wisdom of Insecurity.* London: Rider.

Watts, A. (1961). *Psychotherapy East and West.* New York: Pantheon.

Watzlawick, P. (1976). *How Real Is Real?* New York: Random House.

Watzlawick, P. (1978). *The Language of Change.* New York: Basic Books.

Watzlawick, P., Weakland, J., & Fisch, R. (1974). *Change: Principles of Problem Formation and Problem Resolution.* New York: Norton.

Whitehead, A. N. (1925). *Science and the Modern World.* New York: Free Press, 1967.

Wilk, J. (1980). *Techniques and Theories of Change in Strategic Psychotherapy.* M Sc dissertation, University of Oxford, Barnett House Library, Wellington Square.

Wilk, J. (1982). Context and Know-How: A Model for Ericksonian Psychotherapy. *Journal of Strategic and Systemic Therapies, 1*(4), 2–20.

Wilk, J. (1985). Ericksonian Therapeutic Patterns: A Pattern Which Connects. In J. Zeig (Ed.), *Ericksonian Psychotherapy* (Vol. 2, pp. 210–233). New York: Brunner/Mazel.

Wittgenstein, L. (1934–1935). *The Brown Book.* In *The Blue and Brown Books.* New York: Harper & Row, 1965.

Wittgenstein, L. (1953). *Philosophical Investigations* (G. E. M. Anscombe, Trans). Oxford: Basil Blackwell, 1972.

Zeig, J. (Ed.). (1980). *A Teaching Seminar with Milton H. Erickson, M.D.* New York: Brunner/Mazel.

Zeig, J. (Ed.). (1982a). *Ericksonian Approaches to Hypnosis and Psychotherapy.* New York: Brunner/Mazel.

Zeig, J. (1982b). Ericksonian Approaches to Promote Abstinence from Cigarette Smoking. In J. Zeig (Ed.), *Ericksonian Approaches to Hypnosis and Psychotherapy* (pp. 255–269). New York: Brunner/Mazel.

Zilbergeld, B. (1982). *The Shrinking of America.* Boston: Little, Brown.

INDEX